# WILLING TO BE LUCKY

*Adventures in Life and Television*

By

Andy Friendly

KCM PUBLISHING
A DIVISION OF KCM DIGITAL MEDIA, LLC

# CREDITS

Willing to Be Lucky by Andy Friendly

First Edition

ISBN 13: 978-1-939961-64-8
ISBN 10: 1-939961-64-5

Senior editor: Melissa Grego
Editors: Shayne Shnapier and Christine Schwab
Publisher: Michael Fabiano
KCM Publishing, www.kcmpublishing.com

The KCM logo is a registered trademark of KCM Digital Media, LLC.

KCM Publishing
a division of KCM Digital Media, LLC

# Dedication

This book is dedicated to my huge, far-flung, talented, brilliant, crazy, loving family and to my closest friends – those alive and no longer with us. Especially my parents: Dorothy, Fred, and Ruth, and my loving, talented, beautiful wife, Pat Crowley Friendly.

If I live to be 1,000, I could not begin to thank you all enough.

# PRAISE FOR "WILLING TO BE LUCKY: ADVENTURES IN LIFE AND TELEVISION"

Andy's book reminds me to be grateful not for the material things in life but for the most important thing in life, which is family. Each night before bed, I remind my kids how I feel about them by quoting Andy's father's nightly message to him as a kid: "It's good to be your dad." The response from them is better than anything I can ever accomplish in life. I'm thankful that Andy has passed along these six words that have had such a positive impact on my family.

> — Michael Strahan, Co-anchor *Good Morning America* and analyst NFL Sunday

"I got to see Andy's extraordinary creative talent and strong leadership firsthand, as I watched him build CNBC into a powerhouse. Great leader... great programmer...great strategist...great friend...great man. It's all on display in his honest, teachable new book."

> — David Zaslav, CEO, Discovery Communications

"Communications giant Fred Friendly produced many wonderful programs, two of which were *Hear It Now* on radio and *See It Now* on television. His son Andy has produced a memoir of his trip down the halls of television, which should be called *Read It Now*. His experience with Richard Pryor alone is certainly worth the read."

> — Vin Scully, legendary sportscaster

# Andy Friendly

"In chronicling his own remarkable career in television, including producing shows for talk show icons Tom Snyder and Tim Russert, Andy Friendly delights us with wise, revealing, and often witty tales about these and other television greats. Most of all, he speaks about his devotion to family with a graciousness and passion that is profound and inspiring."

> — Robert Hilburn, best-selling author of biographies on Paul Simon and Johnny Cash and award-winning *Los Angeles Times* critic

"Andy Friendly has given us a remarkable inside history of the television industry. He has generously shared a perspective that few have, and in doing so written a must-read book."

> — Elizabeth Daley, dean of USC School of Cinematic Arts

"From his father, the legendary Fred Friendly, to Tim Russert, Tom Snyder, and the (in)famous King brothers, Andy Friendly has observed and worked with some of the best-known people in television. Here is his take on people we know and thought we knew. Not so much a 'tell-all' as it is a fond remembrance of a life spent in television by one of television's good guys."

> — Bob Singer, veteran producer-writer-director of *Supernatural* and *Lois and Clark: The Real Adventures of Superman*

"With one of the storied careers in the hybrid field of news and entertainment, Andy Friendly has been on the line and in the front office both witnessing and affecting the sea change of broadcast and cable television over the past forty years. In this book, his remarkable memoirs are matched by a wonderful and easy writing style that brings the reader right into the story and keeps your interest from beginning to end. And the chapter about his dad's wartime letter recounting his concentration camp experience and how it affected Andy's life is one of the most emotional things I've ever read. This book was a pleasure to read, made even more of a pleasure because of the person it reflects."

> — Ken Ehrlich, executive producer, writer of Grammy Awards (35 years) and Emmy Awards telecasts

# Contents

# Foreword

Andy Friendly is a generous compassionate man: always curious, open to new ideas, and with a wonderful sense of humor. He's had an extraordinary life, achieved much, and met many fascinating influential people, but you never get a sense of entitlement or having taken things for granted.

He writes beautifully and has the gift of making you feel like you are there with him. He comes from a family with enormous integrity and the ability to observe and listen, something he has obviously inherited.

I never resented Andy for stealing my late husband Allan away for trips to Scotland to play golf, as these sojourns were full not only of freezing windswept rounds but of great conversations, and true friendship.

'Andy Friendly is a BGB,' he would say...a bloody good bloke...high praise indeed from a Londoner. So I do hope you enjoy this BGB...bloody good book.

— Tracey Ullman, award-winning television, stage, and film actress, comedian, screenwriter, producer, director, author, and businesswoman

# Acknowledgements

I started writing this book three years ago with a few ideas scribbled on yellow Post-it notes.

A thousand or so days and about a million (seems like) Post-it notes later, having put it away for months at a time, never quite certain I'd get around to finishing it, I have many people to thank for getting me across the finish line.

First and foremost my Senior Editor Melissa Grego, who I worked with for decades when she was a reporter and top editor at *Variety*, *The Hollywood Reporter*, and *Broadcasting & Cable*. She spent a year getting me to a first draft that never would have happened without her encouragement, patience, and skill.

Because of the three-year timeline and my long periods off, Melissa, while remaining a steadfast partner and consultant on the project, had to return to her many flourishing projects. My friend Christine Schwab, a successful, published author and longtime on-air contributor to *Regis and Kathy Lee* and other shows, picked up the editor reins when I resumed the project. She was invaluable. Her insight and support improved everything I wrote. She, too, was always encouraging and extremely patient. (Anyone seeing a trend here? Yep, I required a great deal of patience.)

Thanks to an introduction by Melissa, *Broadcasting & Cable* ran five excerpts from the book. That was encouraging and gratifying, but after they ran I put the book away again.

A couple months went by. One trusted friend convinced me that more people had read the excerpts in the magazine than read complete books written by people in television and that I didn't have to worry about finishing it. He was kindly providing me an exit ramp if I wanted one.

Other good friends told me to get off my ass and finish it.

One day Melissa called to tell me about her friend Michael Fabiano and his company KCM Publishing. She said he liked the excerpts and was interested in publishing the book.

His five-year-old company had published the distinguished *NBC News* anchor and reporter John Palmer's book, along with about twenty others.

We spoke. I was impressed. We made a deal. Michael, Melissa, and I set some goals and timelines; I got off my ass and went back to work.

Melissa and Christine were busy working on their own books and other projects, and that's when Shayne Shnapier joined our little clambake as the book's third and final editor, to bring it home.

Recommended by my nephew Noah Mark, the co-executive producer of Fox Sports' *The Ultimate Fighter*, Shayne is a successful television producer and a whip-smart, tough-as-nails, get-it-done force of nature.

Dealing with a sixty-five-year-old dinosaur, who still has a BlackBerry and an AOL account, can barely send an email, and has little clue about social media can be a challenge. Shayne, too, was very patient.

Over the past few months there was no job, big or small, that she didn't throw herself into 100 percent to help me complete this project. From editing to photo and legal clearance, to research and fact checking, she guided me to the finish line.

Did I mention she, too, was very patient?

Like Melissa and Christine, Shayne was a taskmaster. All three challenged me to do better, and stood up to me when I was wrong, which was often. They encouraged me when I was unsure.

I will always be in their debt.

I also want to thank my friend Pam Bloch, who was our art director back in the early days of *Entertainment Tonight,* for helping us locate, scan, and archive the many photographs, letters, articles, and other graphics in the book. In the printed version of the book the photos are in black and white, and some are faded. In the digital version they are clearer, and in color.

I want to thank my wife, Pat, who supported me, encouraged me, and listened to my doubts and frustrations along the way. Always giving me time and space, she made me feel it would all be OK.

Publisher Michael Fabiano turned out to be the perfect partner. While visiting me at home one day, he saw the picture of me at age five on my dad's shoulders, taken by my mom Dorothy, and said, "That's your book cover." We had been going back and forth over several ideas. Michael, as with everything else, saw it, understood it, nailed it.

Along the way, everything he said would happen happened. Every suggestion he made was smart and on point. (They don't give out diplomas at Harvard and Columbia, his two schools, to dopes.)

My close friend and lawyer for over thirty-five years: David Nochimson (another dumb guy: Yale, then Columbia Law) guided and encouraged me through the entire process as he has on pretty much everything I've done. As always, I am deeply grateful to him.

As I am to David Zaslav and Bob Hilburn, without whom this book would not have happened.

Many more people contributed to this book in so many ways. I'm thankful to family, friends, and colleagues who took time to read early sections and drafts, who reminded me about facts, dates, and events, and made invaluable suggestions that improved the book significantly.

Here are their names:

Ruth Abrams, Pam Burke, Skip Brittenham, Paul Cantor, Rich Cervini, George Christy, Andy Cohen, Elizabeth Daley, Harriet Ehrlich, Ken Ehrlich, Rick Ehrman, Andrew Friendly, David Friendly, Lisa Friendly, Maddie Friendly, Ruth Friendly, Anne Greene, Maura Harway, Dade Hayes, Will Hookstratten, Mark Itkin, LaWanda Katzman-Staenberg, Aaron Mark, Jon Mark, Michael Mark, Noah Mark, Richard Mark, Karen Schneeberger-Mineo, Bill Nathan, James Nicholson, Christopher Nicholson, Ramona Orley, Eddie Osher, Kate Osher Fay, Steve Paskay, Tony Peyrot, Marc Rosenweig, Herman Rush, Rus Sarnoff, Shelley Schwab, Vin Scully, Bob Singer, Larry Stein, Michael Strahan, Joel Tator, Zak Taylor, Gretchen Theobald, and Debbie Vickers.

Thank you, all.

# Introduction

A s I write this on a beautiful, eighty-degree day in Los Angeles in January, I cannot possibly complain.

I have a wife and family I adore, all in mostly good health, and some really amazing friends.

I'm headed to the links at Riviera to play nine holes—on a balmy, perfect Southern California winter Wednesday. That's something a Bronx kid, who endured New York winters growing up and worked steadily for almost forty years in an office or windowless studio, will never take for granted. (It is eight degrees and sleeting in New York right now.)

After a lifetime of working in TV starting at 21, for the most part my days now go easy. There are no ratings to sweat over or disrupt my sleep, no corporate infighting. No angry bosses are looking for me, and no freaked-out hosts or producers are on my case.

So when my longtime friend, colleague, author, esteemed *Los Angeles Times* critic, and music editor Bob Hilburn urged me to write a book collecting tales from my experience in life and TV, I thought long and hard about it. I had to weigh the pros and cons.

What could possibly go wrong?

Pros: Remembering and passing on some stories about some of the truly great, iconic people I've been so blessed to know and work with...and maybe some bits of advice to the younger generation of my family, along with friends, colleagues, and a few others who might find it interesting. It might even help some high school and college kids studying TV, considering a career in our crazy business. And to that end, any modest profits I might derive from my share of the sale of the book will go toward the Pat Crowley/Andy Friendly Student Scholarship at my alma mater, the USC School of Cinematic Arts; to S.H.A.R.E. (the organization Pat headed and remains dedicated to, which benefits mentally challenged children); to the Shoah

Foundation at USC; and to the Saban Community Clinic, the latter two for which I serve on the board.

Also, I like a challenge. Taking this on would mean applying myself to something entirely new after all these years. Sure, I learned to write on the local news in New York, wrote many of the shows I worked on over the years, and consider myself a capable enough writer to get the story across. But a book?

I do have the time these days, while slowly shepherding a few passion projects for TV, doing charitable and board work, playing golf, and hanging with the grandkids, nieces, and nephews.

The cons: Some of the best stories I have to tell also have the most potential to piss off a lot of people. But as my great pal and mentor Tom Snyder used to say toward the end of his career: "What are they gonna do, fire me?"

Or… I may just bore the hell out of people. (Too late?)

Then there are the "haters" (as the kids say). Over a forty-year career, fighting to become an executive producer or a high-level executive in a major media company or network, you're gonna "wrassle" with a bunch of people (as my friend and golf bud, the late, great Al Stoddart, used to say.)

And I did.

Things occasionally got ugly. In 1996, a few months into my job heading programming and production at King World, my boss, CEO Michael King's assistant, came into my office, closed the door and, ashen-faced, handed me an anonymous, unsigned, typed letter to Michael from someone claiming to be an industry exec who had allegedly overheard me at an industry function calling the King Brothers and some of our biggest stars "fat, stupid losers."

It went on.

Sheila, a good friend, had luckily intercepted it and never showed it to Michael, but the writer (I knew immediately who it was) was a "hater" I had battled with and stood up to in the past.

I had long ago moved on but he clearly had not and was determined to get me in hot water with my boss. Maybe even get me fired.

Of course it didn't work. I went on to spend six great, productive years at King World, including a promotion to president of programming and production from executive vice president.

(Well, maybe five great years and one shitty last one. More on that in the next chapter.)

Even if Michael had seen the letter, it wouldn't have worked, as we were close, trusted friends and he'd have known that I didn't believe those things—just the opposite. And that I would never say anything like that in public. I wanted to sue the guy, but my lawyers talked me out of it.

My publisher Michael tells me we'll need to start a Facebook page for the book, along with other social media. There may be trolls, like the guy who wrote the letter, and ugly, made-up "alternate" facts or generally mean comments, as there are for almost every book.

I know what you're thinking: "This book has a publisher?"

Michael also tells me there will be some good comments. Like the ones that appear a few pages earlier, called "blurbs," which mean the world to me.

As my dad used to say to family and friends about his detractors and critics: "If you can handle it, so can I." As Teddy Roosevelt said, "It's not the critic who counts..."

I feel the same about my family and close friends. If they can take it, so can I. Just be ready, people. And to quote the brilliant, contemporary poet Taylor Swift: "Shake it off."

Among the many things my dad taught me that I'll share in this book (including its title) are: When I was five years old, he bought me boxing gloves and taught me to fight. He was a tough guy and wanted me to be, too. He saw an older kid in the neighborhood named Chris bully me, and he didn't like it.

He would make me spar with the toughest neighborhood kids. Bigger, stronger, older kids like our neighbors Ferdy Valdez and Freddy Montillo, who were my buds and looked after me.

Usually I got my ass kicked, but in time I held my own and learned to stand up for family, my friends, and myself. Especially to the bullies. A lesson that stayed with me through my career and to this day.

I learned to "Be Brave!" as the old man would always yell to the firemen as they sped by with sirens blazing on their way to a fire near our home in the Bronx.

I've stood up to some pretty tough guys. Physically and otherwise.

From Dad himself (yes he could be tough at times, as has been widely reported) to mentors and stars like the great Tom Snyder and Richard Pryor; brilliant but "weapons grade" tough bosses like Roger Ailes, and the King brothers: Michael and Roger.

At my going-away dinner at CNBC as I was heading to King World, Geraldo Rivera, whom I brought to CNBC and whose show I executive produced for three years at the network, said in his toast that night: "What greater tribute to a man than to say that he is up for every challenge that the world has for him. To go from Roger Ailes to Roger King, I mean the guy's got balls."

Got a nice laugh, even from Roger Ailes, who was there.

I even "wrassled" with Donald Trump in 2004 when he tried to have ABC fire me from a primetime special on which I was profiling him. He failed. I'll tell you more about that later.

Anyway, I've learned it takes courage to write a book about your life. (Or maybe stupidity.)

Some people are going to laugh. Some are going to hate. There will, of course, be trolls.

But as Dad and his partner, Ed Murrow, said in a famous broadcast on CBS in 1954, "We are not descended from fearful men."

WTF, let's do this.

While my book is not a tell-all, I have much to say about learning both the hard—and fun—way, things that I took with me from my parents or learned from so many other mentors: great teachers, colleagues, and family and friends I was fortunate to know and work with.

For the most part, I'm going to keep things on the lighter side.

But I'll also be candid—as much about the trying times and giant, heartbreaking, soul-sucking failures as I will about the blessed, surprising victories.

Looking back over the past few years at the so-called journey of writing all this, I realize how lucky I am to have been born healthy and into a smart, caring family that gave me the tools and inspiration to live an exciting and productive life. To experience and share love with friends and family.

The process of writing this has put me back in touch with so many experiences, memories, and emotions I had not focused on for decades, and has helped me put them in greater perspective. It also made me appreciate and have gratitude for all of it, even the bad stuff.

So far it's been, overall, a very positive experience. I say so far, because soon the book will be published and a few people may actually read it.

As my dad used to say, "Take your shot, Andy" and, quoting the author E.B. White, "You've got to be 'willing to be lucky.'"

It really has been the recurring, abiding principle of my life and I thank my dad for teaching it to my sister Lisa, my brothers Jon, Michael, David, and Richard, and me from an early age.

To sum up, the overriding takeaway for me is that I was, and still am, just a guy.

A guy at school, at camp, in sports, high school, college, on TV crews, in lame rock bands, in poker, in the community, and in a great family.

Along the way I got to do a lot of cool things and meet a lot of amazing people, including some of my greatest heroes.

Did plenty of dumb things, too. Things I'm not necessarily proud of.

I'll tell you about some of this in the pages that follow, but in the end, the real joy for me is…I was one of the guys.

One of lots of guys who were around the halls of NBC, CBS, ABC, and other major networks and studios, and who over a forty-year career in TV somehow, through a lot of luck, far exceeded my parents', teachers', and my own expectations. (Along with plenty of screw-ups.)

But while I'm content to be just a guy, I did get to experience true greatness, even TV royalty.

Some say I was born, and married, into it. I agree. And I certainly got to be around it. From my dad, Fred, and Ed Murrow to early mentors like Tom Snyder and Ralph Edwards to the giants: Richard Pryor, Paul McCartney, Dan Rather, Vin Scully, and Tim Russert, to my amazing wife, Pat Crowley, and so many more I will tell you about.

So…I just want to say…though this book may be about my life and experiences, it's really about the people I've been blessed to know and love, including my brilliant, talented, far-flung family and friends. And even some I battled and learned from.

Just a very lucky guy…"willing to be lucky."

OK. Now it's a party.

AF, 2017
Los Angeles

# WILLING TO BE LUCKY

"Writing about yourself is a funny business. But in a project like this, the writer has made one promise, to show the reader his mind. In these pages, I've tried to do this."

– Bruce Springsteen,
from his autobiography *Born to Run*

# 1

## THE $3.2 MILLION FREEZE-OUT

*February 2001, 9:30 a.m. CBS' Eyemark/King World of-*
*fices, Westwood, Calif.*

My large, marble-and-wood corner office at the merged, CBS-owned Eyemark Entertainment/King World in Westwood, California, in 2001 offered skyrocket views to the ocean and Beverly Hills. But as I sat at my desk at 9:30 a.m. early that year, I couldn't stop staring at the CNBC ticker scrolling across the wide-screen TV on the wall in front of me.

I realized I never paid any attention to the ubiquitous stock ticker that ran all day long while I was head of primetime programming at CNBC. For five years, from 1990-95, I executive produced eleven shows with the likes of the great Tim Russert, Tom Snyder, Geraldo Rivera, Dick Cavett, Charles Grodin, Charlie Rose, and Phil Donahue. Six years later in 2001, long away from CNBC, I just couldn't take my eyes off that ticker. Not for a second.

I was president of programming and production at King World, one of the biggest television companies in the world.

King World produced and/or distributed *The Oprah Winfrey Show, Wheel of Fortune, Jeopardy!, Hollywood Squares, Inside Edition,* and *Roseanne,* along with *American Journal, Martin Short, Rolonda, Curtis Court,* and others.

Three years earlier I had been promoted from executive vice president to president and, in addition to our current on-air hits, I supervised the

1

development of a wide range of projects for the company. In the press release announcing my promotion to president, King World CEO Michael King said, "Andy has proven to be an invaluable asset to King World. Since joining the company, he has played a major role in keeping our existing programs on top of the ratings charts....We are confident in Andy's ability to continue to develop and produce quality programming, and it is our pleasure to reward him with this well-deserved promotion."

Working with my tremendous team of producers, writers, directors, and fellow executives, the ratings and resulting profits from our shows, in fact, were higher than ever and we had more than a billion dollars cash in the bank, which made us an attractive target for acquisition by CBS.

But in the boardroom on the floor above, less than a half-hour before, the company chairman Roger King (Michael's brother) told me to leave the senior staff meeting. For years Roger, who as chairman was responsible for sales and business decisions at the company, had (in my and many others' opinions) been frustrated that his brother Michael ran the creative areas of development, production, and marketing as CEO.

When CBS bought us, Roger got his way. Michael was out and now every department reported to Roger, including mine.

I was viewed by Roger's East Coast-based sales team as "Michael's guy" and, despite the huge success we'd had with *Squares, Inside Edition, American Journal,* and *Roseanne* (just being able to keep Roseanne's show on the air and keep it from imploding was a herculean effort that allowed the company to collect more than $50 million in revenues), I was now in Roger's sights.

The powerful, six-foot-four chairman of our company wanted me gone so he would have no one between him and our shows, our stars, our development, and the hundreds of talented people who worked in my area.

After reviewing several sales and distribution issues in the normal agenda of the semi-regular gathering, Roger asked for my report. Before I could tell him about a few new program ideas for development consideration, he interrupted me.

Roger said it really didn't matter, because over the past six years I hadn't really done anything for the company and that he was sure I had nothing worth hearing about. A distinct chill fell over the room as my colleagues visibly cringed with apparent embarrassment for me. And them.

Having heard similar lines of accusation from Roger in the six months since his brother had left the company, I was not totally surprised to hear this sort of thing. I had learned to keep my cool, and I did so, amid my colleagues cringing all around me.

As Roger continued his assessment in the conference room, I tried to muster a slight, professional-grade smile, despite my stomach turning and churning like a roller coaster.

Calmly I said, "Roger, I'm sorry you feel that way and would be happy to discuss my performance with you anytime, maybe just not in this forum. Maybe we could talk privately at your convenience."

We had been friends and colleagues for over a decade before the sale of the company. He and his wife, Raemali, had come to our home for dinner. Pat and I had enjoyed spending time with them at many family and company events.

Before others poisoned our relationship, I genuinely liked and respected Roger and tried my best to figure out and fix what had gone wrong.

Perhaps naively, I still held out hope that if we could talk privately, which he had refused to do for months, we could work things out. I wrote him a letter. I tried to see him. No response.

In the boardroom, I added that I felt good about all we'd accomplished over the past six years as well as our development prospects, at which point Roger stood up and screamed at me to "just get out."

I looked around to see the other executives staring down in stunned silence. Then slowly I stood up and said, "I'm sorry you feel this way, Roger. I'll be in my office if you need me."

He bellowed, "Good, get the hell out of here."

I took one last look at Bob Madden, Roger's senior vice president of operations and trusted "right hand," and Bob gave me a quick look that said to me, "Just go, we'll talk later."

We did talk later. More on that in a moment.

Six months prior, after years of courtship always to be left at the altar by several major media companies, including Turner Broadcasting and New World Entertainment, our company was acquired by CBS, sending our sinking stock from below my $17 strike price (wherein my stock options had any value) to a mind-boggling $46 per share in a matter of days. I owned more than 250,000 options.

But, as mentioned, in the process, my boss and friend Michael King (who had essentially built and run the company with his brothers Roger and Bob) was out.

The multiple hit series, many programs in development, and the five hundred-plus employees who reported to me were now under Roger's charge.

For reasons I believe had mostly to do with the fact that I reported to and was close with his brother, Roger clearly no longer wanted me around.

Roger and his sales guys were based on the East Coast. It was a classic, internecine turf war within the company.

It didn't help that, in the merger, CBS' in-house syndication and production division, called Eyemark, was folded into King World with all programming, development, and production reporting to me.

Here are excerpts from a companywide email sent by CBS CEO Leslie Moonves to announce the changes in January 2000.

### CBS MEMORANDUM

From: Leslie Moonves
To: ALL CBS EMPLOYEES

*January 19, 2000*
*Today we announced our new organizational structure for CBS Television's worldwide distribution operations. This union brings together King World Productions, Inc., Eyemark Entertainment, and CBS Broadcast International into a distribution group that makes the most of our great, complementary assets in management, programming, and sales.*

*All program development and production will be managed by Andy Friendly, named President, Programming and Production.*

As with any merger, there were people who were not happy with the new reporting arrangement. Not everyone in our newly combined production and distribution group liked the new arrangement, and the sniping and backstabbing started immediately.

Breaking news: No one likes losing power and control.

A real shit show of rivalries, lies, and leaks aimed at ingratiation to Roger ensued. I was already in Roger's crosshairs, and the added "incoming" directed at me was fatal. There were even attempts, some successful, at turning my top stars and producers against my team and me through a series of troll-style lies, innuendo, and character assassination.

Nice business.

I knew exactly who was doing it and why, and seriously considered hiring a team of the best detectives and lawyers in the country to go after them. In the end, for a range of issues and at the advice of my most trusted friends and advisers, I decided not to pursue it. I'd be lying if I didn't admit that a big part of me wishes I had. To this day I have kept documents and other evidence related to these events in a safe deposit box. I still think about this because of the damage it did to relationships I cared deeply about.

Once Roger took the reins, he began "managing me" with dialogue along the lines of what we all heard in that conference room, froze me out on one of the talk shows we were producing and distributing, and declined to invite me to key meetings.

But if these things were designed to get me to quit or provoke me into committing a fire-able offense, whereby he wouldn't have to pay me, the strategies failed. I continued to carry myself professionally and maintained my (outward) calm through all of it, even after the humiliation of being thrown out of the senior staff meeting.

Sitting in my office alone after that meeting, I felt oddly OK. Once I settled down and caught my breath, it dawned on me, "It's now the end and all the pain will soon be over." It was surreal; more relief than angst, in a way.

And I continued to stare at the CNBC ticker on my TV and in particular at the CBS symbol.

CBS' stock was already up five points and steadily climbing after just three hours of trading on strong rumors that Viacom was about to buy the company.

"On paper," as the expression goes, my remaining stock options (I had previously cashed in a large share of them after CBS bought us) were up over $1.5 million on the day, and again it was just 9:30 in the morning.

By the end of the trading session, the stock was up more than $10 a share as Viacom and CBS indeed announced the sale.

My remaining options had gained some $3.2 million in value in one day. It was almost dramatic enough a leap to distract me from any remaining queasiness from the staff meeting and all the other challenges to my resolve to stick it out these last few months.

The fact did not escape me that in 1973, my first full year as a junior researcher/writer at WNBC TV News at the age of 21, I earned just $8,000.

Or that in the last year of my dad's pioneering, wildly successful seventeen years at CBS, before resigning as CBS News president over a matter of journalistic principle, he made $100,000.

It was clear that any day now I, too, would be "resigning" from CBS at just about the same age my dad did, also as president of a programming division.

After a few days went by, and I still hadn't quit or done anything to warrant being fired, Roger King sent Madden to see me (so, yes, we did "talk later"). Bob told me it was over. I'd be paid in full, but Roger wanted to "go in a different direction."

For the first and only time in a more than thirty-year career in television to this point, I had been fired.

I wrote an upbeat, positive exit letter to my team of over five hundred, thanking them for all we'd achieved over the past six years and assuring them their best work was ahead of them. I said similar things to the press and "took the high road," as CBS communications head Chris Ender wrote to me in a thank-you note.

I also had a nice conversation with Leslie Moonves, who throughout the merger and my subsequent challenges was always willing to meet and talk with me, and was always kind and supportive.

He, too, thanked me for staying cool and for taking the high road by not litigating or going public with my experience to the press.

But while I lost the job I had once loved, I also gained something: As the poet Rudyard Kipling wrote in his famous poem "If," the hard-won lesson that keeping your cool means keeping some dignity…and in this case, my stock options as well. Here's part of Kipling's wonderful poem:

> *If you can keep your head when all about you*
> *Are losing theirs and blaming it on you,*
> *If you can trust yourself when all men doubt you,*
> *But make allowance for their doubting too;*
> *If you can wait and not be tired by waiting,*
> *Or being lied about, don't deal in lies,*
> *Or being hated, don't give way to hating,*
> *And yet don't look too good, nor talk too wise…*
>
> *…Yours is the Earth and everything that's in it, And -*
> *which is more - you'll be a man, my son!*

I'll be sharing the entire poem with you later in this book.

Despite how it ended, I had many great, productive, fascinating, wild and crazy times and experiences working with Michael, Roger, and the gang at King World over a fifteen-year period, first as a producer and later as an executive.

Wouldn't trade them.

Well, maybe that last six months.

I look forward to telling you more about them in the pages to follow, and also about the close friends and advisers who guided me through the rough ending, and about some of the strategies I learned that got me through this and many other mostly positive adventures in TV, and in life

OK, let's light this candle.

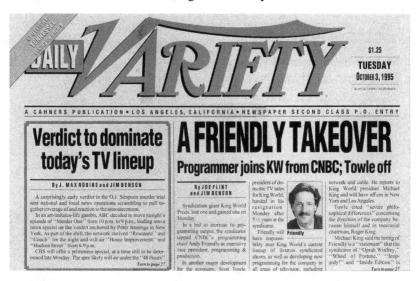

*The front-page Variety story that ran the day I was hired as executive
vice president of programming and production at King World*

*Leslie Moonves, me, and Whoopi Goldberg*

*Bernie Brillstein, Roger King, Martin Short, Michael King, and me at a press conference announcing The Martin Short Show at the 21 Club in New York*

*Roger King, Roseanne, Michael King, and I at the 21 Club in New York announcing Roseanne's talk show*

*Whoopi Goldberg, Cara Stein, Elton John, and me at the
NATPE convention, where Elton performed and we announced
Whoopi as the center square on Hollywood Squares*

# 2

## THEN, NOW, AND THINGS TO COME

The first of three kids, I weighed in at a healthy 7.5 pounds when I was born on November 6, 1951. That's the same week my dad's documentary series *See It Now*, with Ed Murrow, premiered on CBS. Harry Truman was president. We were at war with Korea, having triumphed in World War II just six years before. The Cold War was on and Julius and Ethel Rosenberg were sentenced to death for espionage. TV was brand new and only in black-and-white. It was the so-called Baby Boom following WWII. My generation is now called "Boomers." No wonder we created the counterculture and rebelled in the '60s. Boomers? Really? Not Gen Xers, or Millennials, or something cool?

And they wonder why we drink. (A classic Tom Snyder line.)

In the early 1900s my mom's parents, Louis and Anna Grynstein (their name was later changed to Greene), fled anti-Semitic oppression during a time of terrible pogroms and emigrated from Poland to Providence, Rhode Island. Louis escaped to America first, on a ship called the *Statendam*, in 1904. Shortly after, he sent money for his wife and son to join him: In 1906 Anna and their young son, my Uncle Sam, also fled to America.

*My mom's parents: Louis and Anna Grynstein*

Fourteen years later, following the births of several more siblings, my mother, Dorothy, was born.

My father's family on his mother's side, the Freundlichs (Friendly in English), came to the United States from Germany in the 1840s and eventually were one of the first Jewish families settled in the great Northwest, in Eugene, Oregon.

My great-grandfather Sampson Hiram Friendly (I was named for him, Andrew S.H. Friendly), started a successful general store and then became a supporter and benefactor of the University of Oregon, where a hall was named after him. He became the first mayor of Eugene.

Sampson's daughter Therese married traveling salesman Sam Wachenheimer from Providence and had my father, Ferdinand, in 1915 in New York, where they lived in a small apartment on the Upper West Side of Manhattan.

*The S.H. Friendly General Store, founded by my*
*great-grandfather Sampson Hiram Friendly, second from right*

My dad was an only child with severe dyslexia, which was not understood at the time. Despite showing signs of talent and creativity, and being a strong athlete, he struggled in school and was thought of as "slow" and a troublemaker, getting into scrapes with other students and teachers when frustrated by symptoms of dyslexia.

He had enormous energy and intelligence that went undetected until he began a career in radio. After attending junior college, he joined the U.S. Army, where he thrived as a reporter and a master sergeant and came into his own, both as a journalist and as a man. More on that later.

After the war he began a career in radio in Providence and changed his name from Ferdinand Wachenheimer to the more broadcast-ready Fred Friendly (his mom's maiden name) and went on to a distinguished career in broadcasting and education.

Of all his many achievements, nothing stands out more to me than the letter he sent his mother at twenty-nine, while he was as an army sergeant in WWII, helping liberate the Mauthausen concentration camp in Austria.

As a family we read his letter on the Jewish holidays, a tradition we've passed on for generations. I will be sharing his letter with you later in these pages.

After returning from the war and radio jobs in Providence, he moved to New York to pursue his career in the media capital.

That's where he met and married my mom, Dorothy. My mom, a talented writer and artist, was a researcher and reporter at *Time/Life* at the time. I came along a few years later, followed by my sister Lisa and brother David.

*Above, my parents, Fred and Dorothy, are pictured together aboard the Queen Mary ocean liner on a trip to Europe shortly after they were married in the late 1940s*

My dad, Edward R. Murrow and their team went on to pioneer TV news and documentaries at CBS, including those on Joe McCarthy, the plight of migrant workers, the war in Vietnam, the environment, and many more over a long and distinguished career during which he was also president of CBS News.

My dad famously resigned from CBS News over the network's decision not to carry critical Senate hearings on the Vietnam War; instead they ran a rerun of *I Love Lucy*.

A true pioneer of television news, he was portrayed by George Clooney in the 2005 feature film *Good Night, and Good Luck*, about the famed Murrow/McCarthy broadcast, which many feel led to the downfall of the Wisconsin senator. I will tell you that story in the pages to come. Now more than ever, I feel it must be repeated and passed down for future generations. I believe my dad would want me to, especially in today's political climate.

*This is me as a baby with my dad, Fred Friendly, at our family apartment in Peter Cooper Village, on the Lower East Side of Manhattan*

Mom was by Dad's side in the early years, but in time their marriage felt the pressures of Dad's job and nearly obsessive approach to work, which was key to his career success but challenging to marriage and raising three kids.

They both tried their best and were smart, caring parents and somehow, despite many ups and downs, including their eventual divorce and my mother's breakdown when I was thirteen, we kids survived and went on to live full and interesting lives.

As a kid I hung around the CBS Broadcast Center in Manhattan watching Dad and Murrow work, and later went to NBC at Rockefeller Center to watch Johnny Carson tape *The Tonight Show* and Dick Cavett tape his great late-night show at ABC down the street (I was lucky enough to get to know them both and produce Cavett later in my career). When I was thirteen, I became hooked on TV.

*In 1951, the year I was born, Chevrolet cars looked like this (© Image courtesy of General Motors)*

Over forty years of writing, producing, directing, and overseeing television shows and movies as an executive, I've pretty much had the career I dreamed of.

I worked at and produced programs for almost every major network and studio, including NBC (fourteen years), CBS, ABC, Discovery, PBS, King World, Paramount, MGM, Westinghouse, and others.

Along the way, I got to know and/or work with a wide range of some of the greatest names in entertainment, news, sports, and politics, including Richard Pryor, Tom Snyder, Jimmy Cagney, Clint Eastwood, Paul McCartney, Johnny Carson, Edward R. Murrow, Walter Cronkite, Tom Brokaw, Mike Wallace, Tim Russert, Dan Rather, Charlie Rose, Howard Stern, David Letterman, Billy Crystal, Robin Williams, Elton John, George Clooney, Oprah Winfrey, Roseanne, Whoopi Goldberg, Vin Scully, Robert Zemeckis, Muhammad Ali, Jim Brown, Michael Strahan, Tracey Ullman, Jane Fonda, and Garry Marshall, along with U.S. presidents Harry Truman, Dwight Eisenhower, Jimmy Carter, George H.W. Bush, Bill Clinton, and yes, Donald Trump.

I will be telling you about many of them, and many, many others in these pages.

Along the way, I've been blessed to be able to give back a little by teaching at my alma mater, the USC School of Cinematic Arts, lecturing at Stanford and UCLA, and raising money for and serving as president of the board of the L.A. Free Clinic, now the Saban Community Clinic.

In addition, I got to serve on and be president of the board of the venerable Hollywood Radio & Television Society. Former presidents include legends way beyond my status, such as Leslie Moonves. I also raised money for the Heroes Golf Course at the VA in Los Angeles, where vets play and work as part of their rehab and healing. I owe thanks to my friends, the legendary producer Steven Bochco and his powerhouse wife, Dayna, who got me involved and have done so much for the cause.

At my alma mater, my wife, Pat, and I fund a scholarship to help minority students at the USC School of Cinematic Arts. And with my friend David Zaslav, I have joined the board of Steven Spielberg's Shoah Foundation at the University of Southern California, dedicated to preserving the video testimonies of more than 53,000 survivors of genocides from the Holocaust to Rwanda, among others. With the team at Shoah, I'm working on a documentary about the liberators of the Nazi concentration camps in 1945, which will include my dad's letter from Mauthausen.

I've found life in my sixties, now far away from the center of the showbiz universe, to be a creative and satisfying time. After sixty-five trips around the sun, I look forward to sharing much of this with you in the pages to come, starting with Dad and Ed Murrow's seminal CBS broadcast on Senator Joseph McCarthy.

# 3

## TV NEWS COMES INTO ITS OWN: DAD AND EDWARD R. MURROW'S MOST IMPORTANT BROADCASTS AND *GOOD NIGHT, AND GOOD LUCK*

After struggling to get his career going after the war, my dad found his calling when he partnered with the legendary Edward R. Murrow, widely considered the most significant reporter in the history of radio and then television, along with Walter Cronkite.

Of all their groundbreaking work, none was more important than their *See It Now* programs on Sen. Joseph R. McCarthy. The story of those broadcasts was told in George Clooney's brilliant, Oscar-winning film *Good Night, and Good Luck*.

Here's a piece I wrote for the Hollywood Radio & Television Society (HRTS) Annual Year book about the *See It Now* March 9, 1954, report on Senator McCarthy, when I was president of the organization. It was published on the front page of *The Hollywood Reporter* as well.

I feel it bears repeating now, more than ever, as a reminder of what broadcast journalism was, is not now, but must be again in our endangered democracy.

Andy Friendly

*The Hollywood Reporter, Oct. 10, 2004*

## *See It Now* Flexed TV's Newfound Civic Muscle
## Program helped expose McCarthyism

*Editor's note: Today marks the 51st anniversary of CBS News' landmark* See It Now *broadcast that heralded the beginning of the end of the McCarthy era. The following is industry veteran Andy Friendly's perspective on that seminal television moment.*

*By Andy Friendly*

*I was born in November 1951, the same year the legendary Edward R. Murrow and my father, producer Fred Friendly, launched the pioneering documentary series* See It Now *on CBS. Television was in its infancy as Murrow, along with Jack Benny, Milton Berle, and a host of others, made the transition from radio to a brand-new medium.*

*As a kid, I grew up shining shoes at the studio, watching the team at* See It Now *and CBS Reports put together groundbreaking programs about the plight of migrant workers, the atomic bomb and a wide range of important issues as they learned how to use this exciting and daunting new tool called television.*

*Among their many award-winning programs, none were more important or required more courage than their reports on Sen. Joseph R. McCarthy in 1954, and one preceding it in 1953, about Air Force Lt. Milo Radulovich.*

*To set the scene for those who weren't born or may not have studied it, America in the postwar early '50s was in the grip of a national paranoia over a so-called communist threat. The idea that communists had infiltrated our governmental, cultural, educational and professional institutions and were about to take over our democracy was fueled and exploited in large measure by the cunning Junior Senator from Wisconsin whose last name inspired the term McCarthyism.*

*Still in its infancy, television news had yet to tackle major controversial issues. At this time, as my dad wrote in his*

19

*memoir after leaving CBS,* Due to Circumstances Beyond Our Control: *"The central nervous system of the vast broadcast and entertainment industry, including movies, television and radio, was conditioned to respond to blacklists and self-appointed policemen as though they were part of the constitutional process."*

*Hundreds of the industry's best producers, directors, writers, actors, and composers lost their careers and livelihoods because their names appeared in the insidious blacklisting book* Red Channels, *which was on the desks of top industry executives.*

*Most of those listed had little or no association with the Communist Party and were loyal, patriotic Americans who believed strongly in democratic ideals. They may have at one time in their youth attended a meeting or had a relative who went to a lecture or rally about communism or read a so-called subversive publication or may have been members of the American Civil Liberties Union, which McCarthy erroneously labeled as a front for the Communist Party.*

*As he and his minions continued to exploit this national paranoia for their own political benefit, McCarthy became more powerful and more feared in Washington, in Hollywood, and on Madison Avenue.*

*Against this backdrop of fear that had spread across the country, Murrow and Friendly risked their own careers by quietly setting out to look for a small story that would illustrate the bigger issue. They found it.*

*On Oct. 10, 1953, in their weekly program* See It Now, *they reported on the case of 26-year-old Air Force Lt. Milo Radulovich from Dexter, Mich., who was losing his commission because his father and sister were accused of being "left-wing sympathizers."*

*When the lieutenant refused to resign, the Air Force ordered his separation as a security risk. Producer Joe Wershba convinced Radulovich to go on camera. The young lieutenant said, "The Air Force has not questioned my loyalty in the slightest—only that my father and sister have read subversive newspapers. The only charge against me is that I have maintained a close relationship with them."*

*The Air Force was offered an opportunity to respond but refused. Instead, they sent senior officials to meet with Murrow and his team to try to get them to drop the broadcast, subtly reminding them that up to this point, they always enjoyed great access to the Air Force.*

*The producers informed CBS of their intention to go with the Radulovich program and invited network officials to view it before it aired. They declined, saying that they preferred to see it when it aired. The network declined as well to promote the broadcast, and Murrow and Friendly spent their own money to take an ad in* The New York Times.

*The tension was palpable that Tuesday night as the red light came on above Murrow's camera at CBS' Studio 41 in New York's Grand Central Station; live to the nation, Murrow launched into his summation following the interview and report on Radulovich.*

*"We believe that the son shall not bear the iniquity of the father, even though that iniquity be proved beyond all doubt, which in this case it is not. But we believe, too, that this case illustrates the urgent need for the armed services to communicate more fully than they have so far done the regulations and procedures to be followed in attempting to protect the national security and the rights of the individual at the same time. This is Edward R. Murrow reporting. Good night and good luck."*

*The phone lines at CBS stations around the country were overloaded with calls, ninety percent of which were supportive of Murrow and the broadcast. It was as if the tension of a nation had finally been broken.*

*A few weeks later, Radulovich was fully reinstated as a lieutenant, and Secretary of the Air Force Harold E. Talbott issued a lengthy and supportive statement.*

# Willing to Be Lucky

The New York Times *wrote:*

*The program marked perhaps the first time that a major network, CBS, and one of the country's most important industrial sponsors, Alcoa, consented to a program taking a vigorous editorial stand in a matter of national importance and controversy.*

*During the next few months, encouraged by the reaction to the Radulovich program, Murrow and his team continued putting together their seminal broadcast on McCarthy, exposing him mainly in his own words as the ruthless demagogue that he was.*

*The broadcast is widely acknowledged as the beginning of the end of one of our country's darkest period: McCarthyism, blacklisting, and the so-called red scare. Television news had arrived and had set a standard in courage and integrity that is considered a benchmark to this day.*

Thirteen years after writing that article I believe we as a nation, and the institution of the press (or the "fourth estate," as our country's founders envisioned it), are more vulnerable than ever.

It is important to add here Murrow's closing lines from the broadcast, written with my dad. Their words: cautionary and more critical than ever.

*We must not confuse dissent with disloyalty. We must remember always that accusation is not proof and that conviction depends upon evidence and due process of law. We will not walk in fear, one of another. We will not be driven by fear into an age of unreason, if we dig deep in our history and our doctrine, and remember that we are not descended from fearful men–not from men who feared to write, to speak, to associate, and to defend causes that were, for the moment, unpopular.*

To me, those words ring truer than ever right now, looking at the political landscape and our current president who has said, "The corrupt media is the enemy of the American people."

I'm often asked, "What would your Dad think about the way TV news covers the world today?"

I think he'd be horrified by the dearth of in-depth documentaries and reporting on the major networks, and by the blatantly political point of view of some cable news networks and anchors playing to their audiences' political stances for ratings alone.

I know he'd be asking where is the next Ed Murrow, Walter Cronkite, Bill Moyers, Tim Russert, or Gwen Ifill, with the credibility, trust, and courage to examine the important issues of our day the way Murrow held a mirror up to McCarthy or Cronkite explained Vietnam (which forever changed Americans' view of that unjust war).

*Ed Murrow and my dad working in their office at CBS*
*(CBS Photo Archive/CBS/Getty Images)*

I know he'd appreciate the work PBS is doing with its *NewsHour* (formerly *The MacNeil/Lehrer Report*) and *Frontline* series, and some of the good work still being done at broadcast and cable networks when serious breaking news happens. He'd also appreciate some of the fine documentaries being done on Showtime, HBO, Amazon, Netflix, ESPN, and others.

But apart from that, there are virtually no serious in-depth documentaries on the major broadcast networks today, and that would not please the old man.

In short, to quote a phrase: He's likely "rolling in his grave." In talking about what Dad would think about the state of news today, I can think of no better answer than my brother Richard Mark's: "He'd be urging the media to do better, of course, but then he would probably go out and invent some new method of communication, fit to the moment, to help a mass audience understand the big ideas. *See It Now* took a bunch of camera folks skilled at newsreels and invented the TV documentary. The Michele Clark program for minority journalists opened up opportunities in media for people of color and changed the face of TV and print, bringing it that much closer to the communities being reported. Who would have thought that the Media and Society Seminars (which Dad created with Columbia University for PBS, and are still airing to this day) would be engaging TV and become THE forum for ideas in the '80s and '90s? I think if he were alive, he would dream up some idea for communication in the democracy that would start out sounding nutty and end up being real and powerful. He'd be the one to figure out how to create a social network that would make people value and want real news and communication over empty calories. But since he ain't around, it's up to us."

In 2005, when George Clooney and his talented producer Grant Heslov decided to make *Good Night, and Good Luck*, their film about the *See It Now* McCarthy programs, our family and many of Dad's friends and colleagues were excited and knew it was in capable hands but a bit nervous nonetheless.

Movies, after all, are famous for sometimes taking "liberties" and "creative license" with facts when dealing with historical events.

To Clooney and Heslov's credit, they could not have been more meticulous about sticking to the facts and getting it right.

They and their team were welcoming and inclusive to our family and proactively asked us for notes on their script. In an early draft they had Dad, played by Clooney, smoking; while Murrow famously smoked three packs a day, Dad didn't smoke at all. We let them know and they corrected that detail about my dad; just one small example of how they reached out to us, Milo Radulovich, Dad's close friends and fellow producers Joe and Shirley Wershba (who were on set and of course featured in the film), and anyone else they could find to make sure what went up on the screen was as accurate as possible.

George directed the film and brilliantly chose to do it in black-and-white, which, among other things, allowed him seamlessly to cut in the actual black-and-white footage of McCarthy in his vile speeches and congressional inquisitions rather than trying to cast an actor. At the first table read with the cast, he told me he felt no actor could match the senator's persona of pure evil as well as the man himself. The result created a true sense of realism and drama.

While he could have easily cast himself in the bigger, more heroic role of Murrow, Clooney chose to cast the talented actor David Strathairn in that role instead and cast himself as my dad. He even put on a bunch of weight for the role and heard many jokes about how he wanted to play the more handsome guy. Clearly the opposite.

George and Grant wanted our input on their mannerisms, dress, and speaking styles, and invited us to the first table read of the script with the entire cast, followed by a tour of the meticulously accurate sets they had designed and built re-creating the 1954 CBS broadcast facility to a tee on their sound stage.

George, who had co-starred early in his TV career with Pat on an episode of CBS' *Murder, She Wrote*, could not have been nicer and made a huge deal about her when she joined me at the table read.

During filming, a studio team shot a behind-the-scenes feature about the making of the film, which you can see as a bonus feature on the DVD, if you're interested. It provides an in-depth look at the meticulous process of making *Good Night, and Good Luck*.

*Me, Pat, and George Clooney on a visit to the*
*set of "Good Night, and Good Luck"*

Here are a couple of excerpts from the making-of film, including comments by George Clooney, Grant Heslov, Ruth Friendly, and myself:

*Ruth Friendly: It was a fearful time when people were afraid what would happen to them. What could you say or couldn't you say. That's hard to translate in today's world. Until then, there hadn't really been a controversial program on CBS.*

*George Clooney: This was real. People were terrified of their neighbors, they were terrified of the nuclear bomb, they were terrified of losing their jobs, and to have somebody step up and go "everybody walk out of the shadows that's not afraid right now" and suddenly it was seventy percent of the country, and they had no idea.*

*Grant Heslov: Back then there weren't any shows like this. It was at this period of time that Murrow, who was a journalist, a real journalist, who decides that there are not two sides to every story; they're going to take a side on a story and they're going to editorialize. And that was a huge thing then.*

*Andy Friendly: They were, as Murrow said, not descended from fearful men, and they were very aware of their heritage. Yes, their lives and their futures were at stake, but more important to them than that, even, was that they knew what was at stake for the country, and that if they missed, if they in any way got the story wrong... the country could be subjected to ten or fifteen more years of escalating McCarthyism.*

When the film was finished and just before it opened, George invited us all to his beautiful home for a festive dinner and screening of the movie.

Our whole family, Milo Radulovich, the Wershbas, Ed Murrow's son Casey, along with all my dad's friends and colleagues, could not have been more proud of the film, or more pleased with the entire experience.

The film garnered rave reviews as well as many high-profile award nominations, including Oscar nominations for Best Picture, Screenplay for George and Grant, Lead Actor for David Strathairn, and Best Director for George.

Pat and I occasionally bump into George and Grant at functions around town and always thank them on behalf of Dad, Ed, and our families for their brilliant, important film, which in my view is more crucial now than ever.

If you haven't watched it lately, I urge you to do so, and to remember Murrow and Friendly's courageous and pioneering use of the television medium back in 1954 at its inception, and the vital role that TV news holds in our democracy.

That would be Dad's wish.

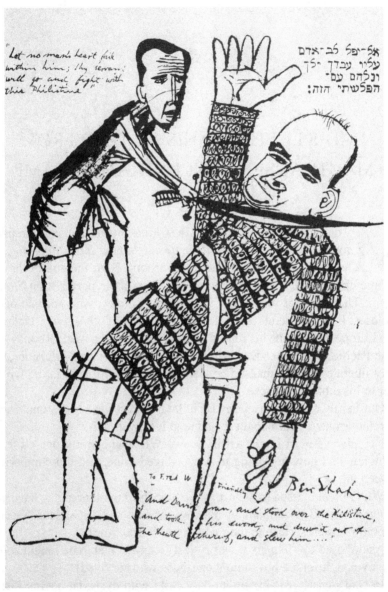

*A drawing by the great American artist Ben Shahn, which he gave to my dad after the McCarthy program aired*
*Art © Estate of Ben Shahn/Licensed by VAGA, New York, NY*

# 4

## DAD'S LETTER TO HIS MOTHER FROM MAUTHAUSEN CONCENTRATION CAMP

My dad spent most of the war in the China-Burma theater as a reporter for the Army newspaper, the *China-Burma-India Roundup,* and as a motivational speaker to the troops. Near the end of the war, he came up with the idea of swapping places with a reporter from *Stars & Stripes.* That reporter turned out to be Andy Rooney, who became one of his closest lifelong friends and a decades-long star of *60 Minutes.* Dad went on to Europe to continue his reporting for *CBI Roundup*, while Rooney went to the Pacific. Soon after Dad witnessed the 11th Armored Division of the Army liberate the Mauthausen concentration camp in Austria, he wrote a letter to his mother, Therese.

Our family reads it during Jewish holidays every year. Over time, friends and relatives have heard about it, and read it as well.

I've always been interested in how WWII changed my dad's life and worldview and how not going to war changed mine, and the comparisons between the two.

While I feel blessed to have drawn a high draft number and to have gone to college instead of Vietnam, in many ways I envy my dad and his "Greatest Generation" their service to their country in World War II.

As opposed to Vietnam, it was a "just" war that had to be fought and, as with my dad, it forged boys into men (those who survived).

In Dad's case, growing up an only child with dyslexia, having lost his dad at 11, and facing the challenges I described earlier; the Army, he said, "made a man out of me." He had just two years of junior college and self-deprecatingly referred to the Army as "my Rhodes scholarship."

Here is the letter:

*May 10, 1945*

*Dear Mother:*

*In just a few days I will be in an airplane on my way back to the APO to which you write me. Before I leave Europe, I must write this letter and attempt to convey to you that which I saw, felt and gasped at as I saw a war and a frightened peace stagger into a perilous existence. I have seen a dead Germany...If it is not dead it is certainly ruptured beyond repair. I have seen the beer hall where the era of the inferno and hate began, and as I stood there in the damp moist hall where Nazidom was spawned, I heard only the dripping of a bullet-pierced beer barrel and the ticking of a clock, which had already run out the time of the bastard who made the Munich Beer hall a landmark. I saw the retching vomiting of the stone and mortar which had once been listed on maps as Nurnheim, Regensburg, Munich, Frankfurt, Augsburg, Linz, and wondered how a civilization could ever again spring from cities so utterly removed from the face of the Earth by weapons the enemy taught us to use at Coventry and Canterbury. I have met the Germans, have examined the Storm trooper, his wife and his heritage of hate, and I have learned to hate – almost with as much fury as the G.I. who saw his buddy killed at the Bulge, almost as much as the Pole from Bridgeport who lost 100 pounds at Mauthausen, Austria. I have learned now and only now that this war had to be fought. I wish I might have done more. I envy with a bottomless and endless spirit, the American soldier who may tell his grandchildren that with his hands he killed Germans.*

*That which is in my heart now I want you and those dear to us to know and yet I find myself completely incapable of putting it into letter form...I think if I could sit down in our living room or the den at 11 President, I might be able to convey a portion of the dismal, horrible and yet titanic mural which is Europe today. Unfortunately, I won't be able to do that for months or maybe a year, and by then the passing of time may dim the memory. Some of the scenes will live just so long as I do—some of the sounds, like the dripping beer, like the firing of a Russian Tommy gun, will always bring back the thought of something I may try to forget, but never will be able to do.*

*For example, when I go to the Boston Symphony, when I hear waves of applause, no matter what the music is, I shall be traveling back to a town near Linz where I heard applause unequaled in history, and where I was allowed to see the ordeal which our fellow brothers and sisters of the human race have endured. To me Poland is no longer the place where Chopin composed, or where a radio station held out for three weeks–to me Poland is the place from which the prisoners of Mauthausen came, when I think of the Czechs, I will think of those who were butchered here, and that goes for the Jews, the Russians, the Austrians, the people of 15 different lands–yes, even the Germans who passed through this Willow Run of death. This was Mauthausen.*

*I want you to remember the word...I want you to know, I want you to never forget or let our disbelieving friends forget, that your flesh and blood saw this. This was no movie, no printed page. Your son saw this with his own eyes and in doing this aged 10 years.*

*Mauthausen was built with a half-million rocks, which 150,000 prisoners–18,000 was the capacity–carried up on their backs from a quarry 800 feet below. They carried it up steps so steep that a captain and I walked it once and were winded, without a load. They carried granite and made eight trips a day...and if they stumbled, the S.S. men pushed them into the quarry. There are 285 steps, covered with blood. They called it the steps of death. I saw the shower room (twice or three times the size of our bathroom), a chamber lined with tile and topped with sprinklers where 150 prisoners at a time were disrobed and ordered in for a shower which never gushed forth from the sprinklers because the chemical was gas. When they ran out of gas, they merely sucked all the air out of the room. I talked to the Jews who worked in the crematory, one room adjacent, where six and seven bodies at a time were burned. They gave these jobs to the Jews because they all died anyhow, and they didn't want the rest of the prisoners to know their own fate. The Jews knew theirs, you see. I saw their emaciated bodies in piles like cords of wood...the stench of death, of decomposition of human flesh, of uncontrolled body fluids, of burned, charred bones. I saw the living skeletons, some of whom, regardless of our medical corps work, will die and be in piles like that in the next few days. Malnutrition doesn't stop the day that food is administered. Don't get the idea that these people were all derelicts, all just masses of people...some of them were doctors, authors, some of them American citizens, and a scattered few were GI's. A Navy Lt. still lives to tell the story. I saw where they lived; I saw where the sick died, three and four in a bed, no toilets, no nothing. I saw the look in their eyes. I shall never stop seeing the expression in the eyes of the anti-Franco former prisoners who have been given the job of guarding the S.S. men who were captured.*

*And how does the applause fit in. Mother, I walked through countless cell blocks filled with sick, dying people–300 in a room twice the size of our living room and as we walked in–there was a ripple of applause and then an inspiring burst of applause and cheers, and men who could not stand up sat up and whispered though they tried to shout it–Vive L'Americansky... Vive L'Americansky...the applause, the cheers, those faces of men with legs the size and shape of rope, with ulcerated bodies, weeping with a kind of joy you and I will never, I hope, know. Vive L'Americansky...I got a cousin in Milwaukee...We thought you guys would come...Vive L'Americansky...Applause–gaunt, hopeless faces at last filled with hope. One younger man asked me something in Polish which I could not understand but I did detect the word "yit"...I asked an interpreter what he said–the interpreter blushed and finally said, "He wants to know if you are a Jew." When I smiled and stuck out my mitt and said "yes"... he was unable to speak or show the feeling that was in his heart. As I walked away, I suddenly realized that this had been the first time I had shaken hands with my right hand. That, my dear, was Mauthausen.*

*I will write more letters in days to come. I want to write one on the Russians...I want to write and tell you how I sat next to Patton and Tolbukhin at a banquet at the Castle of Franz Joseph. I want to write and tell you how the Germans look in defeat, how*

31

*Munich looked in death, but those things sparkle with excitement and make good reading. This is my Mauthausen letter. I hope you will see fit to let Bill Braude and the folks read it. I would like to think that all the Wachenheimers and all the Friendlys and all our good Providence friends would read it. Then I want you to put it away and every Yom Kippur I want you to take it out and make your grandchildren read it.*

*For, if there had been no America, we, all of us, might well have carried granite at Mauthausen.*

*All my love,*

*F.F.*

Quite a letter. At twenty-nine, his ability to paint word pictures, first developed in his early radio work in Providence at WEAN before the war, which would be the hallmark of his future work, was clear. This letter is the memorial of my dad bearing witness to the Holocaust, and passing it on teaches future generations to remember the horror of the Nazis and the bravery of the "Greatest Generation" who stopped them.

After the Germans surrendered, Dad returned to New Delhi, where as a reporter for the *The China-Burma-India Roundup*, he recounted what he had witnessed in Europe along with stories of the continuing war in Asia.

Top generals brought their officers together to hear Dad lecture on his experiences. By then he had become a master sergeant and had developed quite a reputation as a dynamic, larger-than-life speaker and reporter.

After one presentation surrounded by soldiers, the company commander invited Dad to join him and other top brass for lunch in the officers' mess hall. His lifelong friend and army bud Bob Bernstein, former president of Random House, recounts this story in his book, *Speaking Freely*. In this story, Bernstein says it was the colonel in charge who invited FWF to eat with the officers. "He told the colonel he was honored but he was an enlisted man and felt he should eat with the enlisted men. The colonel looked shocked, but he didn't make it an order. When I asked Fred about it, he said, 'I think it's important that the enlisted men have a chance to ask me questions and talk to me about what happened, rather than just a few officers." One of my favorite Fred stories.

Inspired in great part by my dad's letter, written seventy years ago, it is one of the great challenges of my life and an honor to serve on the USC Shoah Foundation Board of Councilors, dedicated to preserving the video remembrances of more than 53,000 victims of the Holocaust and genocides all over the world, throughout history.

*My father, U.S. Army Master Sergeant Fred Friendly, in Delhi, India, during World War II Photo Credit: U.S. Army Signal Corps*

*My father's mother, Therese Friendly-Wachenheimer*

# 5

## MOM

My mom, Dorothy, was a talented painter and sculptor, a skilled writer, and extremely smart and stylish.

She was Dad's equal producing partner when at twenty-eight, and with little money, she and Dad moved from Providence to New York City to embark on careers in broadcasting and journalism.

Mom graduated from the prestigious Rhode Island School of Design and throughout her life painting, sculpting, and mosaic work remained her passion.

But at the time, to help pay for their tiny East Side studio apartment, while Dad was trying to get something going, she landed a job at *Time/Life* as a researcher. She became the breadwinner and also worked after-hours as a creative equal and writing partner to my dad on various radio, TV, and movie projects they were trying to sell.

She was quiet and graceful with a fun laugh and provided a calming, stabilizing effect on my dad, who was always the loudest, most excited, and at times boisterous person in the room.

In the early years of dating and first few years of marriage, they were a great complementary team.

When my dad pitched Edward R. Murrow on doing a record album documenting the greatest historical moments of the 20th century, he and my Mom worked together on it.

With the advance money from Columbia Records (they only got the deal because there was a musicians strike going on and CBS needed something to keep its empty studios going), Mom and Dad moved from their tiny studio apartment to a new family apartment development in the East 30s called Peter Cooper Village.

There, in their relatively large one-bedroom apartment, they held dinner parties with Murrow, Columbia Records president Goddard Lieberson, and many of the top writers, authors, artists, and producers of the day.

The album entitled *I Can Hear It Now* was a success, again partly due to the dearth of music being sold as a result of the strike, along with Murrow narrating it. He was a giant star on radio for CBS in the war years, and just before the advent of TV. CBS, Dad, and Murrow made a deal to do several more, which led to my parents' first sense of financial stability. It also led to a strong partnership with Murrow, which ultimately took them into the new medium of TV.

A year later, the pioneering documentary series *See It Now* was born, and so was I. Within a year or so, with the TV and record deals, we were able to move to a house on Fieldston Road in the Riverdale section of the Bronx, just up the West Side Highway from Manhattan.

Ruth Friendly, my other mom (I never liked the term "stepmom" and consider her a second mom), lives there to this day, and it's great fun to be able to visit and occasionally stay in the home I grew up in, surrounded by family and old friends. It connects my life through the decades, all the way back to childhood, in the simplest, most basic way. I feel very fortunate to have had that blessing throughout all these years.

We moved to Riverdale in 1953, when I was two. Shortly after, my sister Lisa came along, then my brother David. Life was good in a *Leave It to Beaver* (classic, early family sitcom) kind of way.

By then Dad's career in partnership with Murrow was off and running, and Mom, while still involved with Dad's work, spent most of her time taking care of us. She had help from Dell, a wonderful, big, tough Jamaican woman who took us to church with her in Harlem on occasion. Dell cooked, cleaned, and kept us kids in line. Big time. In today's parlance we'd have told you, "Dell don't play."

In the summers we rented a house in the fishing village of Menemsha on the tiny island of Martha's Vineyard, off Cape Cod, Massachusetts. Mom, Lisa, David, Dell, and I spent several summers there, with Dad flying up on weekends to be with us.

Our next-door neighbor in the Vineyard was the brilliant, legendary composer and lead conductor of the New York Philharmonic Orchestra: Leonard Bernstein. His daughter Jamie was my first girlfriend/crush at age six. We'd go clamming and swimming together with our families.

When Dad was there, we'd hitchhike into the village and buy swordfish and lobsters right off the fishing boats as they came into dock. On the way home, we'd stop at the local vegetable stand and buy fresh corn. At night, a bunch of neighbors and friends would hit the beach below our houses for clambakes.

Back in New York, Mom took the three of us kids to school, swim and tennis lessons, and we went skiing and sledding at nearby Van Cortlandt Park.

My favorite memory of my Mom, and I can see it as clearly now as if it just happened, is being dropped off by the carpool from the Dodge Nursery School a few blocks away on a fall day when all the leaves on our tree-lined street were in full color. She was wearing a long, red, plaid skirt and stood with her arms open to welcome me home from school. I remember feeling completely safe and happy as I ran across the lawn and jumped into her arms. That's the memory of my mother I'll always choose first, because as the years went by so did some of the safe and happy times.

Mom and Dad grew apart, in great part due to his nearly complete attention on his work, and also to her being left alone with us kids most of the time, away from the work, the adult and social interaction that marked their early years together. Mom became isolated, lonely and somewhat resentful as Dad's career skyrocketed and he spent more and more time at the office, and around the world, with Murrow and his colleagues at CBS News.

The impact of Dad's focus on work on my parents' relationship and on Mom's relationship with us kids was major. She fell into a depression and eventually ended up in a breakdown. She was hospitalized for a couple weeks at the Montefiore Hospital nearby, and my saddest, scariest memory of her was when we went to visit her there.

In time, and with the help of her doctors, she improved; but there was irreparable damage to the marriage, and a year or so after Mom's breakdown my parents divorced. Mom was not able to take care of us in her fragile condition, so it was decided that the children would stay in the house with Dad, and Mom got an apartment in Manhattan, where we visited her a couple of times a week.

As she improved, she returned to her artwork and enjoyed living in the city, right next to Lincoln Center, where she attended concerts and opera with us kids, her sister Irene and brother Bob, and several old friends she kept throughout her life. She retained her great sense of style and quiet dignity.

Sadly, she never quite seemed to get over my dad. He and the bitter divorce, to an extent, appeared to be always in her thoughts. She never remarried. Often she brought up the divorce to us kids, even into her later years, which led to pressures in our relationship. I'd always hoped she'd get over it and tried to get her to let it go, but she just couldn't.

She always worried about money and what would happen to her if the alimony checks ended. If he died, would she have to move out of her rent-controlled apartment? As Lisa, David, and I began to find some success, we reassured her we'd never let that happen, but I don't think she ever felt completely secure.

When her apartment converted from rentals to condos, the first thing I did was buy it for her with pretty much all the money I had managed to save. She seemed to finally believe, I think for the first time, that she'd be secure and would never have to leave. I was very happy to be able to do that for her.

She lived there until her death at the age of eighty-two, of heart failure. It came suddenly and, thankfully, she did not suffer. We held a celebration of her life at the small swim club on the Hudson River in Riverdale where she took us to swim and play tennis when we were kids. It was a loving appreciation of her, attended by many friends and family members.

Many wonderful memories were shared, and at my request, Ruth's middle son, Michael Mark, a talented professional musician, sang James Taylor's moving ballad "You Can Close Your Eyes."

Pat and I keep several of Mom's beautiful watercolors in our home, and I see them and think of her every day. I love you, Mom, and I miss you and your red plaid dress.

The thing I'll always appreciate most about my Mom is that she always made me feel like a winner, even when I struggled with math in middle school or screwed up in any number of ways growing up.

I believe that's the most important gift a parent can give a child, and I try to do the same with my gang of nieces, nephews, and grandkids.

Mom's unwavering support and love, along with her great intelligence and sense of style, were her greatest gifts to Lisa, David, and me.

*Me, Lisa and Dell on vacation in Jamaica*

*Pat and me in front of my childhood home in
Riverdale on a visit a few years back*

# 6

## THE MERGER

My family and closest friends are the most important people in my life.

That's hardly a groundbreaking statement, I know.

I grew up in the 1950s watching the first family sitcoms and dramas, like *Leave It to Beaver*, *Ozzie and Harriet,* and *Father Knows Best*, but my family life turned out to be anything but the traditional, all-American, Norman Rockwell portrait of family bliss.

When my parents' marriage broke up in the mid-1960s, divorce was nowhere near as common as it is today, and there was a real stigma attached to it for all but especially for the children involved.

This, combined with my mother's depression and my dad's sixteen-hour, seven-days-a-week work schedule at CBS News, led David, Lisa and me into an early independence. It was very different from the way I see kids growing up today.

By age thirteen, I was off with my friends playing sports, taking the IRT subway to Manhattan to hang out in the Village, going to Knicks games, and trying to sneak into the Metropole and other clubs to get a glimpse of rock bands and strippers.

As opposed to kids growing up in the digital world today, some of whom are in touch with their parents pretty much all the time, my Mom and Dad rarely knew what we were doing.

This was by no means unique to the children of divorced parents. There were, of course, no cell phones or Internet then, and kids in general were much more independent. The general rule then: Be home by dinner or let your folks know if you won't be.

# Willing to Be Lucky

By the time I went off to Stockbridge School, a small, progressive boarding school in Stockbridge, Massachusetts, to escape the mess at home when I was fourteen, I was pretty much on my own.

With famous alumni such as Chevy Chase, Christopher Guest, and Arlo Guthrie, Stockbridge was a small, cool, co-ed school that fostered independent and creative thinking and study outside of the strict and often too-difficult (for me) curriculum I faced in math and science at Riverdale. I prospered there in my schoolwork, on the basketball and tennis teams, and socially, along with my close friend Andy Cohen, whom I'd grown up with in Stockbridge, where our families had summer cottages on the lake near Tanglewood, in the Berkshire Mountains.

Under the visionary leadership of headmaster-founder Hans Maeder, it was the kind of school where, if you did your schoolwork and chores, you were rewarded with independence and freedom.

You could even build your own "log cabin" in the woods and hang out there on weekends if you and a few pals were willing to chop down trees and do the work to build it. Andy and I did…and we, along with our buds, had big fun. (Did I mention it was co-ed?)

After striking out for nearly all of my sophomore and junior years, a classmate named Nancy finally let me be her boyfriend when I was a senior. A pretty and smart "teen goddess" to me, she had been going with a (since-graduated) senior for two years and was much more "experienced" than me. Let's just say that my education that year extended beyond the classroom. To quote Sir Paul: "Well, she was just seventeen. You know what I mean."

A couple nights a week I'd sneak out of my dorm and climb a ladder to her dorm window and spend a couple hours furthering my "education" before returning to my dorm before dawn. As Dan Rather, the legendary CBS anchor, used to tell me when I profiled him on a documentary for PBS: "This story has the added advantage of being true."

Needless to say, at seventeen, it was a very good year.

After graduating from Stockbridge (Dad was the graduation speaker and delivered a truly inspiring speech), I went off to college in L.A., at Occidental, where President Obama spent his first two years of college before transferring to Columbia, and then I went on to USC Film School.

I'd talk to my folks once a week or so. I'd come home for winter, spring, and summer breaks and reconnect with the gang. Sometimes I'd bring home one of my student films and play them for my family.

One we made about a Vegas showgirl named Sunny dancing nude among burned-out, rusted cars in the desert in a sincere but lame homage to the great New Wave Italian director Antonioni left my wonderful step-grandmother Henrietta in shock and I'm certain my parents wondering why they were spending so much money on my fancy education. To their credit, they never voiced anything but support and encouragement as always. Sorry, Grandma.

Hey, I'm not necessarily proud of this crap, people.

The only good thing that came from my parents' divorce when I was fourteen was my dad getting remarried a couple years later to Ruth Mark, a bright, upbeat, attractive fifth grade teacher from Scarsdale, New York, just up the road from where we lived in the Bronx.

Recently widowed, Ruth brought with her three terrific sons: Jon, Michael, and Richard.

Jon and Michael were a couple years older, and Richard was a couple of years younger than me. Smart, talented, caring, great guys with whom Lisa, David, and I bonded quickly, and for life.

They had lost their beloved Dad, Sandor, to a sudden heart attack and were bravely adjusting to their new life and family, as were Lisa, David, and I.

Naturally it was a bit awkward at first and a major adjustment for all, but due to Ruth's wonderful teaching and parenting skills and her ability to relate to Lisa, David, and me so well, while being a steadying and calming force for my dad and all of us…family life improved and for the first time in a while I got to see what a happy family could be.

I remain extremely close to Ruth, still going strong now at ninety-three, still driving around Manhattan, going to theater and opera. Still active in her many charitable and civic groups. Still "getting it done." Sharp as a tack. Always there for her friends and all of our family. I treasure her.

I'm closer than ever with the three great brothers she gave me and consider them, their wives, and kids, along with the rest of Pat's and my wonderful, growing family on both coasts among the greatest gifts of my life.

*Here is a shot from Ruth's 90th birthday party with the Mark/Friendly clan, New York, February 2014*

*Pat was under the weather and could not make the long wintertime trip to New York but called in a wonderful toast.*

*L-R: Catie Mark, Alice Mark, Lisa Friendly, Noah Mark, James Nicholson, Maddie Friendly, Christopher Nicholson, Priscilla Friendly, David Friendly, Maura Harway Mark, Richard Mark, Ruth Friendly, Michael Mark, Mary Mark, Ronen Kohn, John Kohn, Aaron Mark, Andrew Friendly, Jon Mark, B.K. Mark, Andy Friendly, Hannah Mark, Ramona Orley, Jason Orley*

*Pat and I celebrating our 30th wedding anniversary with our gang, 2016*

*L-R: Bob and Ann Osher, Will Hookstratten, Gabbi Chickering, Eddie Osher, Kate Osher and fiancé Will Fay, Marion, Erin and John Hookstratten, Erin's fiancé Rob Kelley.*

*Ruth and I at my nephew Noah Mark's wedding to Catie Haub, 2016*

# 7

## THE BEATLES LIVE IN BOSTON

The best times growing up were in the summer.

My first seven summers were spent in the tiny fishing town of Menemsha on Martha's Vineyard.

At age eight, I started going to Camp Robinson Crusoe next to Old Sturbridge Village, an hour up the Mass Turnpike from our new summer cabin in Stockbridge, Massachusetts. The new cabin was a couple hours from New York so Dad could drive up from the city on weekends. When we were on the Vineyard, he had to fly up.

For two months in July and August for six consecutive summers, I was the ultimate camper. Away from the pressures of schoolwork, the growing stress in my parents' marriage, and the bitter winters of New York, I found complete happiness.

Swimming, boating, camping, baseball, tennis, campfires with s'mores, folk songs, and spooky stories told by cool counselors were all part of seemingly endless summer days and nights on scenic lakes in the gorgeous Massachusetts foothills just east of the Berkshires. And it was co-ed!

I held hands on a walk in the woods with my first real girlfriend, Ellen, a pretty brunette with a pageboy haircut. That lasted all summer and picked up again for the next two summers; after she left camp, the equally adorable Lisie became my girlfriend as we entered our teenage years.

Camp was my oasis. At the demanding Riverdale Country Day School, attended by Jack and Bobby Kennedy decades before me, I did OK with English and history and did well in sports, but I struggled with math, science, and language. (I was much more interested in girls, rock 'n' roll, and sports, I'm afraid.)

But I was in my element at camp.

Tall and a decent athlete, a guitar player in the camp rock band that performed at the weekly dances, I was a leader of sorts. Along with my best friend, Paul Cantor, I was elected co-president of the camp when I was fourteen in my last summer, the summer of 1966.

Life couldn't get any better–as the senior members of the camp, we ruled!

We were the oldest, the coolest, and the best athletes. Over the years our band had become pretty good and we rocked the sounds of the Young Rascals, The Byrds, The Rolling Stones, The Beatles, and The Standells ("Dirty Water").

My brother David and his buddies, who were in a group of campers four years younger (Lisa had come for a year but went on to riding camp), would sneak out to hear us play. David also rooted me on when I played number two or three singles and doubles in tennis matches against other camps. As always, I included him in all I did and looked out for him as he did for me.

As the summers went by, we gained more and more independence and lived farther out in the woods and relied more on ourselves for everything. We chopped our own wood and made all our own meals on wooden stoves. There was no electricity or indoor plumbing except at the "canteen," the rec hall a few hundred yards away.

Bob Hill, who ran the camp he took over from his father, believed in camping as a way to turn young boys and girls into strong, self-sufficient, self-reliant teenagers.

Along with cooking, cleaning, chopping wood, and other chores, we went on brutal and difficult camping and canoeing trips for days on end down the Connecticut River, sometimes in bad weather, cold, and rain with just the gear and food we could take with us. No shortcuts, no hot showers, no early returns, no side trips to McDonald's. Girls and boys together, often filthy, tired, hungry. And with hormones raging at fourteen.

One sunny, gorgeous, blue-sky day, paddling down a winding river, with my girlfriend Lisie in her bikini in the front of the canoe, I felt like life couldn't get any better. And then it did.

Upon returning from a five-day canoe trip in late July 1966, we got the coolest, most mind-blowing news of our young lives. We were going to see The Beatles, live at Suffolk Downs Race Track near Boston, on August 18 … and we were going to be in the second row directly in front of the stage. The father of a camper in our group, Patti Burnham, was one of the promoters of the concert and arranged tickets for us.

As they were for many of our generation, The Beatles were an existential, supernatural force in our lives. They were gods.

From the first time I heard "I Want to Hold Your Hand" coming from the little AM radio in my dad's red Mustang in January 1964, as we were coming back from a sleigh ride on the snow-covered golf course at Van Cortlandt Park in the Bronx, the music of The Beatles literally changed my life.

Many others have said this much better than I can, but there was something so exciting, so liberating, and so cool about that single song, followed by "She Loves You," "All My Loving," and on and on.... It was truly explosive.

It was unlike any of the music we had heard. While we loved The Four Seasons, The Beach Boys, and other great American bands, the sound coming from Liverpool, England, was different. The beats and melodies were sharper, hipper, and somehow more dangerous. The sound, the look, the style of the "Fab Four" signaled a spirit of hipness and sexuality as we were making our way through adolescence; a kind of rebelliousness in my friends and me that was beyond exciting. It was empowering. These guys were cool and we could be, too, if we grew our own Beatle cuts.

I learned to play the guitar and played a few of their songs and tried to dress and act like them. Then I saw them perform on *The Ed Sullivan Show*, and heard them in their press conferences. I was taken by the way they dressed, talked, thought, and acted; irreverent, funny, making fun of grown-ups and the establishment.

It opened up the world to me and millions and millions of my contemporaries.

When I heard I'd be going to see The Beatles live, in the second row no less, I thought my head would explode with excitement. My friends Paul, Alan, my girlfriend Lisie, and the rest of our group were beyond excited. It was a kind of anticipation I can't really begin to describe except to use words like "delirious," which we were, and "pure joy," which we experienced. My whole body buzzed with anticipation as we boarded the yellow school bus and headed up the Mass Pike to Boston on the afternoon of August 18.

By the time we arrived at the racetrack, just outside of Boston, my heart was pounding. When we walked past the sold-out crowd of 25,000 to our center-stage seats in the second row, we were literally coming unglued.

We sat directly across from the giant stage that had been constructed on the infield of the racetrack, just in front of the finish line. The track itself was all that separated us from the stage as four or five fantastic opening acts breezed through their polished sets. They included The Remains, a great local band; Bobby Hebb ("Sunny"); The Cyrkle ("Red Rubber Ball," "Turn Down Day"); and the fabulous, Phil Spector-produced Ronettes ("Be My Baby," among other hits).

*Me with a Beatles haircut, wearing my uniform on the
last day of school at Riverdale Country Day, 1966*

*Note the ankle-length white Levi's, which were
all the fashion rage at the time.*

*(Were we expecting a flood?)*

I had been to a couple small concerts before but nothing like this. This was amazing!

When The Ronettes finished at around 9:30 p.m., the stage was reset. The giant Vox amps and Ringo's Ludwig drum kit were set up, and the crowd was going insane.

When the crew had completed its work, from the far corner of the racetrack, where the starting gate for races would normally be, emerged a long, black Cadillac limousine.

As the fans spotted the limo and pointed it out to each other, the crowd exploded.

Slowly, at maybe five miles per hour, the limo made its way around the track as the anticipation built and built and the screams got louder and louder.

By the time the limo arrived at the stage, there was sheer pandemonium.

John, Paul, George, and Ringo jumped out of the limo and bounded up to the stage, guitars already strapped around their necks, and with Ringo's drumsticks in hand.

They were dressed in emerald green suits with black velvet collars as they plugged into their amps, stepped up to their mikes, and went right into a mind-blowing, screaming cover of Chuck Berry's "Rock 'n' Roll Music."

They followed that with "She's a Woman," which was followed by "If I Needed Someone," "Day Tripper," then "Baby's in Black," "I Feel Fine," then "Yesterday." They played "I Wanna Be Your Man," then "Nowhere Man," "Paperback Writer" and an encore of the classic Little Richard song "Long Tall Sally," with Paul on lead vocals.

Eleven songs, about three minutes each, a total of thirty-five orgasmic minutes of pure bliss for my friends and me and 25,000 others who, like me, no doubt experienced the single greatest show of their lives.

Lisie, Paul, and the rest of us must have looked just like all those kids you see screaming, jumping up and down, girls crying and tearing their hair out in old *Ed Sullivan* clips of The Beatles.

Thirty-five minutes is certainly a little different from today's big shows, when Springsteen, the Stones, or U2 play for three and sometimes four hours. But at the time, that was the norm, and we left there 100% elated and satisfied.

What an incredible way to wind up my camp experience. I'll always be grateful to Patti Burnham and her dad for making it happen. How lucky I am to have that memory. I can see it, hear it, smell it, and feel it right now as I write this and know I always will. My brother David, sister Lisa, and I always regretted not getting to see them in one of their iconic *Ed Sullivan*

*Show* appearances. In discussing this recently, David said, "To this day I am still angry with our Dad for not taking us to see The Beatles live on *The Ed Sullivan Show*. He was president of the news division at CBS, which aired *The Ed Sullivan Show*, so it would've been easy. Truth is, he was worried about much bigger issues at the time, and in hindsight we can only respect him for his priorities. But how cool would it have been to say we were there?"

I got to work with Paul McCartney and see him perform several times later in my life, even sat behind him (thanks to my friend, Grammy producer Ken Ehrlich) on the stage at Coachella a few years ago, in front of 70,000 screaming fans, as he and his band played and sounded as close to the actual Beatles as could be. Got to spend a few minutes with him and Ken backstage as well. (Now I'm just showing off.) But honestly...pretty cool.

Nothing can ever top August 18, 1966, but one thing came pretty close: In 2002, Paul came to L.A. for his first major concert in decades and essentially did a Beatles show at Staples Center. I was determined to get tickets so I could ensure that our gang could tell their grandkids someday that they had seen a living Beatle perform live.

Through David Nochimson, I was able to get fourteen great tickets, and it was almost as cool to witness the master and his amazing band through the eyes of our family, as Paul sang many of the same songs in his now two-and-a-half-hour show that he played on that August night in 1966.

A couple of years ago, the wonderful bookseller Taschen published a magnificent book of Harry Benson's iconic black-and-white photographs of the 1966 American tour.

Of course I had to own a copy. When I brought it home and delved into it, toward the end of the book, laid out on two full adjoining pages, I discovered a photograph of John, Paul, George, and Ringo shot from behind, instruments around their necks, walking from the limo to the stage at Suffolk Downs. The exact moment I described earlier.

I couldn't believe it. A chill went up my spine when I saw it and I leave the book open to those pages on a table in our living room and see it every day. It fills me with joy, every single time I look at it with ultimate wonder and gratitude for the miracle of having experienced it.

*Harry Benson's iconic photograph of The Beatles
taking the stage at Suffolk Downs Racetrack in Boston,
guitars strapped on and ready to go, 1966*

*L-R: George Harrison, John Lennon, Ringo Starr, Paul McCartney*

*Our gang on the night of the Paul McCartney concert, 2002*

*L-R: Me, Jon, Marion, and Clare Hookstratten, Cole Kickliter, Gail
Nochimson, Pat Crowley, David Nochimson, Erin Hookstratten, Kate
Osher, Bob Osher, Will Hookstratten, Ann Osher, Eddie Osher*

```
ST1028   119      9   15      B-BAND  EST1028
Event Code  Section/Box  Row  Seat   Admission  Event Code
  259.25  ENTER AISLE M26        259.25  CN 49494
    Price                                CA 305
   119                                     119
Section/Box      PAUL MCCARTNEY      Sec
 CA  26»       BACK IN THE U.S.        606STP
  9   15        STAPLES CENTER      Row    9
Row  Seat
606BSTR        NO CAMERAS / RECORDERS  B  259.25
230CT02       MON OCT 28, 2002 8:00 PM Seat   15
```

**Postscript**: I recently learned that The Beatles, who were big fans of Elvis, had a chance to meet The King during their 1965 U.S. tour during which they played the Hollywood Bowl. Their manager, Brian Epstein, and Presley's manager, Colonel Tom Parker, arranged a meeting late on August 27 at Presley's rented house in Bel-Air, just a few doors down on the same street where Pat and I have lived for over three decades.

It was reported to be an awkward meeting because Elvis was somewhat condescending to these up-and-coming potential heirs to his throne, who were in awe of him. But, by the end of a very long evening, they were joking and even jammed together, which I imagine I can hear in the wind as our dog Bonnie and I pass the house on our nightly walk.

Too cool.

**P.P.S.:** One of the perennial fun debates among my family and close friends is which are the top Beatle tracks of all time

Recently I forwarded writer Bill Wyman's (not the Stones bass player) discussion-provoking ranking of all 213 tracks and asked everyone to send me their top five or ten. I got many interesting responses, including this one from my great friend and colleague Bob Hilburn, who as the *Los Angeles Times'* chief pop music critic for twenty-five years is widely considered the dean of rock critics worldwide. His upcoming, highly anticipated biography of Paul Simon will no doubt be as insightful and compelling as the critically acclaimed one he wrote a few years ago about Johnny Cash.

I asked Bob if I could share his Beatles top ten and he said yes.

**Bob Hilburn:**

*Of course, these Top Ten lists change hourly as you go over all the choices, but here's my list for today...smile.*

*In the beginning, I liked The Beatles, mainly because they were bringing back old rock 'n' roll during a time when real rock had largely disappeared from the airways. I think "Norwegian Wood" and "Nowhere Man" were the first time I really started thinking of them as great songwriters, and of course John was greatly influenced at that time by Dylan. Then it was the adult undercurrents of "Penny Lane" and "Eleanor Rigby" that really convinced me they were special; it was very dramatic to hear a rock band talk about adult figures. Saying that, I have to put in a couple of earlier tracks that I just loved.*

*So here are my ten favorites, chronologically.*

*"All My Loving"*

*"Yesterday"*

*"Norwegian Wood"*

*"Nowhere Man"*

*"Eleanor Rigby"*

*"Penny Lane"*

*"A Day in the Life"*

*"Hey Jude"*

*"Ballad of John and Yoko"*

*"Across the Universe"*

Have fun comparing them with your own and let the debate continue.

# 8

## SHIPPING OUT TO SEA, THE "GOAT," AND ROCKING THE WHO

It was the summer of 1968. I had just seen The Beatles during my sixth and final, glorious year at Camp Robinson Crusoe in Sturbridge, Massachusetts, and I was returning to Stockbridge School for my junior year.

While it was a tumultuous time in our nation's history, with protests and division over our involvement in Vietnam, race relations, the sexual and cultural revolutions, and other issues, my life at sixteen was thankfully calming down following my parents' divorce and my mom's illness. Mom was doing better and Dad was now as happy as I'd seen him in many years with his wonderful new wife, Ruth, and her three great sons, Jon, Mike, and Richard Mark, who were all now part of our family.

My life and studies were improving as I made the adjustment to the less rigorous yet intellectually and scholastically stimulating curriculum at the Stockbridge School.

Along with our studies, my childhood buddy Andy Cohen (not the Bravo network host) and our classmates continued to learn self-reliance as I had in camp, doing daily chores like garbage collection and kitchen patrol, and on weekends working on the little log cabin we built from scratch in the forest behind the school's beautiful campus.

The cabin wouldn't pass the most liberal building inspection but served as our gang's little "clubhouse," and much fun was had there, including the loss of my virginity that year to a lovely senior from California whose name I would never mention as I would not want to embarrass her. The whole thing was over in seconds and was pretty much a disaster.

She rightfully left me in the dust and moved on to a more experienced senior. I couldn't blame her for a second.

Otherwise, school was going well. I was learning life lessons along with my schoolwork, playing on the basketball and tennis teams, and playing rhythm guitar in our little rock band.

Christmas vacation was spent at my pal Peter Morton's parents' estate in Miami Beach. Peter sang and played the Hammond organ in our band. He had real talent; sang and played like a young Felix Cavaliere, the lead singer/songwriter of The Young Rascals, the seminal New Jersey band whose songs we covered.

Halfway through the school year I started to long for my normal yearly ritual of summer camp. There was just one problem: The maximum age for campers was fifteen. I called my best camp bud, Paul Cantor, and said: "What are we gonna do with ourselves this summer?"

After a few conversations about how we needed to get jobs and make some money, Paul called with a truly inspired, truly far-fetched, implausible idea dreamed up by his incredibly cool father, Dick. Hands down, Dick was the dad all the kids looked up to as the hippest dad in our group.

His idea? Paul and I should try to join the United States Maritime Union and ship out to sea for the summer.

What???

"That's right, you private school, bourgeois, spoiled, tennis-playing, expensive-camp-going, fresh-faced, Beatle-haircut-wearing little brats." I'm paraphrasing a little. He was actually very nice about it but that's the message we heard, and rightfully so.

He suggested we go down to the union hall, apply for a membership… hopefully get our cards, then sign up and try to catch a job sailing anywhere in the world that we could, to learn about real work and how to make a buck.

He threw in: "Might even help get you into Harvard." We would be applying to college in the fall and Paul, a top-notch student, had Harvard on his list.

After somehow getting my folks' approval, and with a little help from our neighbor, labor negotiator Ted Kheel, we joined the union.

Each day we went down to the union hall in Manhattan, put our names on a list for a job, and waited. With the lowest seniority, it took about eight days, but on that eighth day, we were assigned our first jobs.

For the next seven weeks Paul Cantor and I shipped out to sea on the *SS Independence*, one of the major cruise ships of its day, sailing from New York to the Caribbean and back.

I know what you're thinking: "This is bullshit. No way would their parents let two sixteen-year-olds do this."

Amazingly, this story has "the added advantage of being true."

On an early evening in July 1968, we pulled out of the ship's massive dock next to the West Side Highway on 45th Street in Manhattan and, escorted by several tugboats, sailed past the Statue of Liberty and out to the open sea.

My job was "baker's utility." On the bottom level, ten decks below sea level, in a tiny oven-lined room as tourists partied on deck on their way to paradise, for ten and sometimes twelve hours a day I scrubbed the dirty pots and pans used by the bakers to make thousands of pastries and desserts for passengers.

Paul's glamorous title was "crew porter." His job was even worse than mine. He scrubbed the toilets for the crew. Poor guy was prone to seasickness to begin with, and this didn't help matters.

We were the only high school kids on the crew of hundreds. There were a few college kids who took us under their wing, showed us the ropes, and looked out for us.

The crewmembers were mostly older, tough, seasoned pros from around the world. Many did not speak English. Few of them found the presence on their crew of two teenagers with Beatles haircuts amusing.

Paul and I took our meals with them in the crew mess, and shared tiny rooms with metal bunk beds and a single locker for our possessions, four men to a room at the bottom of the ship where all crew bunked, way below deck. I shared a room with three guys in their thirties and forties, only one of whom spoke English. Paul was in a room down the hall in similar circumstances.

They fed us well, and at night we got to hang out in the fresh air on the crew deck with our college buds drinking beers and trading stories. A college kid named Jack warned me to always be aware and ready to defend ourselves around a crew of nearly all men living at sea for the better part of a year. We knew we were in vulnerable positions, especially at night when alcohol was being consumed.

One night when I was alone in the bakery cleaning up at the end of my shift, an older guy in his forties approached me and slapped me on the butt. Remembering Jack's advice, I immediately turned around and took a swing at the guy. Missed badly. He laughed and walked away as I yelled some half-assed warning that I'd kick his ass if he ever came near me again.

Thankfully, it never happened.

At the end of each week, including overtime, Paul and I each collected checks for around $150 after taxes were taken out. In today's dollars that's about $1069. By far the most money we'd ever made, or even seen.

We saved most of it, but we did spend some when the ship stopped for twenty-four hours in San Juan, Puerto Rico, and St. Thomas in the U.S. Virgin Islands before heading back up the coast to New York.

While the passengers went on guided tours of the islands and enjoyed fine dining and time in the glamorous casinos, the college guys, Paul, and I had our fun as well.

To say that the local bars and the beautiful young ladies we met in them were welcoming would be accurate.

Underage, we managed to get served as much fine Puerto Rican rum and beer as we wanted and sneak into the fancy casino at the Caribe Hilton, where we gambled away some of our hard-earned pay at the blackjack tables. A two-dollar bet was a big deal to me at the time. I had never been inside a real bar without my parents, let alone a casino.

At the end of the evening we'd head back to the ship, get a few hours of sleep, and head back out to sea, usually sporting a serious hangover but happy as any sixteen-year-old could be.

Two weeks into this routine, Paul decided to meet friends in Europe and signed up for a job on the *USS United States*. While there, he visited with Dad and Ruth in London, who were there on a trip.

I missed Paul but my college pals and I enjoyed the rest of the summer of our proverbial coming-of-age. I even got a promotion to bellboy in the last weeks and got to wear a little white linen outfit and serve drinks with umbrellas in them to passengers, for nice tips.

I'll always be grateful to Dick Cantor for the great idea and to my folks for allowing me to go through with it. They must have known that somehow I could handle it and it might be just what I needed at the time. And of course to Paul, whom I visit regularly on summer trips to Stockbridge along with my other best buds growing up: Andy Cohen and Bill Nathan.

When summer was over we headed back to school, a bit older, wiser, tougher, and ready to rule as seniors a year away from college.

Paul ended up going to prestigious Brandeis University in Massachusetts, where he played on the tennis team, before attending law school. He now practices law and lives in Providence, Rhode Island, with his great family. He remains a ranked tennis player in his age group.

I headed west to college at Occidental and then to USC in Los Angeles, which I'll tell you about in the next chapter.

*Paul Cantor, Andy Cohen, Bill Nathan, and me on a recent
trip to the Friendly/Mark summer cottage in Stockbridge*

Before I left for college I had a great final year at Stockbridge, and then
one fantastic final summer at our beloved Camp Robinson Crusoe, this time
as a junior counselor along with my other childhood and great friend to this
day, Bill Nathan.

We had grown up as campers on the lake at Stockbridge together with
Andy and Paul; now we were hilariously teaching ten-year-olds to play
tennis and do all the other fun camp activities we enjoyed at that age.

We shared a tent together and nearly burned it down twice with the
kerosene lanterns we used to light it at night. We read and debated Goethe,
Plato, and Bertrand Russell deep into the night like the two seventeen-year-
old philosophers we were. Bill was a true philosophy student and intellect;
I was just a guy who liked to read a chapter or two and shoot my mouth off
like I knew something.

On days off, we hopped into Bill's dad's Pontiac GTO, one of the great
American muscle cars of all time, known as "The Goat." We cranked up Iron
Butterfly's classic rock anthem "In a Gadda Da Vida" on the stereo at full
volume and cruised down the Mass Pike with newly minted driver's licenses
to visit our families for dinner an hour away in Stockbridge.

On the drive back to camp after dinner, late at night with the top down and no one else on the road, Bill would literally crank that 400cc/360hp engine to 125 mph and then, just to freak me out and hear me scream like a baby, he'd turn the headlights off for a split second.

I wish I was kidding, but I'm not. In the years to follow he'd pull the same stunt driving around the lake at night in Stockbridge with Andy Cohen, my brothers, and me in his dad's green BMW, going 80 mph on winding roads where the speed limit was 30. Lights out and all.

Today he is a serious businessman and devoted dad living in New Jersey, and thankfully he now drives like a normal person.

To close out the summer of '69 after our summer as camp counselors, I got a job as a junior assistant working for the legendary promoter Bill Graham at Tanglewood, summer home of the Boston Symphony, near our cottage in Lennox. Graham was the dynamic promoter who created the iconic Fillmore East and West, and is considered by many to be the greatest rock impresario ever.

A tough-as-nails, super smart business and cultural leader, he was one of the One Thousand Children, a group of mainly Jewish children who managed to flee Hitler and Europe, and come directly to North America, but whose parents were forced to stay behind. Graham was one of the most impressive people I'd ever met. It was a thrill to watch and learn from him as he presented The Who, B.B. King, and Jefferson Airplane that August, right in my back yard.

All the sweeter as I had been unable to go to Woodstock, the seminal music festival that happened weeks earlier just hours away in upstate New York, because I was working at camp. Bill and I made a valiant effort to get off work to go but couldn't make it happen.

Always a rock 'n' roller from the time I can remember, this was beyond exciting for me. To stand on the side of the stage with my thirteen-year-old brother, David, whom I was able to bring with me, while Pete Townshend and The Who and other great artists played live at volumes never heard at historic Tanglewood before or since, was truly mind-blowing. Almost on a par with the live Beatles show I witnessed outside of Boston.

A couple summers later, I returned to work for Mr. Graham, on concerts that included one of my favorite bands: Sly and the Family Stone. When my brother Michael, his wife, Mary, and I drove to Albany, New York, to pick up the band at the airport, there was a slight problem: Sly was not on the plane. The infamous soul/funk master, who had blown the crowd away at Woodstock a few years prior, had missed the flight. With just hours to go before the concert, panic ensued. We called Mr. Graham to fill him in.

Back at Tanglewood, with fans beginning to tailgate and fill the venue, Mr. Graham somehow tracked Sly down and arranged for a helicopter to bring him to the show.

An hour and a half after he was scheduled to go on stage, with the crowd in a near-riot, Sly in his helicopter landed on a grassy field nearby.

We escorted the clearly impaired superstar through the crazed crowd to the stage where his band was waiting. Somehow he delivered an amazing show, and the crowd went home happy. Disaster averted. Hail, hail, rock 'n' roll!

These were the summers of my teen years.

# 9

## COLLEGE MAN

"My final-year approval ratings are going up. The last time I was this high I was trying to decide on my major."

–President Barack Obama
2016 White House Correspondents Dinner

Honestly, it's like I have a twin.

Not the high approval rating part but the other part. And the funny thing is that President Obama and I both spent our first two years of college at Occidental: a wonderful, small, liberal arts college in the Eagle Rock suburb of Los Angeles.

He was there about ten years after I was and went on to Columbia in his junior year. I went to film school at USC, where I graduated in 1973.

In the fall of 1969 at seventeen, my folks put me on a plane to L.A. and wished me good luck in college. There was no advance-scouting trip. No "We're coming with you for your first year, to move you in and make sure you're all set," the way it's done today. It was pretty much: "Here's a few bucks for books and food. Try to learn something and stay out of trouble. See you at the holidays."

I had been away at boarding school in Massachusetts, so no problem. "Let's do this."

I arrived at LAX with suitcase and guitar in hand, found a bus, and within a couple of hours moved into my dorm room where I met my roommate: a smart, shaggy-haired, loud, funny kid from Iowa who loved Led Zeppelin as much as I did. We cranked up "Whole Lotta Love" on the stereo, and kids from all over the country started showing up.

In my seventeen years on Earth I'd never met anyone from Iowa, Kansas, or Texas. These guys knew how to party.

As mentioned, I was never much of a student. I did better in high school and began to enjoy reading and writing at the Stockbridge School. Still, I was nowhere close to being the kind of strong student that my brothers and sisters were.

When I followed my Stockbridge pal Andy Rubin to Occidental, I made myself and my parents a promise: I'd try to get all A's my freshman year.

I had always dreamed of getting away from the freezing winters of the East Coast and fell in love with California on a visit to my dad's cousin Fred Harris in Beverly Hills a few years prior.

"Oxy" is a first-rate school and I thrived there. Beautiful campus, small classes, fantastic, engaging, cool professors like Jim Hosney and Marsha Kinder, who had us studying Norman Mailer, Federico Fellini, and Bob Dylan.

They were not like other teachers I'd had. They were cool. The kind of people you felt lucky to be around: that you'd want to talk to at a party. And party we did.

In today's world, they probably couldn't do it, but Hosney and a couple of other professors let us hang out at their homes, drink beer, smoke an occasional joint, and "rap" about art, culture, politics, and music. They took us to midnight screenings of Godard and Antonioni films and twenty-four-hour Billy Wilder marathons.

We'd stay up all night and dissect and debate Beatles and Stones lyrics, go out for Mexican food and beer, and "rap" some more.

They, along with Arthur Knight and others later at USC, taught us so much.

In 2001, when Dean Elizabeth Daley of the USC School of Cinematic Arts asked me to teach at my alma mater, I modeled my TV Development and Production classes on Professor Knight's.

A film historian and critic for *The Hollywood Reporter*, he would bring top directors, producers, writers, and stars to class each week, to interview them and let us ask questions and interact with them. A screening of their latest project usually followed.

When I taught there, I followed his lead and was lucky enough to get everyone from Vin Scully to Garry Marshall to Tom Snyder and dozens more to come to campus and teach with me.

With the help of my friend Debbie Vickers, we brought my class to a behind-the-scenes taping of *The Tonight Show* after which host Jay Leno spoke with my students.

Much like me thirty years earlier, they loved it.

Back in my Oxy days, I got to work at and host a little music show at the tiny radio station KOXY and became the station manager. It only went to the dorms and the quad, but still, I was "spinning wax," counting down records, and loving it. Worked at the little campus TV studio, too. Played in a cool band. Wrote some lame songs. Smoked some weed and drank some beer but never took acid like some of my pals. I was too scared.

My bandmates and I had dreams of being pop stars someday as we played frat parties, coffeehouses and dive bars near Occidental College. We had big dreams but reality soon intervened.

Our band, including the talented John Rhodes, Dennis Miller (not the Fox news guy), and I, scored a gig to perform at the big Saturday night season-opening talent show in the campus's main auditorium, which seated 1,500 of our fellow students and faculty. By far the biggest audience any of us had played for.

At eighteen we thought we were "all that."

We rehearsed endlessly and, when the big night came, took the stage and seamlessly powered through our brief set of Beatles, Creedence Clearwater Revival, and Who classics. We had a couple of strong voices and players in John and Dennis; I was serviceable on my cherry-red, George Harrison-style Gretsch Country Gentleman rhythm guitar and singing backing vocals.

Opening with The Beatles' great, rocking "Tell Me Why," we felt we had the crowd behind us and our futures were full of rock stardom and all that comes with it. The feeling was short-lived.

The band that followed us, all seniors (we were freshmen), were classically trained musicians. They quietly took the stage and proceeded to blow the roof off the dump with a flawless, perfect, monumental set of much more precise and complex music, including highly sophisticated, difficult originals they'd written along with classics by Poco, Crosby, Stills & Nash, Buffalo Springfield, and others we never would have even dreamed to attempt.

They were perfect. They were cool. They didn't miss a single note or harmony. And... they looked and dressed better than we did.

Back to reality.

We went back to the drawing board, playing local coffeehouses and frat parties for tips. The truly talented older guys went on to careers in the music business, and rightfully so. Our rock 'n' roll career dreams soon came to an end, but the fun of playing in a band continued.

The good news was I kept my focus on my studies. Got to put off math, science, and French for a year, and instead I concentrated on English, history, and film.

When I brought home my report card at the holidays: all A's. In June my pal Andy Rubin and I drove cross-country in his Porsche and delivered another: nothin' but A's.

For the first time, my parents thought there might be hope.

Having proven I could get good grades in subjects that appealed to me, and then having to face the tougher requirements in weaker areas like math and language for the next three years, my grades came back down to earth. I did OK, mostly B's. I could have worked harder, but there was fun to be had.

\*\*\*\*\*

In my sophomore year at Occidental, I experienced and survived my first major earthquake when I awoke in the middle of the night in 1971 to the ground and walls shaking. Through my window I could see electric grids in the distance exploding. I thought L.A. had been attacked and we were being bombed.

My roommate Billy Goldman came out of his room in his underwear, screaming and waving a heavy, metal flashlight.

Thirty seconds later it all stopped.

WTF!!??

Welcome to California. As the brilliant columnist Art Buchwald once told me about the Golden State, "It's either sliding, shaking, or burning."

Holy crap!

Along the way, I made some great, lifelong friends. Made some student films; some cool, some lame. I even got some help on one from the brilliant director Taylor Hackford, who was then working as a young director at KCET, the public television station in L.A.

Taylor went on to make *An Officer and a Gentleman*, *The Devil's Advocate*, *Ray*, and *Parker*. He could not have been kinder or more supportive, even if he knew my little movie, *Sunny Skies*, was the definition of a "student film."

The film school at USC was full of talented, young filmmakers, like my pal to this day Bobby Roth, who went on to make dozens of award-winning films and television series. Then there was my classmate Bob Zemeckis, the genius director of *Back to the Future, Forrest Gump*, and other huge hits, who completely showed me up, along with my other hot-shot classmates, after the screenings of our first little five-minute-long, black-and-white projects. (smile) His was called *The Lift*, and it immediately became a film school classic, one of the first films screened for all first-year film students at USC.

Game over. Thanks, Zemeckis.

Along the way I got my first wheels, which I drove at ridiculously high speeds around the LA freeways until I traded it for a little Datsun convertible that was so old and broken-down I had to park it on a hill and pop the clutch to make it start. The roof leaked so much that I, and my few-and-far-between dates, got soaked anytime it rained, which it did a lot in the winter of 1974.

I wasn't exactly a chick magnet like the frat guys in their brand-new BMWs. Plus I looked like a dork with my shoulder-length, James Taylor "Sweet Baby James" hairstyle. This, plus the fact that there were forty guys and two girls in my class at film school, and I was not exactly getting it done with the ladies.

It didn't help that the film school, which now resembles the finest Hollywood studio (thanks to the amazing work of Dean Daley and her team), was housed back then in a converted horse stable on the edge of campus, isolated from the rest of the student body. It had a couple old 16mm cameras and a couple beat-up Moviolas. Like my car, the roof leaked when it rained.

When I transferred there from Oxy, I was living off campus and fairly removed from all the fun going on around campus. It was also a different time. The war in Vietnam was still raging and dividing the country. We were "film school" people and pseudo-intellectuals, and at the time looked down on the frat boys. Wish I could have a do-over on that.

I did go to a few football games. With my classmate Pat Hayden playing quarterback, and with O.J. Simpson just a few years gone, the famed Trojans were No. 1 in the country, and that was cool but not really my scene. Now I'm a huge Trojan fan, along with many of my family members who went to school there and those who are now attending. I truly regret not participating more.

On my rare dates, I did get to see some of the coolest bands and artists ever emerging on the L.A. scene. With friends like Stuart Birnbaum, Lon Levin, and John Rhodes, I hung out at the famed Troubadour in West Hollywood, where I got to see up-and-coming artists like The Eagles, Jackson Browne, Loggins and Messina, Elton John, and James Taylor.

I wrote reviews of the shows as well as new albums for the *USC Daily Trojan* so I could get free passes and records, which was extremely useful, as

I couldn't afford either. In the summer of my junior year, based on my *Daily Trojan* work (I was a journalism minor as well), I got a job writing music reviews for a cool underground L.A. paper called *The Staff.*

I was also hired by a small radio station in Massachusetts during summer break to cover the Democratic Convention in Miami in 1972 when George McGovern was nominated.

I filed my best "Hunter Thompson gonzo-style" reports on the goings-on at the convention. His classic *Fear and Loathing in Las Vegas* was all the rage at *Rolling Stone* and we all tried to write like him.

My folks listened to me on the radio and Ruth told me the old man was proud, which made me feel good since he was rightfully not too thrilled in general with the results of his expensive and extremely generous investment in my education to that point. (Except for the A's my first year at Oxy.)

As always throughout my early life and, in many ways, to this day, music gave me many of my best times and greatest joy: playing and even (lamely) writing some, and being a DJ, reviewer, and reporter.

I'll never hear music as good as it was then, in such a cool setting, at such a special time of life.

Sadly, I did not work very hard at film school. I did not come close to getting the most out of the great opportunity my parents paid a fortune for me to have.

I wish I could go back and do it differently. I was immature and easily distracted.

I had very little, if any, supervision or guidance such as I see the young people in my life getting now. But in fairness, I probably didn't want much.

That said: My college years were a blast. I'm sure some of it did sink in and that I learned some things that later helped me in my career as a writer, producer, and occasional director.

As the Trojan motto demands...we "Fight On!"

*My dad and Ruth on my Suzuki X-6, while I was home
from Occidental after my freshman year*

# 10

## WELCOME TO 30 ROCK, NBC NEWS, AND THE REAL "ANCHORMAN"

*Dad, my brother David, my sister Lisa, and me at 30 Rockefeller Center on a visit in 1958, fourteen years before I would get my first job there, at WNBC- TV*

My goal as a graduating senior at the School of Cinema and Television at USC in 1973 was to work on a national TV newsmagazine. I never dreamed that a few years later, in 1980, Paramount would hire me to make one from scratch for $25 million called *Entertainment Tonight*.

But first things first.

In 1973, fresh out of school, I found a job as a summer replacement researcher at Channel 4 News in New York. The job paid $150 per week and lasted just two months until the man I was filling in for, a researcher who had been moved up to a summer replacement writer, returned.

Fortunately for me, he was hired away as an associate producer on the local news in his hometown of Cleveland. After working my butt off finding and researching stories on topics ranging from the first female bus driver in New York to the lack of fire safety in local discos, I was given his old job.

It was the one and only job my dad helped me get. He made it clear: "You'd better make it work, this is the first and last time I will get you an interview." Looking back, it was the best thing he could have done for me. I knew he was a hundred percent serious, and I knew I'd better focus and make it work.

The day I left USC was the last time I took a dime from my parents; their choice, not mine. From the days I shined shoes for ten cents a pair in the CBS cutting room to be able to buy a decent baseball glove when I was ten, my parents let me know that while they'd feed, house, and educate me, that was about it.

Friends had help with apartments, cars, clothes, and food, while I was now on my own. I was OK with that. I did appreciate that my mom let me camp out on the living room couch of her one-bedroom Midtown apartment for a month or two until I found a few roommates.

My roommates and I shared a below-ground, broken-down janitor's apartment of a brownstone on East 64th Street for three years. What a dump. The floors were cracked and uneven. There were holes in the walls of the kitchen and the bathroom, and bars on the windows looking up to the street. But it was one of the coolest neighborhoods in New York, and it even had a little slab of concrete in back where we had great barbecues and parties as my buds and I embarked on our adventures in work, relationships, and adult life.

I loved walking down Madison or Fifth Avenue every day and turning right on 50th Street past the iconic skating rink into 30 Rockefeller Plaza and up to the seventh-floor newsroom. I'd then head to my little cubbyhole desk way in the back corner of the newsroom, where veteran researchers Gail Yankosic, Bret Marcus, Eric Denby and production assistant Cheryl Kagan (they had been there maybe a year but to me they were veterans) showed me the ropes, covered my butt, and became my lifelong friends.

I learned to write for the broadcast, starting with the weather, then sports, then hard news. Condensing large amounts of fast-breaking news from the field, wire, and telephone sources, writing it up, marrying it to just-developed 16mm film or two-inch videotape under tight, tight deadlines to make air was baptism by fire. It was by far the best education and training anyone could ever have if they want to be in this business.

I made my share of mistakes. Once I was banished by the news director, Earl Ubell, to the 12th-floor offices of consumer reporter Betty Furness, where for two weeks all I did was return her fan mail as punishment for screwing up and missing a deadline on a story for the six o'clock news. I deserved it and never made that mistake again, though there were plenty more close calls.

To this day, over forty more years of TV, I've rarely experienced more intense pressure than when I had to accurately research, report, write, and edit breaking hard news on the tightest deadline imaginable.

Often I'd be handed a ream of wire copy on a brand-new, complex story, told the film was in the lab and would be ready in ten minutes, and asked to have the piece on the air in fifteen. I feel I owe a great deal to the "older," grizzled producers like Gerry Solomon (he was thirty), and on-air talent like Frank Field and Marv Albert and Chuck Scarborough, who took me under their wing, allowed me to screw up, and patiently taught me to write and produce the news.

It formed a solid foundation for everything I did in television, and later few things ever fazed me.

In time, I got to produce pieces out in the field. Among other things I spent a week documenting life at the infamous Attica prison in Upstate New York following deadly riots there as well as flying to London to produce a three-part series with one of my all-time heroes: Paul McCartney, whom I spent a year trying to book and finally was able to deliver.

The week at Attica was admittedly intense and frightening. My two-man camera crew and I "lived" there with the most dangerous murderers and rapists in the country for fourteen hours a day, for a whole week. To make matters worse, it was the middle of the winter and there was almost no heat and I was suffering from the worst flu I'd ever had, with a fever of 102 degrees.

But we told some strong stories and delivered a compelling three-part series reported by anchor and former Cleveland Mayor Carl Stokes, who gained the prisoners' trust. He got them to open up about conditions in the prison leading up to, and after, the deadly riots there in 1971. It was an exclusive for WNBC and generated a lot of press and ratings. As scary as it was, I developed a better understanding of the plight of some of the prisoners.

I corresponded for a few years with Winston Moseley, the man who killed Kitty Genovese on a Queens street in a case made infamous because of the many witnesses who didn't come forward to help the victim. He was an intelligent, soft-spoken, articulate man who had learned to read and write in prison and had become a model prisoner. It was hard to believe he was a cold-blooded murderer.

I was twenty-two at the time, and the experience left a lasting impression, To this day prisons scare the crap out of me, having seen what I did of the inner workings. I feel sorry for the often horrid, overcrowded, violent places our prisons have become. That goes especially for nonviolent offenders who are sent there to rot and be violated and who become violent and hostile as a result of being there.

The McCartney series was the polar opposite. As with another hero of mine, the great Jimmy Cagney, in a story I'll tell you later, I refused to give up in my effort to secure an interview with Paul. In the years right after The Beatles' breakup, it was a rarity to get an interview with any of the band.

The Beatles were, and are, my favorite band.

At fourteen, my dreams came true when I got to see them perform live in Boston, and now, nine years later at twenty-three, I was determined to pull one of the biggest "gets" imaginable for a diehard Beatles fan. Of course every media outlet wanted McCartney, but after a massive letter-writing campaign to his lawyer, John Eastman (Paul's wife Linda's brother), we got the go-ahead.

Two weeks later, reporter Scott Osbourne and I were on a plane to London (my first trip to Europe), and the night after that I was having dinner at the Hard Rock Café near Hyde Park with Paul McCartney and Leslie West, the outrageously cool and talented lead singer and guitarist of the band Mountain.

I was beyond, beyond excited and couldn't believe this was really happening. I still can't believe it.

The next day we shot the interview with Paul. He couldn't have been nicer, smarter, or wittier. He spoke candidly about The Beatles' highs and lows, their recent breakup, his new life with Linda, and the inception of his new band, Wings. During breaks, he offered us food and joked around with the crew.

Ultimately, the exclusive, three-part series was a big rating and press coup for us and ran nationally on the NBC stations. Twelve years later Paul did another great interview with the award-winning *Los Angeles Times* music critic Bob Hilburn, for our series *The Rock 'n' Roll Evening News* with King World. Twenty or so years after that, I got to meet and hang out with him again, backstage at Coachella, thanks to my close pal Grammy producer Ken Ehrlich. Even in my sixties, I still feel like a teenager and get that same rush whenever I hear an early Beatles song. I'm not often star-struck, but meeting and spending time with "Sir Paul" was, and is, a lifelong thrill.

My first job at WNBC in TV News was a great experience. About a year and a half in, with ratings sagging a bit, the station overhauled the broadcast with a new concept it called *NewsCenter 4*. Anchors Jim Hartz and Carl Stokes were out and new anchors Chuck Scarborough and a hot-shot anchor from L.A. named Tom Snyder, who was also the host of a brand-new, late-night talk show on NBC called *Tomorrow*, following Johnny Carson, were in. My life was about to change forever.

I'll never forget the day Tom arrived at Channel 4. There was great anticipation in the newsroom and all over the metropolitan area. His and Chuck's faces for weeks had been on buses, billboards, and all over the airwaves to tout the new broadcast in the largest-ever promotion of a news program.

It was around 3 p.m., two hours before air on a Monday, when I heard that booming, one-of-a-kind voice in the halls of NBC News, where formality, suits, and ties were the norm. He was wearing plaid golf pants and a bright pink Bel-Air Country Club golf shirt. He stood six foot four and his long hair was at least three colors, including black, silver, and somehow a touch of what appeared to be orange…he was smoking a butt.

Snyder's sharp baritone boomed out across the newsroom as everyone turned around to glimpse the new "savior." As always, he was brief and to the point: "ALL RIGHT I'M HERE…SHOW'S OVER FOLKS, NOW GET BACK TO WORK AND I'LL SEE YA ON TV."

And then that famous laugh…"HA HA HA HA HA"…and he was gone.

But at 6 p.m. and 11 p.m. he was back and on the air, and the magic really worked. He commanded the anchor desk like no one before or since. He seemed to connect to viewers as if he was talking to them alone, and within a few months, he and Scarborough were No. 1. It was a thrill to work for them. Tom taught me how to tighten up my writing, he taught me producing skills, how to be more natural and relate better to viewers. He made us all laugh and enjoy our long, pressured workdays and nights.

Often he'd ignore the scripts and report in his own impromptu words after just reading some wire copy or debriefing a reporter or producer. He was brilliant and gifted, with a magnetism that grabbed viewers right through the lens of the camera and hooked them.

A few months later, his friend and original producer-director of his new NBC late-night network show *Tomorrow*, the brilliant Joel Tator, decided to move to back to L.A., where the show started, and Tom moved producers Pam Burke and Bruce McKay to the executive producer jobs. The move created an opening for a segment producer.

Tom and I had developed a good working relationship; he seemed to like my work and suggested me for the job to Pam and Bruce.

After a round of interviews, I was hired and moved to my first network show, complete with my own office, an assistant, and a nice raise. I could finally move out of the janitor's apartment and get a place of my own.

Leaving my friends and teachers at *NewsCenter 4* was tough but I'd only be moving a few floors away to the *Tomorrow* offices on the second floor of 30 Rock, so we'd be staying close and seeing each other a lot, while taping our show just across the hall in Studio 6A.

I can never thank those folks enough for all they taught me and for putting up with my youthful exuberance and dopey mistakes, and for patiently teaching me the skills that served me for a lifetime in television.

Following is news director Earl Ubell's memo to the *NewsCenter 4* team upon my departure:

*Earl Ubell*

*1/23/76*

*To the Staff:*

*As you may have heard, Andy Friendly is leaving* NewsCenter 4 *to become a segment producer on the* Tomorrow *show. Although I am sad to see him go, this is a wonderful opportunity for Andy and I wish him all the luck in the world in his new adventure.*

*Andy has been one of the creative people we have had with us. His work on The Beatles, the Portchester night club fire, and the Attica prison series are just three of the many important projects that helped move us forward. He has always been willing to help in whatever had to be done and that is no small matter either.*

*Again, good luck, Andy.*

*Earl Ubell*

*Tom and I on the set of Tomorrow, 1975*

*Tom and I at an NBC party while we were
working on his CNBC talk show, 1994*

# 11

## TOM SNYDER: TEACHER, MENTOR, AND PAL

I've been blessed to have giants as mentors. After my dad, there was the aforementioned Tom Snyder, the larger-than-life NBC News anchor and iconic host of NBC's late-night *Tomorrow* show.

I watched Snyder in awe when I was at USC and he anchored the *Channel 4 News* in L.A., and when I went to work for him soon after college, starting at WNBC-TV news in New York, and continuing on and off for the next forty years.

Like my dad, Tom was a big man at six foot four, with a big, loud voice. He dominated any room he entered and every TV set he appeared on.

As a kid out of college, I was mesmerized by him. Aside from his physical presence, he was brilliant, widely acknowledged as one of the most talented writers and talkers in the news and talk business.

We had a long and great friendship for almost four decades. As mentioned, after the local news, he brought me on to his *Tomorrow* show and then hired me to produce his primetime specials on NBC and as a producer on his NBC newsmagazine *Prime Time Live*.

After six great years with Tom, I left for Los Angeles to produce series and specials with others, and we lost touch for a few years. But later we reunited when I talked him into doing a show at startup CNBC, where I was in charge of primetime programming. We became closer than ever and had another good run. We remained close friends until his death in 2007, from complications related to leukemia, at the far-too-young age of 71.

A week after he died, I was asked to write a remembrance of Tom for the publication *TelevisionWeek*.

It follows here:

# Andy Friendly

### *Recalling Snyder as Fearless, Peerless Friend*

*At least once a week, and often every day for the past thirty-five years, I've had the privilege of hearing what Tom Snyder had to say.*

*In recent years, it's been on a weekly phone call, but that sadly ended July 29, when Tom lost his battle with leukemia at the much-too-young age of 71.*

*The first time I saw him was in 1972. I was a student at USC and watched him anchoring the news on KNBC.*

*Wild hair, super-wide tie, cigarette smoke wafting above his head when he came back from commercial. A sparkle in his eye and a voice so strong that he almost came through the lens of the camera into the student lounge, where we were all mesmerized by his no-holds-barred, in-your-face style.*

*He was such a dominant force in L.A. news that NBC gave him his own talk show called* Tomorrow, *which followed Johnny Carson from 1973 to 1982 and pioneered late, late night TV and paved the way for Dave, Conan, Bob Costas, and others, earning multiple Emmys and rave reviews along the way.*

Tomorrow *also broke new ground in the kinds of things you could do on TV. The first interview from a nudist colony. First interview with a real-life Mafia hit man.*

*Also, John Lennon, a young Bono, presidents Carter and Bush (Sr.), Muhammad Ali and the legendary Alfred Hitchcock, of whom Tom asked, "What scares you?"*

*"Policemen," replied Hitchcock.*

*Had that question been asked of Tom, the answer would have been "Nothing." He was fearless.*

*In 1974, when NBC asked him to move* Tomorrow *to New York and anchor the news there to bolster sagging ratings, he opened his first newscast by saying, "I'm the new guy....I don't work for NBC or its executives; I work for you, the viewers."*

*That philosophy got him in hot water on many occasions with top NBC execs like Fred Silverman and the heads of NBC News and, on occasion, with his guests and sometimes in his everyday life.*

*Tom was fearless and often politically incorrect. He asked the tough questions we all wanted answered and he spoke truth to power. He never tried to make himself "commercial" or "sellable." He cared about getting at the truth and cutting through the layers of prepackaged, canned responses that personify most interviews.*

*Sometimes on air or off, the subtleties, the social radar most of us who toil in this business try to employ to keep ourselves in good graces, went by the wayside. Tom was hot, he was cold. He was up, he was down. He was in, he was out, but he always remained Tom, and sometimes that did not endear him to the power brokers used to having their asses kissed.*

*But the cabbies in New York loved him and shouted his praise when he walked by, and so did millions of regular, loyal viewers who appreciated his honesty and his great sense of humor, which was always on display. When Howard Cosell jousted with Tom on* Tomorrow *saying, "Your demise is near and this may be your last hurrah," Tom shot back, "Many more guests like you and it will be."*

*Of course, he wasn't always spot-on. He sometimes had trouble keeping up with the latest pop stars and, as his longtime producer-director Joel Tator recounts, "once introduced the singer Meat Loaf as Meatball."*

*He was a workhorse and could go for hours live if necessary without a script or a road map. Like, the time a fire shut down the CNBC studios in New Jersey in 1994 and his was the only working studio (he was based in L.A.) at the network. He expanded his one-hour show to four and a half hours and broadcast live and by the seat of his pants, brilliantly, until headquarters could get back online.*

*The most fun was his opening "monologue." No writers, completely unscripted. Each night for five minutes or so, Tom would take us into his life and inject himself in ours with stories and observations from his everyday life.*

*The ice cream cone he enjoyed at lunch or the folks he saw protesting at the nativity scene in Beverly Hills or his new yellow T-Bird or some cornball joke he heard from the crew that day... always followed by that one-of-a-kind laugh, made famous by Dan Aykroyd on* Saturday Night Live, *which repeats in my brain daily: "Ha ha ha ha ha"–always five of them, in precise rhythm, always loud and infectious.*

*I got to share those laughs with Tom and so many wonderful friends and colleagues on the local news,* Tomorrow, Primetime Sunday, The Tom Snyder Specials *and* Tom Snyder *on CNBC.*

*Anything I might know about TV, I learned from Tom and colleagues like Pam Burke, Bruce McKay, Ricky Carson, Joel Tator, Debbie Vickers, Dick Ebersol, John McMahon, Barbara Gallagher, George Paul, Gerry Solomon, Steve Friedman, Greg Sills, Katherine Coker, Paul Friedman, Marc Rosenweig, Michael Horowicz, Bob Morton, Pat Caso, Patty Mann, Bob Brown, Tom Chasuk, Carole Chouinard, Sharon Smith, Ellen Deutsch, Kay Wilmot, Kelly Lange and so many other talented people whom Tom brought into his inner circle.*

*I'm so lucky to have known him and learned from him and to have been his pal for the past thirty-five years. He was truly a unique voice. He gave me, and all of us, so much.*

I miss and will always miss Tom a great deal. But I hear his voice every day, imagining what he'd say about topics in the news, a goofy joke he told, or a hysterical rant on what happened at the butcher shop or whatever he'd have been up to if he was still here.

In that sense he is never too far from me.

As this is being written: Pam Burke, Joel Tator, Scott Carlin, Jeff Sotzing and I are working with NBC to bring back *Tomorrow* in its original form on cable or streaming.

We're tracking hundreds of shows that have been rotting away on tape in warehouses around the country and trying to preserve and find a home for the more than 1,500 episodes of Tom's Emmy Award-winning show, including his in-depth interviews with four U.S. presidents, John Lennon, Orson Welles, a young Bono and The Edge, Charles Manson, Alfred Hitchcock, Marlon Brando, and so many more. It is a labor of love.

*Two of my heroes, Clint Eastwood and Tom Snyder, and me on the roof of 30 Rock during a taping of an NBC primetime special Tom Snyder's Celebrity Spotlight, 1979*

*It was one of several specials I wrote and produced for Tom.*

Andy Friendly

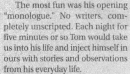

**GUEST COMMENTARY** By Andy Friendly

# Recalling Snyder as Fearless, Peerless Friend

At least once a week, and often every day for the past 35 years, I've had the privilege of hearing what Tom Snyder had to say.

In recent years it's been on a weekly phone call, but that sadly ended July 29, when Tom lost his battle with leukemia at the much too young age of 71.

The first time I saw him was in 1972. I was a student at USC and watched him anchoring the news on KNBC.

Wild hair, superwide tie, cigarette smoke wafting above his head when he came back from commercial. A sparkle in his eye and a voice so strong that he almost came through the lens of the camera into the student lounge,

**TOM SNYDER**

Tom was fearless and often politically incorrect. He asked the tough questions we all wanted answered and he spoke truth to power. He never tried to make himself "commercial" or "sellable." He cared about getting at the truth and cutting through the layers of prepackaged, canned responses that personify most interviews.

Sometimes on the air or off, the subtleties, the social radar most of us who toil in this business try to employ to keep ourselves in good graces, went by the wayside. Tom was hot, he was cold. He was up, he was down. He was in, he was out, but he always remained Tom, and sometimes that did not endear him to the power brokers used to

The most fun was his opening "monologue." No writers, completely unscripted. Each night for five minutes or so Tom would take us into his life and inject himself in ours with stories and observations from his everyday life.

The ice cream cone he enjoyed at lunch or the folks he saw protesting at the nativity scene in Beverly Hills or his new yellow T-Bird or some cornball joke he heard from the crew that day ... always followed by that one-of-a-kind laugh, made famous by Dan Aykroyd on "Saturday Night Live," which repeats in my brain daily: "Ha ha ha ha ha"— always five of them, in precise rhythm, always loud and infectious.

I got to share those laughs with Tom and so many wonderful friends and colleagues on the local news, "Tomorrow," "Primetime Sunday," "The Tom Snyder Spe-

*A portion of the tribute I wrote to honor Tom when he passed, 2007*

# 12

## JOHNNY AND RICK CARSON

One of my greatest memories growing up is of attending a taping of *The Tonight Show Starring Johnny Carson* in the mid-1960s at NBC Studios at 30 Rock in New York.

I had grown up in and around TV studios watching my dad and Ed Murrow do a wide range of historic programs, but as a teenager I was enamored of Johnny Carson's funny, witty, hip-for-the-times late-night series. When my dad was able to get me tickets to a taping, my world changed.

The exhilaration of being in Studio 6B for the taping at 5:30 p.m. is something I can feel all over again just thinking about it.

Ten years later I'd be working in that studio on the local *WNBC News* and then across the hall in Studio 6A on *Tomorrow,* and be taken back to being fourteen.

I'd never felt such a rush as when Doc Severinsen, Johnny's great bandleader, and his famed announcer Ed McMahon warmed up the audience before taping the show that would air at 11:30 p.m. on NBC that night.

They built us up to a near fever pitch in anticipation of Johnny coming out and then at precisely 5:30 p.m., the red light on Camera One flashed. Doc and the band played the opening notes of the famous *Tonight Show* theme and Ed boomed, "And now, heeeere's Johnny."

The monologue, the guests, the band…the hour flew by as if it was five minutes. At the end, I was hooked.

As with my love for Dave Letterman's show, I was pretty much addicted to Carson's. Of course there were no home taping devices or DVRs then, but whenever I was able to I watched at least through Johnny's monologue, which my pals and I discussed and tried to mimic at school the next day (and, as time went on, at work).

So twelve years after that first *Tonight Show* taping, when I found myself playing tennis, swimming, and playing drums with Johnny at his home in Bel-Air (*The Tonight Show* had moved to L.A. in 1972), I was thrilled.

I was there because his middle son, Rick, had become one of my closest friends. Rick, the spitting image of his dad except with the longish hair of the mid-'70s, was our stage manager and then associate director on *Tomorrow*.

Along with Bruce McKay, Debbie Vickers, Pam Burke and a few other twenty-somethings who worked with us, Rick was part of the nucleus of our inseparable gang.

We worked together all day and hung out pretty much every night and on weekends, often joined by our larger-than-life host, Tom Snyder. Rick was a sweet, fun, talented guy who, in addition to his other duties, picked all of the show's great music, which became one of its signatures.

The group shared all the ups and downs of our young careers and relationships with girlfriends or boyfriends. We shared vacations and maybe a little too much partying. Of course, in the mid and late '70s in television, at NBC in New York (and then L.A.), that was pretty much the norm.

In New York, we were taping in the same building (30 Rock) as *Saturday Night Live* and eventually moved to Studio 8G, just down the hall from its famed Studio 8H.

John Belushi, Dan Aykroyd, Chevy Chase, Gilda Radner, and the gang were frequent guests on our show and often just came around to hang out at our "prop bar" after tapings.

It was a different time. Every night before the show, which we taped at 6 p.m. for air later that night, Rick, Bruce, Bob Brown, and I went downstairs to a bar in the bowels of 30 Rock near the skating rink for a pre-show cocktail. I can't even imagine any network or production entity allowing that now.

After the show, we'd open the "prop bar," so called because we kept a full bar in the show's movable prop cabinet, and Tom would hold court with us for a post-show drink and a smoke. We all smoked Marlboros, including Tom, who did so famously in the middle of shows as Ed Murrow had done in his day. Another thing that is unimaginable today.

After that we'd head out to McMasters or Hurley's or another of our favorite hangouts for a bite and some beers. There were other things being consumed as well, including of the herbal and pharmaceutical variety, but that was mostly confined to the weekends. It was a time when network execs, stars, top producers, directors, and studio bosses would be doing the same in their offices right out in the open. Seems impossible, but it's true.

As I said, it was a different time, and for the most part it all seemed fun and "grown-up" and exciting, and everyone was doing it and producing great television along the way. We had a lot of fun for the most part, but there were consequences. My group and I put ourselves in some stupid and dangerous situations and made some seriously bad decisions during this time. We made it through relatively unscathed but for others it became horribly tragic and out of control, and careers and lives were ruined.

I regret some of my behavior and wish I could take that part back. That said, I feel lucky as hell to have made it through ok, and I sincerely apologize to those I hurt or offended during this period on the off chance they might be reading this. I was a jackass at times, especially with several smart, talented, lovely women I dated who truly deserved better.

Rick and I were inseparable. When the show moved to L.A., we got apartments in the same building. Our whole gang hung out there. It was very much like the show *Friends*, but '70s-style and we were in Los Angeles, as opposed to New York.

We taped our show right after Johnny finished his in Studio 1 at NBC in Burbank.

For the first time I had a couple bucks and bought my first nice car. We could afford to eat at nice restaurants once in a while. We'd go to the beach and get together every Saturday night at Bruce and Debbie's house in Beachwood Canyon in the Hollywood Hills to watch *SNL* and party into the night. We'd spend Sunday recuperating, and then it was back to the studio for five more shows starting Monday.

On a few occasions, Rick invited me to his dad's estate in Bel-Air on St. Cloud Road, just a few blocks from where Pat and I live now.

I'll always remember how nice Johnny was to me. I was a decent tennis player, having played on my high school team and my freshman team in college, and Johnny was seriously into tennis at the time.

We'd hit balls intensely for an hour and play some points on his beautiful private court. He was fast and a good player and very intense. It was surreal to pound balls across the net with the man I had seen at NBC hosting *The Tonight Show* when I was fourteen, whom I watched pretty much every night, and whom I idolized.

Later, Rick and I would swim, hang by the pool, and drink beers. Johnny would sit with us for a while sometimes. He was relaxed and funny as hell, as opposed to the many accounts I've read of him being distant and withdrawn in private.

Johnny invited us into his pool house, where he had his drum set, and played for us along with some great jazz on his state-of-the-art stereo.

We did this on several occasions. To this day it was one of the greatest thrills of my life. I'll always be grateful to Rick for including me.

So it's with regret that I now look back on two of the poorest decisions of my life, both related to Rick and Johnny.

Rick and I remained close for years, but when I left *Tomorrow* and we stopped working together, we went in different directions. We had long moved from our shared first apartment building to different parts of Los Angeles. Our group kind of split up and, while we remained friends, we grew apart.

I went on to produce *Entertainment Tonight, This Is Your Life*, and a Richard Pryor movie. I also married Pat. Rick remained single and had a tough time finding his next meaningful work experience after *Tomorrow* ended its run. His love of partying also caught up with him, and he struggled with that as well.

Occasionally we'd talk or get together, but after I headed east to work at CNBC in 1990, we rarely saw each other. Our lives had gone in different directions.

I was executive producing shows at CNBC with Tim Russert, Tom Snyder, Geraldo, Phil Donahue, Al Roker and Dick Cavett, among others. On June 25, 1991, I was sitting in my office going over upcoming shows with the TV on in the background when I learned the most terrible news.

I wasn't paying much attention to what was on the TV until I heard a promo for the local news.

"Johnny Carson's son killed in car accident...tonight at 11," the announcer said.

My heart started racing. I held my breath.

Rick had two brothers. From the promo that ran, I didn't know if it was Rick or one of his brothers, Corey or Chris, who had died. I asked one of our production assistants to check the wire services for more info. My emotions and fears ran wild while I waited for what seemed like hours for confirmation.

A couple of minutes later, a staffer brought me the wire copy reporting Rick's death in a car accident while taking photographs near the Pacific Coast Highway in California. He was thirty-nine.

My eyes filled with tears. I called Tom Snyder, Debbie Vickers, Bruce McKay, and Patty Mann, who had worked with us and had been Rick's girlfriend. We all cried.

They told me there would be a memorial for Rick at a church in the San Fernando Valley near his apartment in L.A. a few days later.

I was in the middle of prepping a live primetime special to air the day after Rick's memorial. I had recently gone from consulting at CNBC to vice president and executive producer of all of the network's primetime shows.

Willing to Be Lucky

In a few days, I would be executive producing my first, high-profile primetime special. I lay awake that night thinking through how I could work ahead and delegate the rest of what needed to be done.

I tried to convince myself I could make it work but there was too much to be done. The timing was just too tough. Ultimately I determined I could not make the cross-country trip without jeopardizing the show. So I didn't go.

I have regretted that decision ever since.

I do think Rick would have understood my decision, but looking back, I wish I had gone. While we were no longer close, at one time we were dear friends and I still cared about him a great deal.

His death, in his late thirties, following a difficult time in his life, was devastating to me, and to all of his friends and *Tomorrow* colleagues.

I wrote a long letter to his dad expressing my sympathy and describing the kind, fun-loving, great person and colleague Rick was.

Upon returning to the show, a few days later, Johnny closed *The Tonight Show* with a heart-wrenching, tear-filled tribute to Rick.

A few days later I received a brief note from Johnny thanking me for my note and for being a friend to Rick.

It was a life lesson and a mistake I would not make again. As much as I despise going to funerals and memorial services, I have not missed another for someone I was close to.

Not long after that day, I inadvertently angered Johnny, or at least Johnny's "camp."

In 1993, after trying for a few years to convince top management at NBC, I was successful in bringing my old pal and mentor Tom Snyder,who had been doing radio, back to tv, with a primetime show on CNBC.

With his old pal and original *Tomorrow* producer-director Joel Tator directing, his friend and former producer Michael Horowicz producing and Tom at the very top of his brilliant game, the show took off. It tripled the ratings in the 10 p.m. timeslot on CNBC.

The press and critics took notice and a series of "love letters," from *The New York Times* on down, praised the return of one of talk TV's most unique and original voices to TV.

Other networks and syndicators took notice, and Tom received offers to move networks for more money, but he loved the freedom and no-pressure atmosphere of CNBC. He said that he thrived in the free and easy relationship he shared with his boss and former employee, yours truly, so he loyally stayed put. That is, until 1994, when he got a call from Dave Letterman.

Following Johnny Carson's retirement as host of *The Tonight Show* in 1992, Dave had moved his show to CBS. NBC, in a well-documented series of events, had decided to go with Jay Leno over Dave as Johnny's replacement.

As part of Dave's deal, his company would control and produce the hour following his own show. The show was to be called *The Late Late Show*.

Since Dave's first appearance on *Tomorrow*, which I'll tell you about in the coming pages, he and Tom had been pals and guested on each other's shows. Dave always admired Tom as a broadcaster and interviewer, and considered Tom a mentor. He offered Tom the hosting job.

As loyal to us as Tom was, and while he was thoroughly enjoying himself at CNBC, it was impossible to not return to the "big tent" of CBS and big-time network television. It was a much bigger paycheck and audience, and it meant the chance to follow and work with Dave and his company, Worldwide Pants.

At that point I had been at CNBC for four years, and Pat and I were looking to move back to our home in L.A. to be with our family full-time. Tom asked me to come with him to produce the new show. That didn't work out, which in the end was for the best, as I never would have ended up at King World a year later.

Tom went on to do his usual brilliant show after Dave's, at 12:30 a.m., on CBS for a few years, until CBS decided it needed a younger host to bring in younger viewers. They hired Craig Kilborn and then Craig Ferguson, who recently handed the reins to British actor-comedian James Corden.

Tom's departure for CBS left a huge hole in the CNBC primetime lineup at 10 p.m., and I didn't have much time to fill it. Just two months, in fact.

Usually networks, as with David Letterman's retirement, plan successions at least a year out, affording them ample time to find and groom a successor and develop the show. In this case, CBS wanted Tom on the air in two months, which left us the same amount of time to scramble and find someone to fill Tom's giant shoes at CNBC.

Marc Rosenweig, my talented senior vice president, along with then-CNBC president Roger Ailes, our team, and I went to work on finding a replacement.

The consumer and trade press were filled with the news of Tom's departure and our search for a replacement. Agents and managers quickly submitted a wide range of possible hosts. They offered mostly the usual suspects: former and aspiring talk show hosts, comedians, actors, and journalists of all stripes.

I resisted talking to the press about it, mostly because we were just too busy and were zeroing in on two or three possible hosts. While trying to get our ducks in a row, in a moment of pure stupidity I agreed to take a brief call from a *New York Post* reporter who asked me a simple question. She said, "If you could pick anyone on Earth to replace Tom, who would you pick?"

Without much thought, I blurted out the most honest answer I could to what I considered a truly hypothetical question.

"Johnny Carson," I said.

It was an honest answer and I thought an innocent, nice shout-out to my all-time favorite talk show host. I added something like, "You never know, he might be bored in retirement, and I know he still has a lot to say, and maybe a show on CNBC, in a low-key setting, might be just the thing for Johnny."

Of course, we had had no discussions with Johnny or his representatives about such a possibility. It was just an honest, I thought obvious, answer to the question.

But when the *Post* editors got ahold of it they went to town and, in true *Post* tabloid style, turned it into a major media frenzy, running a huge headline the next day: "JOHNNY RETURNING TO TV WITH CNBC SERIES?"

The proverbial shit hit the fan. Media outlets all around the country picked up the story and suddenly CNBC, NBC, and all of us were fielding dozens of calls from people wanting to know when Johnny's show was starting, etc.

Of course we explained there was nothing to it, and it soon went away. But I had apparently seriously angered Johnny, or at least his friend and former producer Peter Lassally. Peter publicly, and privately, denounced my comments and claimed I was trying to exploit Johnny and that my comments were completely out of line.

In retrospect, he was partly correct. While I would never have done anything on purpose to upset or exploit Johnny, a hero and someone I looked up to, and had a relationship with years ago through Rick, I should have known better.

I never should have spoken to the *Post* and I certainly should have been smart enough to know how they'd present my well-intentioned answer to what I thought was a back-of-the-book, one-line-in-a-TV-column question.

Was I naive to think that maybe Johnny actually might have been ready to have a forum again in a more low-key way with a little show on CNBC? Yes, I admit I thought my comment might at least get him thinking about it and that as I (and my dad and E.B. White) said, "You have to be willing to be lucky" in life and in television. But I certainly had not planned it in any way. And that doesn't excuse it.

I sent Johnny a note apologizing for the whole mess. I was told he got it and accepted my apology, but to this day I feel like a dope for falling into that trap.

In the end we hired the brilliant actor-writer Charles Grodin, one of Johnny's favorite guests, to take over for Tom.

I'll always value the great times and the many shared experiences I had with Rick and Johnny Carson, both in person and through my TV. While I regret those two decisions and hopefully have learned from them, my overall relationship with both was overwhelmingly positive and I treasure them.

*Tom Snyder, Rick Carson, and I prepare to tape a Tomorrow show at Studio 54, the infamous NYC club, at the height of its run in the late 1970s*

*Johnny Carson with Tom Snyder during Carson's appearance on Tomorrow*

# 13

## BOOKING LETTERMAN ON HIS FIRST NETWORK SHOW, AND PASSING ON ROBIN WILLIAMS

I've only met David Letterman three times, but as my friends and family know, right up until the last day of *Late Show With David Letterman*, I watched him (on DVR) almost daily during workouts. I also liked to repurpose his jokes at my weekly "prayer meeting," aka my Thursday night poker game with the same guys for the past thirty years.

Also, at birthday parties and other events, I annoy everyone with my own lame Top 10 lists. I've been doing these since Dave took over our 12:30 a.m. *Tomorrow* time period on NBC in 1982 (now *Late Night With Seth Meyers*).

For four years, I was a producer on the Emmy Award-winning *Tomorrow*, which followed Johnny Carson's *Tonight Show* for eight years on NBC. *Tomorrow* starred another of my biggest influences and mentors, the great Tom Snyder, whom I've told you about.

In the smallest of ways, I may have inadvertently helped sow the seeds of Dave replacing Tom, because six years earlier in 1976, as a twenty-five-year-old segment producer on *Tomorrow*, I booked Dave on network television for the first time.

I had the idea to do a show on up-and-coming young comics and approached my bosses, executive producers Pam Burke and Bruce McKay, with the idea. They gave me the go-ahead.

The first thing I did was call the legendary talent manager Buddy Morra, whom I had met and become pals with after doing a piece on his client and my favorite comic, Robert Klein, for WNBC-TV news.

Buddy and his partners, Charles Joffe and Jack Rollins, were the deans of comedy managers, representing Woody Allen and many of the top comedy stars of that time. They also represented a bunch of rising young talents, including Billy Crystal, who was just beginning to be known, as well as Robin Williams and Dave. All three were starting their careers at the Comedy Store in Los Angeles.

In a conversation with Billy many years later on his show, Dave affectionately referred to Buddy and his laid-back management style as "the master of the standing nap," a story that Buddy, in his mid-eighties now, loves to recount.

So when I asked Buddy who to book on the young comics show besides Billy (whom I knew and liked a lot), he suggested Robin and Dave.

Tom Snyder had just one rule: If you booked someone on the show, they had better be good talkers. He rarely got mad at his producers if things went sideways, but if the guests you booked were not good talkers, that was big trouble. Good rule for a talk show, huh?

Like producers on most talk shows, the central way we went about finding out if someone was a good talker was through what's called a "pre-interview," usually done by phone. Tom's theory was if they were great on the phone, they'd probably be good on the show. If they were not great on the phone, then the pressure of the lights and cameras, along with a nationwide audience, probably wouldn't help.

Most of the time that worked out to be a good theory. In this one case, yes and no.

Billy was a quick yes and became a regular guest and someone my wife, Pat, and I worked with a few more times. Billy cast and directed Pat as Roger Maris's wife in his wonderful HBO movie *61\**, and Billy appeared on our series *Rock 'n' Roll Evening News* and later *Hollywood Squares* with Robin and Whoopi Goldberg. More on that later.

Dave had never been on network television, but on the phone I found him to be funny and easy to talk to. We chatted about his nightly gigs at the Comedy Store in L.A. and how different L.A. was from his home state of Indiana. He was relaxed, funny, and forthcoming.

I booked him for what became his first network gig. His appearance on *Tomorrow* went well. As he was on the phone, he was glib and confident in a low-key way. Dave, Billy Crystal, Merrill Markoe (Dave's head writer and girlfriend at the time), and Rick Newman, who owned the comedy club

Catch a Rising Star in New York, traded quips and funny stories about the world of stand-up comedy with Snyder.

Soon after, Dave was booked on the first of many *Tonight* shows and his career "blew up," as the kids say. He also was booked as a headliner in Vegas and at comedy clubs around the country. He then became a guest host on *The Tonight Show*.

From time to time over the next twenty years, I saw Dave when I accompanied Tom as a guest on Dave's show on NBC, and later CBS. Dave was always great to Tom, and did a long and moving tribute to him when he passed away in 2007.

On the other hand, Robin, as is the case with many comics when they're not on stage, was practically monosyllabic during our pre-interview. I declined to book him. Soon after, the brilliant writer-director Garry Marshall cast him as Mork on *Mork and Mindy* and his career was off and running. He became a regular on all the major talk shows and "killed" every time.

Clearly passing on Robin was a decision I've always regretted, for as we learned, Robin would have been great on the show.

So while I can brag about putting Letterman on network television for the first time, I also have to admit I passed on Robin Williams.

Fortunately, I got to work with Robin again and was able to tell him the story twenty or so years later when we were doing *Hollywood Squares* at King World, and he did a week of shows with Billy and Whoopi to promote Comic Relief.

I think the reason I took so immediately to Dave, more than any other comedian or host, is that there's a lot of Tom in him. He's so smart, articulate, and interested in the world. He is one of the few guys on TV who, as he demonstrated after 9/11 and countless other events in the news, can speak live on just about any topic. Dave has a natural gift for humor, of course, but he gets that jokes and scripted desk pieces are not enough.

Johnny Carson, Dave's other mentor, had the same ability. He didn't need cue cards or a script to be funny or touch people's hearts.

Talent like that is rare, and one of the great pleasures and privileges we have as viewers. As soon as he retired, I began missing Dave's presence on the air very much. I hope he'll decide to do something else soon to express his unique voice.

A week before his last CBS show, I sent Dave a note and asked him to please keep talking to us in some way—on the radio, a podcast, or a new smaller show on cable or the web. I told him that the country needs his voice. I can't wait to watch his new series on Netflix.

There will be many more Letterman references and jokes throughout these pages but my favorite moment of all was when he had Rush Limbaugh on his show in 1993. You could always tell when Dave loved or didn't love a guest, and in this case it was obviously the latter.

Dave was polite but clearly couldn't wait for the segment to end. After the opinionated master of right-wing radio went on a rant against Hillary Clinton, mentioning that she had put on weight, among other barbs about her, Dave took a beat. Then he looked over at Limbaugh and with perfect timing said, "Well, you can say that because you, Rush, are a perfect human specimen."

God love you, Dave!

But the words that I'll always appreciate most from Dave were the ones he said on his first night back on the air after 9/11.

He was the first late-night host to go back on the air, just a few days after.

From his studio, just north of the fallen Trade Towers, to a city and country still in shock and fear, Dave opened his show with no band, no applause. Just these words:

"There is only one requirement for any of us, and that is to be courageous, because courage, as you might know, defines all other human behavior."

Dave let us know it was OK to get back to living our lives and it was going to be OK.

# 14

## THE GREAT JIMMY CAGNEY, "NO SWEAT, NO STRAIN," AND "ANDY HAD TO GET ON THE HORSE"

In 1978 when Tom Snyder was at his peak, winning an Emmy Award for hosting *Tomorrow* and anchoring for *NBC News* and primetime magazine shows, NBC offered him three primetime specials similar to the Barbara Walters specials on ABC.

Tom asked me to write and produce them, and at twenty-six, after a few years at *NBC News* and *Tomorrow*, I was excited about the opportunity. The gig took me from 30 Rock in New York to the NBC studios in Burbank.

We were lucky to score some major booking coups with then-mega stars Clint Eastwood, Cher, Jack Lemmon, Carroll O'Connor (who was starring in the top-rated television series *All in the Family*) and "It Girl" Bo Derek, star of the movie *10,* among others.

But the one person Tom and I wanted most was the legendary, Oscar-winning actor Jimmy Cagney.

Along with Humphrey Bogart, Cagney was my favorite tough-guy actor growing up, starring in countless gangster flicks such as *The Public Enemy,* but he could also sing and dance and had great comedy chops, as he displayed in films like *Yankee Doodle Dandy* and Billy Wilder's classic *One, Two, Three.*

At this point, he was long retired, and had not appeared on TV or in movies for decades; he was living quietly on a 100-acre horse farm in Upstate New York in a town called Pawling, about an hour and a half north of Manhattan. Pawling, coincidentally, is where Ed Murrow's dairy farm was. It was a place I spent many wonderful times as a kid being taught by Mr. Murrow everything from how to shoot a .22 rifle to how to milk a cow.

For years, Barbara Walters, Mike Wallace, and *60 Minutes*, along with the *Today* show, *Good Morning America,* and just about everyone else had been after the ultimate big "get," an interview with the elusive Cagney. His reps turned down request after request.

My dad used to quote E.B. White's wonderful line, "You have to be willing to be lucky." I was determined to land my movie hero, and I was willing to keep trying through any avenue I could think of.

I got lucky when I took a different path away from the normal agents, PR people, and other regular gatekeepers. I wrote to his housekeeper/nurse, who took care of Mr. Cagney and his wife in their modest stone house on the farm.

After a couple months of letter writing, explaining my and Tom's love and admiration for him and the interview we wanted to do, I received a call from his caretaker, who invited me to come up for a visit. I was thrilled to get the call and shared the news with Tom, who was equally excited. He helped me craft our pitch to the legend.

I drove up the Taconic Parkway from Manhattan to Pawling on a chilly spring day in disbelief that I was about to meet with James Cagney. All the way on the ninety-minute drive north, I went over and over our pitch and why Tom was the best choice: because he was a true student of Cagney's films and his history, how their personalities and senses of humor were simpatico. All the while I kept playing scenes from *The Public Enemy, One, Two, Three,* and *Yankee Doodle Dandy,* three of my favorite classic Cagney films, in my head.

I could not have been more excited to meet another human being.

My palms were sweaty and I could feel my heart beating. I kept breathing in and out in a form of meditation to keep calm and maintain my focus as I rehearsed the pitch in my mind. I had spent six months writing and calling, and now I could see the finish line of what could only be called a major get for Tom, me, and NBC.

Cagney couldn't have been nicer to me: quiet, welcoming, and completely down to earth. He asked me about my hopes for the interview and some of the logistics. He offered me some lunch. We chatted some more about everything from the Yankees to his upcoming appearance in the movie *Ragtime*, his first acting job in many years, which he was excited about.

After lunch he walked me out to my car, down a grass and dirt road. When we got to my car, he casually turned to me and thanked me for coming and said, "Tell Tom I'd be pleased to do the interview."

He said yes! I couldn't believe it. My head was exploding with joy and excitement as I tried to keep my cool and thanked him profusely. He must have known how thrilled I was as he smiled and wished me a safe drive home.

Needless to say, Tom and everyone at NBC were likewise excited, as was the press. Papers across the country ran stories about our upcoming interview. I heard through the grapevine that Mike Wallace and Barbara Walters were pissed.

A few weeks later, the big day came. My crew and I arrived early and set up so that by the time Tom arrived around 1 p.m. we were ready to go.

The interview far exceeded all expectations. Mr. Cagney regaled Tom with wonderful anecdotes from the making of his classic films.

All the while he downplayed his work, saying repeatedly, "It was no big deal; just some singing, some dancing, and some acting. No sweat, no strain."

That became a catch phrase for Tom and me and our crew: "No sweat, no strain."

Safe to say, it was one of Tom's, and of course my, favorite interviews ever. When it was over, we shot some B-roll of Tom and James touring the farm. In post, we edited in some great clips from *Yankee Doodle Dandy* and others, and the net result was one of the best shows we ever did. It got great reviews and ratings and to this day is one of my top five career highlights.

In the TV class I taught at USC, I told that story with the quote about "willing to be lucky" and never giving up on a seemingly impossible "get." How you can't accept "no" from agents, managers, and publicists. In fact, oftentimes you need to open up other avenues, like my letter-writing campaign to the nurse/housekeeper. Just find a way. Any way. This applies to a big interview and, in my opinion, pretty much anything else you really want in life. (I'm talking to the younger folks who might be reading.)

Here's a little story from the shoot you might enjoy. We had finished setting up early and, with a couple hours to kill before Tom arrived. Mr. Cagney generously suggested my crew and I might want to take a ride on his horses to pass the time. Naturally, I agreed.

We followed the attractive young woman who ran his stable over to the barn, and when she asked who'd like to go first, my crew volunteered me. Though I was not a horse person, I felt confident, since I had ridden the old nags in Griffith Park in L.A. once or twice and had no trouble as they slowly walked along the scenic trails.

What could possibly go wrong?

There was just one problem: These were five-year-old, recently retired thoroughbreds, with Eastern saddles and nothing to hang on to like the Western saddles in Griffith Park. The horse they put me on knew instantly that I had no idea what I was doing and took off in a full gallop.

She bolted straight toward a white fence, and I was sure she was going to jump over it on her way to God knows where. So I decided my best hope of survival was to bail. I did so by jumping off. I landed on my left wrist, breaking it.

The crew and I were laughing (and quite possibly the horse, too) as I got up and dusted myself off. What a dope.

I declined Mr. Cagney's offer of a hospital visit (no way would I risk missing the interview), put some ice on it, and waited for Tom to arrive.

By the time Tom got there, my wrist was pretty swollen and I had a bit of a fever. But there was no way I was leaving.

When we finished, the swelling and pain were intense but I was so happy about the taping that it didn't matter. More ice, aspirin, some lunch and a seemingly endless three-hour ride in traffic back to Manhattan followed. On the ride down, Tom decided it would be best to stop for a bite and a couple vodkas to ease the pain...not a good idea.

I arrived in the emergency room at Lennox Hill Hospital in Manhattan about eight hours after my wrist was broken. By now my wrist was as big as my leg. I was running a 103-degree fever, and the doctors told me I was in mild shock.

They fixed me up and a couple hours later I was in a cast. Of course it was all worth it and much, much more.

In Tom's *Tomorrow* monologue the next night, and for months after, he relished telling the story over and over: "Andy HAD to get on the horse." Followed by the famous Snyder laugh: "*Ha ha ha ha ha. Ha ha ha ha ha. Ha ha ha ha ha.*"

I keep the picture of Mr. Cagney and me over my bar and it remains one of my favorite memories.

The word "legend" is often overused. Not in this case.

*In this photograph of Mr. Cagney and me chatting on his porch as we awaited Tom's arrival the day of the taping, you may notice I'm holding my left wrist. That's because it was broken.*

# 15

## THE FIRST BIG BUMP IN THE CAREER ROAD

The four primetime specials Tom Snyder and I did for NBC in 1977 and 1978 marked a turning point in my career.

After cutting my teeth and learning to write, produce, and direct at *NBC News* and *Tomorrow*, I got to be in charge of these four primetime specials.

I'd been involved in more than 500 broadcasts, doing almost every job imaginable, but I'd never been in charge or responsible for the final product as the boss.

Bruce McKay, as co-executive producer along with Pam Burke and Tom, had hired me onto *Tomorrow* from WNBC and was now vice president of specials for NBC.

With his help, we set up a small but talented team in Burbank and began the task of booking and producing *Tom Snyder's Celebrity Spotlight*. Kind of a corny title but that's what NBC wanted to call them.

The conceit was to use Tom's rising popularity and stardom and tremendous interview skills to compete with the highly successful specials Barbara Walters was doing on ABC.

The programs were relatively inexpensive to produce and garnered strong ratings for NBC.

Our associate producer was Debbie Vickers, who started on *Tomorrow* as an assistant and was Bruce McKay's significant other for many years. Debbie was, in her own right, a smart, fun, charismatic leader and producer, who quickly rose through the ranks and went on to become Jay Leno's executive producer for decades. She was part of the small but talented and close-knit team behind the specials. So was Rick Carson, Johnny's son, who was our associate director, a role he filled on *Tomorrow* as well.

We were all in our twenties and learning about life and love and career.

It was a heady time. We worked all day and night and hung out together on weekends. My life and career were going better than I could have hoped.

I got a call from the famed William Morris Agency after the third special saying they had an exciting new series for NBC, executive produced by George Schlatter, the legendary producer who co-created *Laugh-In* with Ed Friendly (no relation), and they wanted to talk to me about it. They wanted to represent me; I saw only more blue skies ahead.

Little did I know, I was headed for the first big fall in my career.

Schlatter had a thirteen-show commitment from NBC to do a weekly series called *Speak Up, America,* hosted by Marjoe Gortner, the former evangelist, and sportscaster Jayne Kennedy. The show would, in his words, combine the humor and cutting-edge wit and production of *Laugh-In* (one of the hippest, groundbreaking shows of the 1960s, which I loved and watched religiously) with timely and topical current events in the news.

Schlatter wanted me to write, produce, and "be his partner." William Morris represented him and wanted to represent me and promised that this was just the beginning of their plans for me.

On top of all that, NBC was going to pay me a whopping $4,000 a week, double what I was making on the Snyder specials. In 1979 dollars, that was big money for a kid in his mid-twenties. It's the equivalent of nearly $15,000 in 2017.

The allure of it all was too exciting. After a tough conversation with my mentor, Tom, and our wonderful team, I left the "nest" so to speak for what I thought were greener, bigger, primetime series pastures, the William Morris Agency, and a big payday.

Within days of moving into the *Speak Up, America* offices on Beverly Boulevard, I realized the only reason I was there was that NBC had insisted Schlatter hire a producer with a news background to appease the affiliates who were concerned that George, while hitting it big with *Laugh-In* and *Real People*, did not have a background in news.

This new series, based on events in the news, needed a producer who could ensure the show would be faithful to the ethics and standards of an NBC News program, even though it was being produced by the entertainment division.

George of course went along with this plan, brought me in, and pretty much immediately stuck me in a downstairs office far removed from him and his real team and basically ignored me for the run of the series.

I went from being part of a great, successful team of close friends and people I loved and respected, doing quality, exciting television, to being a non-contributing, non-participating, albeit well-paid, fancy-titled outcast with nothing to do on an embarrassingly awful show.

When I called my agent at William Morris, who also represented George, I was sure they'd talk to him and all would soon be resolved. How naive I was. They did nothing.

George was a huge client who made millions for the agency in packaging fees on the huge series he'd produced over the years. I was just one of many "up-and-coming" young producers on a salary they couldn't even commission since they represented the "package" and George's company.

The only relief was that the show was a complete bomb and was canceled after just thirteen episodes. I've had naps longer than that.

There was an upside…

I met some talented producers there, including the brilliant Steve Paskay, whom I took with me to my next job, producing and writing the two-hour, 30th-anniversary special of *This Is Your Life* for NBC, then *Entertainment Tonight* and several others.

While it took some time to get over that experience, I later ran into George at some parties and industry events and we got along fine; I even used his edit facilities on a couple of shows. I see him around from time to time these days and I always enjoy seeing him. It wasn't really his fault and it certainly wasn't personal.

He never wanted or needed me for the show. He was just appeasing the network and was always going to do his own thing. He was and is a very talented guy.

It was a wake-up call of sorts for me. I kind of grew up in a sense and became a lot less naive about the business, and hopefully stronger.

I realized that the business was not always going to be fun and that my career would not always be satisfying or perfect, and that things in TV are not always what they seem or what agents tell you they are. It seems so obvious when looking back. How naive and trusting I was at that age. I left the agency and signed with a smart young agent at CAA named Phil Kent, who went on to run Ted Turner's company. A good guy, but never got me any work. He commissioned the jobs I got myself, though. Good gig!

Soon after I decided I'd be better off on my own.

A couple years later I was lucky enough to meet David Nochimson, who's been my lawyer and dear friend for thirty-five years and has negotiated all my deals starting with *Here and Now*, the Richard Pryor movie we produced for Columbia Pictures in 1983. More on David…and Richard in the pages ahead.

Fortunately my next boss, the great Ralph Edwards, and the big *This Is Your Life: 30th- Anniversary Special* we did together for NBC, were the perfect antidote to *Speak Up, America.*

# 16

## *THIS IS YOUR LIFE*, RALPH EDWARDS: PIONEER, LEGEND, GENTLEMAN…AND "DON'T GIVE THEM TOO MANY CHOCOLATE ÉCLAIRS"

In 1980, after the primetime specials Tom and I did for NBC, and despite the less-than-ideal experience on *Speak Up, America*, NBC approached me about a two-hour primetime special celebrating the 30th anniversary of Ralph Edwards' iconic series *This Is Your Life.*

I had enjoyed the pioneering, early black-and-white series growing up, as Ralph surprised stars such as Milton Berle and Lucille Ball. For those of you who may not be familiar with it, the series, through a combination of documentary and usually hysterical and/or moving surprise reunions before a live studio audience, told people's life stories.

The show was created and hosted by a wonderful man named Ralph Edwards, who over the years and several iterations had refined the format, writing, production, and hosting of the show into a precise, fail-safe format.

His company, a tightly bonded group of talented friends and family, worked like a well-oiled machine captained by their kind and distinguished leader, Mr. Edwards.

But he was a little older now, in his mid-sixties, and while he still looked great and was as sharp as ever, NBC decided to bring in the larger-than-life British television host and interviewer David Frost to take over hosting duties from Ralph.

Ralph and his company would still be the production entity. I would write and produce the two-hour special, a combination of highlighted clips from the classic old shows along with two brand-new "lives" at about a half-hour each.

The new segments would be complete with the lavish surprise opening, mystery guests from the subjects' lives, and all the trappings. We brought in the talented English director Bruce Gowers (*American Idol*) to direct and we were off and running.

I'm sure Ralph was not thrilled about turning over the host duties, but as always he handled things with class. Frost was a smart, if at times bombastic, host and interviewer.

He had hosted the very funny and groundbreaking mock-news program *That Was the Week That Was*, and had recently received high marks for his tough and extensive post-Watergate interviews with Richard Nixon.

So there was great excitement and anticipation when Frost flew in from London on the Concorde and walked in to meet Ralph and me and the team in Ralph's stately office in a tall building overlooking Hollywood.

Ralph, dressed immaculately in a navy suit and tie, greeted David warmly. David, after a long day of intercontinental flying and possibly some adult beverages along the way, was in an ebullient mood, to put it diplomatically. "More pinot grigio, Mr. Frost?"

Before Ralph could say "Welcome," Frost took off on a thirty-minute monologue about his view of the old shows, his vision and plan for the new "lives" we were about to produce, and how the special should be booked, written, produced, directed, promoted, and hosted.

As Ralph and the rest of the key team listened, Frost, who had yet to take off his London Fog raincoat, stood up and began pacing back and forth and around Ralph's large office. With his shirt and tie undone and hair a mess, Frost put on quite a show. His presentation picked up even more speed.

After about a half-hour he plopped down in a big red leather chair, told Ralph how lovely it was to meet him and what a fan he was, and then asked, "Well, what do you think?"

Ralph, always the consummate gentleman, and knowing this might not be the moment to explain how the show really works as proven by decades of success, responded, "Welcome, David, it's great to have you. You've clearly thought a great deal about the show, and in the days ahead we look forward to working with you closely."

Some wine and hors d'oeuvres were served and we adjourned.

In the end, David was a fine host, if a bit of a character, and proved smart enough to know that Ralph and his team knew exactly how to write, produce, and host the show, and things went relatively smoothly.

That is, until I had the great idea to surprise our first mystery guest, the legendary actor Charlton Heston, from a helicopter.

At the time, Heston was one of the biggest movie stars in the world. We decided to outfit Frost in a tuxedo, have him hold the famed *This Is Your Life* leather-bound script, and descend from a helicopter above Heston's Beverly Hills estate. He was to land on Heston's tennis court in the middle of his Saturday morning game. What could possibly go wrong?

This was a precarious idea for several reasons. For one thing, it was a very windy day, and the landing area, one side of the court, was dangerously small. Also, Heston was wearing his toupee, and between the wind and the huge gale displaced by the chopper's rotors, there was a good chance his "piece" would fly off. Never mind we could have had a horrible, life-threatening accident. I clearly saw my career coming to an abrupt end right before my eyes at my own hand.

When Heston saw the helicopter and Frost in his tux hovering above his tennis court, he was not happy and tried to wave the chopper off. But his wife and others in the tennis group clued him in to what was going on and that he was being taped for national television. So he relented and went along as our brilliant pilot managed to fight strong winds and land the helicopter safely.

Frost jumped out, book in hand, and ran over to a now "got" and good-natured Heston and exclaimed, "Charlton Heston, this is your life!"

After Heston cleaned up a bit, a limo whisked him to a waiting studio audience and surprise visits from old friends, teachers, and other stars, including the great Orson Welles, at the NBC Studios in Burbank. It turned out to be a great show. And yes, his "piece" stayed on despite the wind and the chopper.

Looking back, it was one of the scariest and probably dumbest things I ever did (among many). But it worked out and made for quite an opening and some great ratings.

The second of our new "lives" was the classic Rodney Dangerfield, at the time among the funniest and most popular comedians in the world.

After Heston, we decided to take a safer route with Dangerfield's opening surprise. We decided to surprise him in his massive dressing room just as he was to take the stage before a sold-out crowd at the Sands Hotel in Las Vegas.

En masse, several cameras rolling, with Frost in his tux and book in hand, we barged into Rodney's backstage dressing room into a dense fog of marijuana smoke. Apparently Rodney liked to get a little "herbed up" before a show.

The weed cloud all but obscured Rodney across the room and made the now even more hilarious "surprise" barely viewable.

Somehow our talented director Bruce Gowers and his guys managed to fight through the smoke, and a truly shocked and apparently baked Rodney came through like the pro he was and gave us a hysterical surprise open and a great show before a thousand or so audience members at the Sands.

Just a week before air, these two new "lives" had to be edited down from more than an hour each of footage to about twenty minutes for air, along with editing decades of highlights from Ralph's early black-and-white classics.

At one point we took over three full edit bays at the top edit facility in Hollywood and worked three shifts of editors, twenty-four-hours a day, for five days straight.

During that time, I slept on the editing room couch an hour here and an hour there as Bruce Gowers, who was doing the same, and I worked straight through, delivering the two-hour special to NBC just hours before air.

The stamina of youth. These days I can barely make it through the day without a nap.

It was a solid ratings and critical success, and a few years later we did thirty-nine new half-hours with NBC for syndication, with my trusty right-hand men and close pals Steve Paskay and Bob Parkinson writing and producing and the talented Bruce Gowers directing.

The best part was getting to work with the great Ralph Edwards.

He taught me that despite my early mentoring by the brilliant but "bulls in a china shop" Fred Friendly and Tom Snyder, it's possible to make good television with quiet grace, patience, and compromise.

Despite putting Frost and our crew's lives at stake, I am happy that fortunately things worked out and Ralph was happy with the result. That is what really mattered, as the show was his baby and he cared deeply.

Over the years we stayed friends.

Ralph taught me a great deal about television and about grace under pressure.

The following is the tribute to Ralph I delivered before I introduced a Hollywood Radio & Television Society "Hitmakers" luncheon to a sold-out industry crowd of 600 shortly after his death in 2005.

*Good afternoon.*

*Before we get started, I want to take a moment to salute one of the pioneers, one of the original "Hitmakers" of our industry, my friend and mentor, Ralph Edwards, who passed away on November 16 at 92.*

*Ralph's charm, wit and one-of-a-kind voice were enjoyed in American living rooms for more than half a century.*

*Starting in radio, he made a successful transition to television in the early '50s, when he created, produced and hosted groundbreaking series like* Truth or Consequences *and his signature* This Is Your Life, *which ran in primetime on NBC for nine seasons and again for many years in first-run syndication.*

*Over his long and distinguished career, Ralph won dozens of awards, including two Emmys and a Lifetime Achievement Award from the Academy of Television Arts and Sciences.*

*I was lucky enough to work with this brilliant and wonderful man when I produced the two-hour 30th anniversary of* This Is Your Life *for NBC and, a year later, thirty-nine new episodes for syndication.*

*Growing up around my dad, Ed Murrow and the professionals at CBS News, and over a career in television, I have been blessed to know and work with many unique and brilliant talents in front of and behind the cameras.*

*I have never known a nicer or classier person nor a finer craftsman than Ralph Edwards.*

*Each word, each sentence, each frame, of every one of the hundreds of programs he made mattered dearly to him.*

*He was a passionate perfectionist who drove himself and all of us who worked for him to their limits to achieve our best.*

*He was relentless but he did it with grace and with kindness. In all the years I worked for him, even under the greatest pressure, I never heard him raise his voice or say an unkind word.*

*He was also a teacher, a philanthropist, giving and raising tens of millions to a wide range of charities and causes over a lifetime of caring for others.*

*Every year since 1950, there has been at least one Ralph Edwards series on television.*

*His legacy will continue with a brand-new version of* This Is Your Life *on ABC next year, along with the continuing* People's Court, *which he produced with his longtime partner Stu Billet, who is with us today along with daughter Barbara, son Gary and longtime producer Bianca Pino, all of whom will continue to run Ralph Edwards Productions for many years to come.*

*A longtime HRTS member and supporter, Ralph will be honored Thursday at a memorial service at Beverly Hills Presbyterian Church starting at 11 a.m.*

*In closing, I just want to say how lucky I feel to have known and worked for this wonderful man.*

*He stood for all that is good about our business. He was one of its pioneers, one of its greats.*

*He will be missed. Thank you.*

**Postscript**: One of Ralph's favorite lines when it came to producing the show and TV in general was: "Don't give the viewer too many chocolate éclairs. Everyone loves chocolate éclairs but you must save them."

He was referring, of course, to those most wonderful, sentimental, heartwarming reunion moments when a guest would be reunited with an old friend, teacher, or relative they hadn't seen in years. A great TV production lesson I learned and stuck by throughout my career. Classic Ralph.

*I keep this photo of Ralph, with his kind inscription, in my study
where I see it every day. It reminds me how lucky
I am to have worked with giants.*

**RALPH EDWARDS**

1717 NORTH HIGHLAND AVENUE

HOLLYWOOD, CALIFORNIA 90028

April 28, 1986

Dear Pat and Andy,

Every once in a while something so darn right and nice happens that you want to jump up and shout "Atta Boy, God!"

We couldn't be happier than if it were our own son (I guess we have a patch of you, at least, Andy) and daughter-to-be. It's going to be a wonderful world for you.

Pat Friendly, as I mentioned into your answer box, has a real inviting sound.

Much love,

*Ralph & Barbara*

*A letter Ralph sent soon after Pat and I were married, which sums up his kind spirit and our close relationship*

*The team at the taping of a show from the 1983-84 syndicated series (L-R): host Joe Campanella, me, Jane Fonda, Mimi Silbert, Ralph Edwards, and my co-producers and loyal right-hand men, Bob Parkinson and Steve Paskay.*

*(Nice '80s beard and mustache, Andy. Honestly, did I even OWN a mirror?)*

112

**NBC**  National Broadcasting Company, Inc.   Thirty Rockefeller Plaza
New York, N.Y. 10020   212-664-4555

Fred Silverman
President and
Chief Executive Officer

March 20, 1981

Mr. Andrew Friendly
838 North Doheny Drive #607
Los Angeles, California  90069

Dear Andy:

Thanks very much for your nice letter.

I know how hard everyone worked on "This is Your
Life" -- and we appreciate that.  It was a good
show.

I hope we'll be doing more together in the future.

All good wishes.

Sincerely,

Fred Silverman

---

**NBC Studios** — Studio 4

3000 W. Alameda Ave., Burbank, California

You are invited to a special presentation of
**This Is Your Life**
30th Anniversary Special
Starring Ralph Edwards, David Frost,
and additional surprises
Audience Will Appear On Camera
Gentlemen are requested to wear coats and ties
Minimum age 14
Ticket distribution is in excess of studio capacity

Monday
February
**16**
1981

Show time
4:30 pm

Guests must
arrive before
3:30 pm

*A note from then-NBC president Fred Silverman, which
meant a lot to me, and a ticket to the NBC taping*

# 17

## *ENTERTAINMENT TONIGHT*…THE STARTUP, BURNOUT, AN EMMY NOMINATION, AND LESSONS LEARNED

In the spring of 1981, I was wrapping up the two-hour *This Is Your Life: 30th Anniversary Special* that I was writing and producing for NBC when I heard about a new day-and-date newsmagazine Paramount was developing about the entertainment business and its stars.

The combination of news, high-profile, big-get interviews, and behind-the-scenes magazine pieces on the issues and inner workings of the industry appealed to me and seemed right in my wheelhouse, given my background. There was a very long and accomplished list of producers vying for the job, many more accomplished than me.

The hiring process was arduous and highly competitive for this first-of its-kind, lavishly expensive, complex series. (This was years before *Access Hollywood, Extra, Inside Edition,* or *The Insider.*)

I had seven intense job interviews, including meetings with Michael Eisner, Barry Diller, and Rich Frank (the moguls who ran Paramount) and Jack Haley Jr., the famed producer of *That's Entertainment!,* who was to be the executive producer. Finally, the day after my final interview with Eisner and Diller, I got a call that I was being offered the job.

Not yet thirty years old, I was facing the biggest, most daunting challenge of my life to that point.

With a then-unheard-of budget of nearly $25 million per year, I was tasked with building a staff, an editorial and production infrastructure, and creating a show architecture from content to talent to newsgathering to establishing bureaus to graphics to music for a show that would be fed live every day to stations around the country, many of which did not yet have dishes to receive satellite feeds. No one had ever done a newsmagazine on a daily basis in syndication. This was brand-new.

When I reported to work on a June morning in 1981, I found there was no functioning office, staff, or infrastructure at all, but rather an empty sound stage at the historic Paramount Studios.

Jack Haley Jr., who was to be my boss, wasn't there. Just the woman hired to be my assistant, Carolyn. She told me straight away that Diller, Eisner, and Frank wanted me to come to lunch in their private dining room.

When I arrived, they got straight to the point: Jack Haley Jr. was out, they said. I would in effect be the showrunner as producer, reporting to the three of them.

They also told me the pilot Haley had produced a few months earlier, featuring light, fluffy, gossipy segments about celebs, was not the show we were going to do, and that we'd be starting over from scratch.

They laid out their vision for a nightly newsmagazine about show business that was part *60 Minutes*, part *Nightly News*; it would be smart and credible and would truly probe the issues and inner workings of the business.

They reviewed my budget and directed me to hire a staff of a couple hundred people, build a production and editorial infrastructure including a bureau in New York, and be ready to go on the air six days a week, starting in three months.

I walked back to my empty office and sat there by myself in a state of mild shock for about an hour, contemplating the reality of what I'd just heard, the reality that so little was in place and that there was so little time before we were to go on the air in September.

At *NBC News*, which already had bureaus, reporters, producers, crews, and vast worldwide infrastructure, it often took six months to a year to launch a new weekly magazine like *Prime Time Sunday*, which I had worked on.

I sat there quietly trying to breathe deeply and not panic as I started to make an initial to-do list. It was so big and so vast. What had I gotten myself into?

When I snapped out of it, I told my assistant Carolyn, "We have some work to do."

The first call I made was to my talented co-producer on *This Is Your Life:* Steve Paskay. All I remember saying was, "Get over here to Paramount, I need you, bud."

For the next six months until I resigned after fifty-two shows, just days before my 30th birthday, Steve and I and the rest of our talented team worked seven days a week, literally eighteen hours a day, under the greatest pressure I'd ever known.

The pressure was not just from the sheer size of the effort but also from the battles between Paramount and its production partners at Cox, Taft, and TeleRep, whose executives had a much more tabloid vision of the show than Diller, Eisner, and Frank did.

For example: In my near daily meetings with Eisner and Diller leading up to the launch, they might suggest a lengthy, thought-provoking piece on media censorship by the government.

When an executive from TeleRep came by the office the next day and saw that segment on a blue index card on my office wall, indicating we were working on that piece, the executive would question me about why we were doing such an esoteric, dull segment and insist we do an exposé on a major celeb's rumored affair instead.

Even with the mixed messages and unimaginable deadlines, I was optimistic.

Here are some excerpts from an article that ran on the front page of the Calendar section of the *Los Angeles Times* before the show went on the air.

### LOS ANGELES TIMES

*"TV SHOW-BIZ MAGAZINE FOR FRED AND MARGE"*
*By Howard Rosenberg,* June 1981

*The next TV newsmagazine scheduled--Entertainment Tonight--is an awesome undertaking and something to keep an eye on. It is among the most ambitious of the genre, a six-times-a-week syndicated program covering entertainment from Asner to Zoetrope, transmitted daily via Westar III satellite to more than 100 subscriber stations, most of which are putting up their own earth stations to receive it.....* *"They do health shows, consumer shows and others, so why not a show on entertainment?"* *asked bearded Andy Friendly, the 29-year-old man to whom has fallen the task of "setting up a news operation in three months with one one-hundredth of the budget of the (network) nightly news." ...*

*Friendly also isn't interested in producing a video trade paper. "I read this, but it all bores me," he said, holding up a copy of* Variety. *"If I couldn't care less, I know Fred and Marge couldn't care less."*

*Fred and Marge?*

*Fred and Marge are a mythical couple in Des Moines, Iowa, Friendly envisions as typical TV viewers....*

*Amid the chaos of rushing to pull things together in only a few months, however, Friendly has recruited an impressive staff of journalists drawn from such sources as network news, 20/20,* 60 Minutes *and Rona Barrett, who has charged Friendly with "raiding" her* Today *staff and has personally complained to Barry Diller, chairman of Paramount Pictures. Although Friendly says he doesn't want Barrett as an enemy, he is more concerned about winning over Fred and Marge."*

I cringe when I read some of the hyped-up, overblown cocky things I said and wrote back then. I was just immature. I had some ability, but not the grace or maturity to either pace myself for the eighteen-hour days and seven-day weeks or calmly handle the pressures and egos I was dealing with.

After a successful launch and fifty-two good shows on the air, the infighting, lack of sleep, and intense pressure led me to quit a show for the first and only time in my career.

Here is how I lamely described some of this in an interview a few years later with Adrienne Meltzer for Andy's Warhol's *Interview* magazine in response to her asking why I quit *Entertainment Tonight.*

*When it came time to go on the air, the other station groups and partners felt very left out of the process. They wanted the show to be much more like a fan magazine and they may have been right. Who knows?*

*But I was working for Diller, Eisner, Frank, and [Randy] Reiss, and I didn't know that the partners had a real right to contribute. Of course, the attitude of Paramount was, "Let's be deferential, let's listen to them and be polite." So I was caught in a holy war when the show finally aired.*

*I was getting so many mixed signals in trying to produce the show six days a week, where you literally had to be in the studio at 4 a.m. and had to remain until midnight seven days a week.*

*The process of producing a show like that with a small staff... It's not like NBC News, where you have bureaus all over the world and decades of history and tradition. We were 200 young kids, average age 25 years old. But we were smart and energetic. We were finding our way, but we were not allowed to do our best work by way of this feud–this total divergence of attitude. We were called into meetings and political discussions and luncheons, and it was enervating, and after 52 shows that looked good, I was ordered to do a couple of things that I did not want to do. I just said, "I'm too tired, I'm too burned out, I've achieved what I came here to achieve. I put the show on the air."*

Not that it would be easy today, but I often think how I could have handled things better if I had some of the coping skills I've learned over the years.

But that's who I was then and, for better or worse, that's what happened.

When I look at an article I was interviewed for that ran in *Variety* on the show's 16th anniversary, I realize that I gained perspective over the years, and my early contributions have been recognized and are part of the historical record.

Looking back, it was an incredible experience, and I got to work with an amazing team of talented people, to whom I'll always be grateful.

On the day I resigned I met with the staff of over 200 people, along with Paramount executives, on our stage at Merv Griffin's TAV Studios in Hollywood, to tell them I was leaving, to explain why, and to thank them.

It was an emotional gathering, but I tried to keep it positive and assure the team that their best work was ahead of them and that I knew the show would survive and prosper.

And that it did. A few months later the show, and I as its originating producer, received the first of many Emmy nominations, and the show is now thriving in its 36th hugely successful year on the air. In my view the show will stay on the air, much like the *Today* show, forever.

In the end the show became, and is, much more the breezy, tabloid series Paramount's partners and Al Masini, who ran TeleRep and came up with the original idea, wanted it to be.

It has spawned a bunch of successful imitators, such as *Access Hollywood* and *Extra*. It is a huge moneymaker for CBS, which owns and produces the show, closing in on the start of its fifth decade on the air.

Andy Friendly

Following is my somewhat plaintive, but sincere, letter of resignation to then-Paramount president Michael Eisner, dated October 29, 1981, seven days before my 30th birthday.

```
                        ANDREW FRIENDLY



                        October 29, 1981




Mr. Michael Eisner
President, Paramount Pictures

Dear Michael:

I must respectfully submit my resignation as producer of
"Entertainment Tonight" effective Friday night, October 30,
1981.

I feel I've taken this program a very long way in a very short
time...and if I had the creative freedom a good producer ought
to have...I think I could make "Entertainment Tonight" an out-
standing show in the months ahead.  But that's a big if.

Since June fifteenth when I started working here...I've had eight
or nine voices pulling me in every conceivable direction...I
don't have to list for you the constant and often contradictory
directions I've received from the partners who don't really agree
among themselves and from all of you.  The result is plain.  I'm
really not producing the show.

The show will be o.k. without me here because I've set up a
system that's easy enough to follow.  There are a bunch of
dedicated, bright people here who'll continue to produce
"Entertainment Tonight" effectively.

The most difficult part for me will be leaving them.  They're some
wonderful people.

Michael, I have a lot of respect for you...But if I thought you
were a puppet controlled by nine other voices...that you did
things you didn't think were right because those voices ordered
you to I could not respect you.  I can't allow the professionals
on my staff to view me that way.  I hope you, Barry, Rich and
John understand.

                            Sincerely,


                            Andy Friendly

AF:cg

cc:  Barry Diller
     Rich Frank
     John Goldhammer
```

My *ET* boss Michael Eisner, who went on to run the Walt Disney Company, delivered an important speech at an HRTS luncheon in 2005, which I introduced when I was president of the organization.

In his opening remarks, Michael said these very kind things about me, which I'll always appreciate:

*"Andy, thank you very much. Working with Andy on* Entertainment Tonight *twenty-five years ago was extremely exciting, it was a new technology: satellite-delivered programming on a daily basis, with a gifted young producer."*

I'm thrilled every time I see the show or a promo for it and hear the wonderful theme music my brother Michael Mark wrote for it thirty-six years ago, beating out Henry Mancini, Mike Post, and other top Hollywood composers, who also submitted themes. Every time those famous notes are played anywhere around the world, my brother Michael gets a little check. That money has helped pay for his kids Noah and Ronen's educations, and much more, which puts a smile on my face. Nice going, Michael. Good gig!

On the day we finally launched the show in September 1981, we were all celebrating with champagne in the studio after the first episode was taped and fed out to our network of stations when our associate director informed us that he had mistimed the show and it was two minutes "light" (or short).

Several stations aired the show in early fringe time periods, before their local news at 4 p.m., which meant we had exactly thirty minutes to fix and re-feed the first episode.

Celebration turned to mild panic, but we went back to our offices and found a two-minute profile we had just completed, shot a quick introduction with anchor Ron Hendren, edited it into a new version of the show, and got it up on the "bird" (satellite) to stations just in time.

We had a little more champagne, and then we went back to work on show two. It was an auspicious beginning.

## ACADEMY

### OF

## TELEVISION ARTS & SCIENCES

*Honors*

# ANDY FRIENDLY
PRODUCER

ENTERTAINMENT TONIGHT

SYNDICATED

*Nominated for*
OUTSTANDING INFORMATIONAL SERIES

1981-1982
TELEVISION ACADEMY AWARDS

*President*

*My Emmy nomination for Entertainment Tonight, which hangs in my study*

# 18

## A FEW COPING SKILLS I WISH I HAD KNOWN
## THAT MIGHT HELP OTHERS

One thing I know for sure is that life, while incredibly rewarding, amazing, interesting, beautiful, and fun, can also be tough on each of us. Over my sixty-five (and a half) years I've learned a few coping skills, which I wish I had learned much earlier. They've helped me a great deal and maybe they can help you young peeps (and older peeps) in the tougher moments of life, and especially in the workplace.

Hey, I'm no Dr. Phil, (smile) and I certainly don't claim to know everything, so you can take 'em or leave 'em. They come from many sources.

Phil Stutz is a well-known L.A. shrink whom I consider to be one of the wisest men I know. I saw him a few times in the late '90s when I was having some difficulties at work, as described in the opening chapter of this book.

In addition to Stutz, I've drawn these lessons from quite a range of people and sources: from smart friends and family to my brilliant friend and twice-monthly therapist.

I started going regularly almost two years ago. It's great to have someone smart, whom you trust, in your corner. Someone you can truly be open with in ways you can't with others. Even your closest friends and family. I enjoy and appreciate it a great deal and urge all to try it.

Other sources for this chapter range from the poet Rudyard Kipling to the writer Roger Rosenblatt (more on them soon) to good, old-fashioned experience.

Here, in my own, much less articulate reconstruction, are some of the things I've tried to learn and live by (although not always successfully).

# HAVE AN IMPREGNABLE SELF-IMAGE

Stutz says you must have self-generated authority. You must have an impregnable self-image.

If you rely on others to give you authority or make you feel happy or good about yourself, you only make yourself more vulnerable and insecure. Stutz calls these negative feelings "part x."

# TAKE RESPONSIBILITY

Stutz says once you turn thirty you can no longer blame your troubles on others; not your parents, your family, your boss, your friends, your enemies, bad luck, or anything else.

You have to accept full responsibility for your actions, your life, and your happiness.

# FIND A FEW GOOD PEOPLE

It's great to have lots of friends but in my experience, you must have a few truly best friends.

Trust and love them and treat them better than you treat yourself. Treasure them. Never, ever lose them. They will get you through the tough times and you will do the same for them. And you will truly share the great times as well.

Throughout your entire life.

You obviously can't go out and instantly make a best friend, but if you're conscious of the goal and work hard and invest in people you truly like, trust, and respect…in time, it will happen.

Some lucky folks have them from childhood. Others find them in the middle or even the latter part of life. In my case I've been lucky to have all three. I truly cherish them, as I believe they know.

# RENOUNCE THE BAD PEOPLE

Conversely, you must completely renounce, as Phil Stutz says, the bad people in your life.

You can't ignore bad co-workers, friends, family members, bosses, etc. You must deal with them if they're in your life but you must learn to "manage" them, as Stutz says, while at the same time totally renouncing them in your mind.

How do you implement these ideas and make them part of your life strategy?

First you have to understand the concepts, and then you have to train your brain to put these coping skills into daily use. I do it by writing stuff down on yellow Post-it notes and sticking them in a kind of journal I read regularly. Sometimes I email them to myself as reminders on my phone. (This sounds lame but works.)

Also I try to think about them daily, as a mantra of sorts.

Not easy by any means but doable if you commit to it.

Most of us have to work to make a living. I did for about forty years.

I had the great luck and fortune to have worked with many brilliant and talented people.

Along the way there were some very difficult people and situations, and while I had some success, plenty of situations and opportunities blew up, and I'm sure I could have avoided many of them and handled them better had I learned some of these techniques.

## WRITE THE LETTER BUT DON'T SEND IT

When you're angry and upset, write the letter or email but do not send it. Great advice from close friend/lawyer David Nochimson, paraphrasing Abe Lincoln.

"Write it; get it all out of your system. Have it in a file for future reference and for the record. But DO NOT PUSH SEND!"

I confess to not always having followed this rule. There are times when you have to press send, but in general it's a smart rule.

## UNDER-REACT

In the workplace, a board meeting, at a family gathering, poker game, golf club, dinner party with friends, or pretty much any other setting you can imagine, things can go south and get ugly in a heartbeat.

The reasons for this are wide and varied. They range from underlying disagreements, politics, egos, hurt feelings, power and turf wars, and jealousies, to just plain nasty people or bullies: people who enjoy picking on those who are weaker physically, emotionally, intellectually.

Then there are those who just like to stir things up, whose very comfort can only be attained by churning up the waters, creating tension and unhappiness. You see this a lot in our business and, of course, in politics, unfortunately. These people are only comfortable when others are uncomfortable. They can wreck any project, outing, or dinner party. They can wreck our country.

When things are going smoothly, these folks are instinctively compelled to cause trouble, create crisis, and generally disrupt things.

"Power players" (a Stutz term), are strong and smart enough to see what's going on, size up the various personalities, and, as David Zaslav taught me in two brilliant words twenty-five years ago at CNBC: "UNDER REACT."

It's a way to stay "chill" (as the kids say).

I've shared this technique with a few friends and family members, including my nephew Chris, who is a brilliant guy but who was having a hard time reining in his emotions at work when people challenged him. He'd overreact, lose his cool, and end up out of a job.

He and I worked on some of these techniques for a year or so, and now I'm pleased to say, thanks to his effort and focus, he has employed these concepts and is now under-reacting and doing well in his political consulting business. I'm extremely proud of him for the huge effort and turnaround, and I know he will maintain these techniques for life.

It is not an exaggeration to say these techniques, strategies, have actually saved careers, friendships, and lives.

Here's another good one.

## REMEMBER: NO ONE IS THINKING ABOUT YOU!

Another key coping skill I learned is from a great little book Ruth Friendly gave me, by *Washington Post* writer Roger Rosenblatt, called *The Rules of Aging*, in which he says in chapter two, titled "Nobody is thinking about you":

> *"Yes, I know, you are certain that your friends are becoming your enemies; that your grocer, garbageman, clergyman, sister-in-law, and your dog are all of the opinion that you have put on weight, that you have lost your touch, that you have lost your mind; furthermore, you are convinced that everyone spends two-thirds of every day commenting on your disintegration, denigrating your work, plotting your assassination. I promise you: Nobody is thinking about you. They are thinking about themselves—just like you."*

I first read this about ten years ago and have found it to be very liberating and ultimately the truth. I try to remember this every day and suggest you try it.

It's truly empowering and makes us laugh at ourselves, which is half the battle—not to take ourselves, or our problems, too seriously. As others have said, take your work, your community, and your friendships seriously, but not yourself.

And try to make fun of yourself and your dopey worries as much as possible. I've found these concepts are truly helpful.

## GET AND KEEP A SENSE OF HUMOR

Develop and cultivate a good sense of humor about the world, about others, and mostly about yourself.

I do it by reading and listening to funny people. Starting in junior high and straight through today, I watch and read as much humor as possible and try to come up with my own takeaways to apply in my life.

When I read or hear something funny I try to write it down and put it in a little journal I keep. I'll retell it at poker or dinner with friends, family, etc.

I've found that the more I do this, the more my brain comes up with my own original thoughts, observations, and material, some of which, surprisingly (to me) is pretty good. Some is lame as hell.

I believe developing a good sense of humor will make you happier, and make you more fun to be around. And guys (nephews, grandkids, and others), here's a little tip...the ladies like guys who can make them laugh. You can thank me later.

## NOBODY LIKES A BULLY

It took me until my mid-twenties to discover this last part. It was one of my early mentors, Tom Snyder, who first showed me how to use a sharp one-liner to defend and protect myself from bullies in the workplace and beyond.

In a public setting, at an NBC press function, a reporter was giving Tom a hard time about rumors he might be jumping ship to another network. The reporter was pretty snarky, even bullying, in his tone and implied that Tom was manipulating NBC for a raise. Tom, rather than take the bait, just smiled and said, "I guess Will Rogers never met (reporter's name)." For those who may not know, Will Rogers famously wrote, "I never met a man I didn't like."

Tom calmly went on to deny the rumor, which was not true, but he taught me a great lesson: Rather than respond with anger, he used humor and the reporter's negative energy and turned it around on him and made him look like the snarky dope he was in front of his colleagues.

I have used this technique countless times in the workplace, at my thirty-year poker and golf games, at dinner parties, press conferences, and countless other settings.

It seems there are always snarky, mean-spirited a-holes in just about every crowd, and they feel compelled to take shots. But you can defeat them with humor every time. Getting angry or upset just makes you look weak.

A good comeback makes you look cool, funny, and in control.

Like when Letterman told Rush Limbaugh on Dave's show, after the bloviating, overweight pundit implied that Hillary Clinton was fat: "Well Rush, you can say that ...because YOU are a perfect human specimen."

Or at a dinner a few years ago when a particularly nasty, mean-spirited producer was making awful comments about other dinner guests and I asked, so all could hear, "How is it possible you're still single?"

The guy turned beet red and finally shut up.

Of course, as with all these techniques, they require work, discipline, and practice. You've got to train your brain to under-react, stay cool, and stay funny.

If you do, you'll soon notice, bullies will look elsewhere for their targets and leave you alone, as they don't want to risk you coming back over the top on them.

My other favorite way to stand up to bullies is by implying a physical response but with humor, like the time a well-known "super" agent I was partnered with on a project tried to intimidate me into a subservient role on the project at our first meeting. He had a reputation as a nasty bully and I knew I had better shut it down immediately, so I interrupted him early in his rant before a group of staffers to say, with a big smile: "You know, if you keep this up, you and me may have to wrassle." (Doing my best Southern accent and confident smile.)

As with almost all bullies, he immediately backed off and his tone became, and stayed, respectful. I have found that most bullies are weak, insecure cowards who will back down if stood up to almost every time.

## CONTROL YOUR OWN NARRATIVE

I learned this one at the age of twenty-nine when I left *Entertainment Tonight*.

As I told you earlier, the decision to leave was mine and came as a surprise to my bosses, including studio heads Rich Frank, Michael Eisner, and Barry Diller.

No one was sure at that point if the show would work or last, but when it (and I) was nominated for an Emmy and the ratings started to take off, a wide range of people started taking credit for the launch and success of the show.

In various interviews and press generated by the show I was rarely, if ever, mentioned.

The old saying "Victory has a thousand fathers, but defeat is an orphan" was in play.

I got it...but refused to accept it. I thought it was fundamentally unfair. I had worked too damn hard, contributed too much. I did my own press and spin, claiming what I believed was my rightful role in the launch and success of this now thirty-six-year juggernaut. On anniversaries when the studio and producers took ads and did press touting their success, I did some, too.

That pissed them off but I felt it was fair and right. I was building a career and I refused to stand idly by and accept being left out of the acknowledgment I felt I deserved.

I didn't need a lot. Just a mention would have been fine. When that didn't happen, I did it myself and have tried, mostly with success (sometimes not), to control my own narrative ever since.

If you deserve it and have the courage and energy to do it, you can take on any powerful studio, network, or other institution or person and get what is rightfully yours. At least some of it.

If you don't deserve it, you most likely won't get it. Reporters will know the difference and most often will side with you if you are telling the truth against the giant spin machines of the powerful. Good reporters will.

Takes some guts and belief in yourself but it can and should be done. And not just with press but in life in general.

Don't allow anyone to tell or control your story. Not your rivals, or your enemies. Not so-called friends or even family who, while they may like or even love you, have agendas of their own.

I have seen great, talented, wonderful people marginalized many, many times by foes and "friends" alike; especially when they've gotten a little older or lost a little cachet in their careers.

This is bullshit. Your life's work and accomplishments over the decades can never be taken away.

You don't have to accept it. Not at any age or any point in your life or career. Keep growing, learning, contributing to people and causes around you and your community.

Carry yourself with strength, humor, kindness, and dignity.

Never, ever let others control your narrative. YOU control it with your actions and behavior.

I'm not saying it's easy or that I've always been able to do it. I've failed many times. But for the most part, I feel I've been able to do it, and believe that you can too.

OK, so much for my little Dr. Phil advice chapter.

By the way, Dr. Phil seems like a smart, good guy, and is great on TV, but as Dave says about him: "I'd like to see the paperwork on that degree."

**Postscript**: As I'm doing a final edit of the book, I am reading my friend Steven Bochco's terrific book *Truth Is a Total Defense*, which tells the story of his brilliant career creating some of my favorite television shows ever, like *Hill Street Blues*, *NYPD Blue*, and many more seminal, Emmy-winning series.

He also writes about his brave battle with leukemia, which almost took his life. Through his great courage and the support of his wife, Dayna, and many loving friends and family, he continues to recover with dignity and grace, and his usual wicked sense of humor.

In his candid and brilliantly written book, Steven writes that he, too, has benefited greatly from the wisdom of Phil Stutz, who has helped him through his battle. Steven quotes several of what he calls "Phil's Rules for the Road" including No. 1: Embrace uncertainty. Looking for certainty will only result in terror. Another great Stutz "rule."

I am always learning about more people who have learned from, and been inspired by, Phil's unique and brilliant insights.

Steven and I have worked together on HRTS events, the Saban clinic golf tournament, and the Heroes golf course at the V.A., and are fellow members at Riviera, where we had lunch recently. He looked and sounded great and was his usual whip-smart, funny, "take no prisoners" self.

He was encouraging about me finishing my book and wrote a beautiful inscription to me in his book, which I will always cherish along with his friendship, bravery, and his ever-lasting and, in my view, unmatched contributions to the quality and influence of the television drama. I look forward to many more great lunches with Steven.

I urge you to read his brave book.

*With Steven Bochco and Norman Lear at a Hollywood Radio & Television Society event I produced featuring these two legendary Hall of Fame producers, 2001*

# 19

## LIFE AFTER *ET*...AND 30

The three most interesting calls I got after I left *Entertainment Tonight,* days before my 30th birthday in November 1981, were from Pierre Cossette, the veteran producer of the Grammys and many other important variety series and specials; from *Playboy* boss and founder Hugh Hefner; and from Fred Silverman, who had run all three major networks, including NBC while I was there in the '70s.

After a week recuperating in Hawaii and celebrating my birthday, I returned to meet with all three, rested and ready to figure out my next steps.

My first meeting was with Cossette, a larger-than-life, old-school Hollywood impresario and a real character. He had his office in the penthouse of the famous ICM building on Beverly Boulevard, where the Hollywood hot spot Madeo is now.

I was ushered into his massive corner office only to find no one there. I looked around and from behind an open door I heard the sound of someone relieving himself. I remember thinking to myself, sounds like Seabiscuit's peeing in there. Interesting way to start a meeting.

Within seconds, Pierre bounced out from his private bathroom, still zipping up his pants, and extending a big smile and hearty hand to shake. This was before Purell, so no help there, I'm afraid.

He charmed me with war stories from his long career and explained he wanted to do a version of *ET* based purely on the soaps and wanted me to produce it. He explained that this would lead to other opportunities in his vast empire, possibly including working on the Grammys. He was a kick and it was tempting, but I wasn't a "soap" person and had little interest. I thanked him and declined.

My next meeting was at the iconic Playboy Mansion with the famous "Hef," a godlike hero to every red-blooded American kid who grew up in the '50s and '60s sneaking looks at his famous *Playboy* magazine.

Some of my earliest memories of the opposite sex were studying the centerfold cutouts hung on the walls in the cutting room at *See It Now* and *CBS Reports*, where I spent weekends shining shoes and hanging out as a ten-year-old with my dad. Can you imagine Human Resources allowing those centerfolds to be displayed on the walls of a CBS facility today? No way.

I was excited and curious as I drove up to the massive gates of the mansion in Holmby Hills. The guard directed me up the long, winding driveway past wandering peacocks and other exotic birds that lived on the sprawling, exclusive property between Beverly Hills and Bel-Air.

When I pulled my car into the fountain-lined circular drive filled with Ferraris, Rolls-Royces, and the like, I was greeted by a large security guard and ushered into the living room of the mansion. After a few minutes, the man himself arrived, accompanied by two beautiful blond Playboy Bunnies. Hef was clad in his famous burgundy silk pajamas, black leather slippers with a big, gold "H" embossed on them, and a burgundy, crushed velvet robe; in his mouth, his ubiquitous pipe.

The meeting went well. He was a bit more serious and laid-back than I expected, a sharp contrast to my meeting with Pierre Cossette. Hef explained that he was looking for someone to expand his efforts in television around his famous brand and work with him, his daughter Christie, and the rest of his team to develop series and specials and oversee his burgeoning adult entertainment programming.

To a single, thirty-year-old man—especially in those wild and crazy party days—it sounded like a dream job.

I just couldn't do it. I knew, despite his insistence that he wanted to develop all kinds of legit programs, that there would be porn involved. I would never be able to go back to news or any kind of serious programming. I also knew it would break my parents' hearts.

A few years later they approached me again about getting involved, but it just wasn't for me. I did get to go to a few of the famous movie screenings and parties at the mansion along the way, and that was fun. One in particular for Howard Stern years later was especially memorable with naked Bunnies in the grotto...the whole nine yards.

In the mid-'90s, a good friend of mine, former syndication executive Jim Griffiths, became president of Playboy Productions and he invited me out to his Glendale offices/studios for lunch and a tour of the facilities. When we stopped by one of the sound stages, there was a full-on porn film being shot. I found it fascinating and really nuts that in the middle of a busy business district in Glendale in what looked like a shopping mall, this film was being made. I realized I had made the right decision years earlier…at least for me.

Jim is a great guy, confirmed bachelor, and Riviera bud, who had run MGM and other major television companies. He loved it and did a great job. Different strokes, as they say.

*Hugh Hefner and I at the Playboy Mansion when we profiled him for a Life of Luxury special I executive produced for ABC, 2004*

*My team on the specials included the talented co-executive producer Krysia Plonka, my trusty line producer going back to Entertainment Tonight days, Jim Ziegler, and my nephew Noah Mark, who was then a twenty-three-year-old associate producer and is now co-executive producer of the hit Fox Sports series The Ultimate Fighter.*

The last of the three job meetings was with Fred Silverman and his partner, the veteran variety show producer Bob Finkel. They were looking for someone to produce a new variety show called *The World of Entertainment* as part of a deal they had with MGM.

Fred was a god to me at the time. As president of CBS, ABC, and NBC over the past decade, he was the first TV executive to be featured on the cover of *Time* magazine.

He was my far-removed boss when I was at NBC for most of my twenties, and I had only met him once. It happened in the control room in Studio 3A at 30 Rockefeller Plaza in New York during a live airing of the NBC newsmagazine *Prime Time Sunday*, which Tom Snyder anchored and on which I was a young field producer, doing profiles of mega Hollywood producer Jerry Weintraub among others.

It was a huge deal that Fred had come by to show his support, and all of us, including Tom, were buzzing with excitement.

As part of the show, which was broadcast live, going in and out of breaks we showed the workings of the massive control room, including executive producer Paul Friedman giving orders to the team. Paul, a wiry, smart former *Today* producer during some of that show's earlier ratings struggles, had thinning hair and a mustache and a somewhat dour look about him.

During a break, Silverman came over to Tom and asked, "Who's the guy with the mustache giving orders? He looks like an undertaker."

Without skipping a beat, Snyder shot back, "Well he should be, he buried the *Today* show." Of course this wasn't true, just a funny line Tom couldn't resist, typical of the boys-will-be-boys humor that pervades newsrooms. In truth there were many reasons, unrelated to Paul, for the ratings decline on *Today*.

I digress...Paul was a good guy who gave me some of the best advice of my career a few months later when NBC asked me to move to L.A. to produce Tom's primetime specials. I was torn between the great opportunity to be in charge of something for the first time and my lifelong goal of producing on a network newsmagazine, which I'd just recently achieved.

When I discussed the opportunity with Paul, he told me, "If you stay in news, no matter what you do, you'll always be in your father's shadow. This is a chance for you to move into the entertainment division of NBC, produce your own show, and be your own man. You should do it." It was the right call and I'll always be grateful for the advice.

Years later, when I was running primetime programming at CNBC, I got a call out of the blue from Paul. He was a news producer at CBS then. He said in his best Godfather, former boss voice: "Fifteen years ago I hired you onto *Prime Time Sunday* and now you're going to hire my son David, who's looking for his first job in the business."

I felt like responding "Yes, Godfather" but did not. I agreed to meet with David, a bright young man, and ended up finding something for him. He did well and went on to be a successful producer of *Late Night* and other shows at NBC.

One last note while I'm on the subject of *Prime Time Sunday*: I shared an office there with one of the show's young reporters, Chris Wallace, whose dad, Mike, was the legendary anchor and star of *60 Minutes* and a lifelong friend of my dad's.

Chris is now host of *Fox News Sunday* and moderated one of the presidential debates between Trump and Clinton in 2016 to wide, bipartisan acclaim. He's widely considered one of the best in the news business.

End of digression, back to *The World of Entertainment*.

The idea behind Silverman and Finkel's series was to do an electronic version of the old *Ed Sullivan* variety show, which ran for many years on CBS and showcased a wide range of performers, from The Beatles to Richard Pryor to circus acts. The difference was that rather than having them come to a studio, we would go all around the world and record them on location.

Being a huge fan of *The Ed Sullivan Show* and excited to work with Silverman and Finkel, I signed on to produce.

We wanted a host with international stature, and with a huge stroke of luck, were able to sign a living movie and stage legend, the great Gene Kelly. He co-hosted along with football god Joe Montana, former Miss America and actress Mary Ann Mobley, and one of my all-time TV crushes and future wife: actress Pat Crowley.

We made a good pilot, and Bruce Gowers directed it brilliantly. We shot on location all around the world, including Paris and Vienna, where Pat hosted segments featuring the can-can at the Moulin Rouge and the famed Vienna Boys Choir in concert.

The special did well, but it was an expensive show to produce and MGM could not clear the show in enough major markets for enough money, so we didn't go to series. It was a disappointment for sure, but a great first project after *ET*.

Working with Gene Kelly was a pure pleasure. He was fun, generous of spirit, and a team player. Montana, Mobley, and that Crowley girl were great.

Pat and I stayed close to Bob Finkel and his lovely wife, Jane, until their deaths. He was a great friend and a great television producer I learned much from.

His top production executive, Bob Parkinson, a colorful and fun-loving guy who worked with us closely on the pilot, became a good friend as well as my producing partner on a number of shows.

I stayed in touch with Fred Silverman as well and ended up in the same office building with him in Brentwood when I was running production and programming at King World in the mid to late '90s. Fred would come in and pitch us shows regularly, and we tried hard to find something to do together, but it never happened.

I could never quite get over the fact that this man, whom I used to see as a TV god, who then became my uber-boss, was now sitting in my office pitching his heart out to me.

Same feeling as when I got my former boss and mentor Tom Snyder to come back to television with a series on CNBC in 1993, and he called me his "Boss," a label I always refused.

The cycle of life in a forty-year career in TV.

# 20

## AND NOW, THE *PENTHOUSE* MILLION-DOLLAR PET OF THE YEAR CONTEST!

While I grew up in and around news and spent my first seven years at NBC writing and producing news, talk, magazine shows and specials, in 1979 I left the pure, rarefied world of NBC News in New York and headed to L.A. to produce Tom Snyder's primetime celebrity interview specials: *Speak Up America, This Is Your Life,* and *Entertainment Tonight,* all of which aired on NBC. (*ET* was syndicated but aired on many NBC stations.)

In 1982, my career took an interesting turn after I met Bob Parkinson on *The World of Entertainment.* Bob was our associate producer on that show and on a number of primetime specials for the network. He was a skilled production guy with a strong grasp of the technical and budgetary aspects of production, which were not my strength, so we complemented each other well and decided to partner on a few projects.

Bob was bright, fun-loving, flashy, good-looking in a John Forsythe-on-*Dynasty* kind of way… (Sorry for the dated reference. Look it up, young people.)

He drove a Rolls-Royce, and always had a perfect tan, great hair, handmade Italian suits, and the best jokes. This guy was nothin' but fun, and I loved being around him.

Pretty much everyone loved "Park," as he was affectionately known, especially by the ladies. At six foot four, he literally turned heads when he walked into Ma Maison or any of the other top Hollywood hot spots he frequented.

As a kid from the Bronx I couldn't get enough of this super flashy, fun Hollywood guy. Best of all, he got the joke and didn't take himself too seriously, always making fun of himself.

I brought him on as associate producer on a new syndicated version of *This Is Your Life* I was writing and producing along with my close friend and talented writer-producer Steve Paskay.

We also did a pilot for a business magazine show called *Taking Advantage* for Paramount and McGraw-Hill, on which I again hired Ms. Crowley as a feature reporter. Much more on that young lady in the next chapter.

I brought in Bob on that one, too, as my associate producer. Among the many big, primetime specials Bob had worked on were the Miss Universe Pageant and other major beauty contests. He knew this world well and was highly respected as a producer in the field.

One day he came in my office and told me that *Penthouse* and its famous founder, Bob Guccione, had approached him about turning their signature magazine cover feature, "The Million-Dollar *Penthouse* Pet of the Year," into a big, glitzy TV special.

He asked if I'd be interested in producing with him as partners.

I had turned Hef down at Playboy but that was for a full-time job.

This was a one-off, primetime special for broadcast television, which by definition could not contain any nudity, let alone any porn.

Again, what could possibly go wrong?

We flew to New York and met with Guccione in his magnificent double brownstone on 63rd street off Park Avenue, filled with artwork by Picasso and Degas. He threw us a big party, ordered up a major article about the show and us in *Penthouse*, and most importantly opened his checkbook and told us he wanted the biggest and best in every category in front of and behind the cameras.

He and his partner, Kathy Keeton, were very cool, surprisingly intellectual, artistic, sophisticated, and nice people. Not anything like the image I previously had of them.

Once on board, we brought in Andy Gibb, the youngest Bee Gee brother and a major pop star at the time, to host. Walter Miller, longtime Grammy director, was hired to direct. Tony Charmoli, the brilliant choreographer, was brought in to teach the fifty or so "Pets" coming in from around the world to dance.

We arranged for award-winning set designer Tony Sabatino to do the sets.

The best of the best, Guccione was true to his word. He let us hire the best people in Hollywood, whatever the cost.

On the first day of pre-production we flew to New York, where our first meeting was at the famed Americana hotel on Seventh Avenue, to check in on the fifty Pets doing their wardrobe fittings.

Keep in mind, Bob was a seasoned veteran of this world. I, a complete neophyte, was simply following his lead. I had no idea what to expect…but it certainly wasn't what I was about to behold.

When we walked into the ballroom of the hotel, fifty beautiful *Penthouse* centerfolds from around the world were bustling around in various degrees of undress: many totally nude, climbing in and out of gowns, swimsuits, and other outfits for the show that the dozens of designers, fitters, tailors, and wardrobe people scurrying about had picked out for them.

If they noticed us at all, it was clear they could not care less that two guys they didn't know and had never seen before had just walked in to see them *au naturel*.

I'd pay good money right now to see the look that must have been on my face. Bob just laughed and said: "Follow me, let's go say hi."

After a few days rehearsing on sound stages in Manhattan, we moved the entire production to the Sands Hotel in Atlantic City, New Jersey. Our brilliant, hilarious director, Walter Miller, ran the girls, Andy Gibb, and our entire team through rehearsals for a week, leading to a flawless two-hour special that aired around the world and accomplished all Mr. Guccione hoped, to build and show off his brand.

As the saying goes, if you live long enough, you'll see everything.

At thirty-two, this was my first and last beauty pageant, but I'm really glad I did it and I had a blast.

My only real reservation was my parents. Ten good years into my career this was clearly a left turn, and not their proudest moment.

It weighed on me, but after discussing it with them, they said they understood and gave me their blessing. I assured them I'd return to other projects and make them proud again; that this was a one-off.

A few weeks into pre-production, the trade publication *Variety* ran a nice story about the show. Thinking it might somehow add some legitimacy and help to assuage my parents' concerns, I sent them a copy.

I will never forget the letter Dad wrote me a few days later. It hangs on the wall of my study.

If you want to know about my dad, this letter is all you need to know.

He hated that I did this show; that I left his sacred, beloved world of journalism.

It was bad enough that I left the so-called "priesthood" of NBC News to do primetime specials and *Entertainment Tonight*. But this?

The letter tells you what kind of father he really was. And, in my humble opinion, serves as a beacon of selfless parenting and putting your kids above yourself no matter how galling or humiliating their youthful, misguided indiscretions; of true love and support. My two moms, Dorothy and Ruth, were totally supportive as well.

I like to think I made good on my promise when I went on, over the next decade, to produce and direct projects with Dan Rather, Tim Russert, Charlie Rose, Bob Hilburn, and other "high priests" of broadcast and print journalism. My folks told me often that I did.

In any case, as I told my dad as a young kid when he tucked me in and said, "It's good to be your Dad"…

It's good to be your son.

And to both my moms, Dorothy and Ruth, who were equally supportive: I'll always be grateful.

Here is Dad's letter. It's all you need to know.

**FRED W. FRIENDLY**

March 17, 1983

Dear Andy,

Ruth and I enjoyed the profile of Andy Friendly in <u>Daily Variety</u>.
You have a lot on your platter, young man. You seem to have all
of the occupational defects of your old man of not being able to
say "no." Sorry about that - or maybe it should be congratulations.

On the subject of Guccione, I am moved by your concern for my
sensitivity to your working on such a project, but don't let it
bother you. I'm very proud of you, Andy, but that's partly because
you are your own man. You're not Fred Friendly, and you don't pre-
sume to be that person any more than I tried to fit into the
Murrow mold -- or he, mine, for that matter. He went his own way
on "Person to Person", and who is to say that that wasn't the right
decision for him to have made at that time. You should also remember
that the old man started his network career doing a quiz program
called "Who Said That?". We all try to get a rung on that
slippery ladder whichever way we can, and as long as you can live
with what you're doing, so can I. I know you'll always give it
your best shot, and I know that your commitment will not only be a
maximum one in energy but in integrity as well. You've already
demonstrated that.

So make it the best, the most imaginative "Woman of the Year" program
you can, and Ruth and I will be ready to celebrate at the victory
party. As with all of you kids and your activities, we'll also be
present for the occasional temporary stumble, *As You do ours*.

We had a great party a week ago when Lisa and Tim were here. Everyone missed you and talked of you with the pride and exuberance you
deserve. Give our best to Pat. Ruth and I hope to see you both
soon.

Always,

# 21

## THE WOMAN WHO SAVED ME

I'm not sure of the first time I saw Pat Crowley on television but I'm pretty sure it was on the classic *Twilight Zone* episode she co-starred in with the great Burgess Meredith.

In the episode, titled "The Printer's Devil," she plays a feisty reporter working for Meredith, who per Rod Serling's brilliant script makes a deal with the devil to save his troubled newspaper. The editor uses the demonic linotype machine to create the next day's news by writing it the night before. The episode is considered one of his best and is included every year in the annual Twilight Zone marathon.

It was either that or co-starring with Gene Barry on another of my favorite primetime series of the '60s, *Burke's Law*, or maybe it was on the pilot and premiere episode of *The Man From U.N.C.L.E.*, opposite Robert Vaughn, another one of my all-time favorites as a teenager.

Whichever of those it was, and later on her own series on NBC, *Please Don't Eat the Daisies*, and then on countless series from *Rockford Files* and *Police Story* to *Love Boat*, *Charlie's Angels*, and *Hotel*, plus numerous appearances singing and dancing on variety shows with Dean Martin, the Righteous Brothers, and so many more, she was always one of my fantasy crushes. One of the most beautiful, sassy, classy women I had ever seen.

So when I met her for the first time at a small dinner party at Tom Snyder's house in Beverly Hills, when I was producing his specials for NBC in the late '70s, needless to say I was, as the kids say, blown away.

She was married to Tom's lawyer/agent, Ed Hookstratten, who also represented Tom Brokaw, Bryant Gumbel, and many other famed broadcasters, athletes, and coaches. I had met Ed a couple times before with Tom, and he was there along with my close friends Bruce McKay and Debbie

Vickers, and Pam Burke, Tom's longtime producer and "companion," as he referred to her lovingly.

I had invited Sean Derek, Bo Derek's younger sister, as my date. Bo was the current "It" girl starring in the hit film *10* that year, and I'd booked her on one of Tom's specials.

I had been in a three-year relationship with a lovely girl named Wendy, who moved with me from New York when *Tomorrow* moved back to L.A.

We had lived together, but she was ready to settle down and have a family and I was an immature dope who wasn't anywhere close to settling down. That relationship had recently ended.

Sean was a fun, smart girl. But my attention was elsewhere.

I could not believe that I was at a dinner party with Pat Crowley. I was impressed by her charm and easy-to-be-around manner—despite being a major television star—and of course by her mind-boggling beauty.

Mostly, I just couldn't get my head around the fact that I was having dinner with one of my all-time teenage "fantasy goddesses." And she was even more charismatic and beautiful than on TV.

It was a fun, loud, vodka-fueled evening.

Reminiscing about it recently with my lifelong friend Debbie Vickers, who went on to be Jay Leno's executive producer for two hugely successful decades on *The Tonight Show*, I realized that in my platonic (at that time) fascination with Pat that night, I was probably guilty of ignoring the lovely Sean on this, just our second date. I even recall telling Sean about my teenage crush on Pat and "that if I ever met someone like that, I'd get married in a heartbeat." Probably not the best thing to tell your date. That was the end of that relationship. Like I said, I was a dope.

The years went by and I saw Pat a few more times at parties. I ran into her and Ed at the Super Bowl in Pasadena once. Ed was then helping me with some of my deals and was instrumental in getting me into the running to produce *Entertainment Tonight*.

Pat was always the model of the perfect woman as far as I was concerned. There was no romantic interest due to our circumstances, yet I think that subconsciously, unfairly, and impossibly, I measured every woman I dated (and there were many, most of them better than the likes of me deserved to be with), by Pat.

By my mid to late twenties and into my early thirties, I had become a fairly successful producer, with a couple bucks in my pocket for the first time, and miraculously I was dating some pretty amazing women, including well-known actresses and models such as the lovely, fun, and talented Rita

Wilson. I had also been in a yearlong relationship with a lovely "California girl" named Linda, followed by Kathy Gallagher, a Ford model and Hollywood hot-spot restaurant owner, while I was producing *Speak Up, America* for NBC and then launching *ET* for Paramount.

I remember during each relationship having dinner with Pat and Ed, and afterward, telling each girl the same thing that I'd told Sean Derek: "If I ever met someone like Pat, I'd settle down and get married." I guess I was trying to let them know what I was looking for in a wife, but again, it may not have been the smartest thing to say. Slow learner.

The other thing I distinctly remember was some coolness, even some angry and at times ugly arguments between Pat and Ed at each of those dinners.

I was not totally surprised when, a few months later, I learned they had separated and were getting a divorce.

My relationship with Kathy had recently ended and I needed a date for the opening of Peter Morton's new Hard Rock Cafe in the Beverly Center. I had made plans to go with my friend, producer, and later MGM studio head Roger Birnbaum and his then-girlfriend, the actress Teri Garr.

Kathy and I had recently split up, so I asked Pat, with whom I was working on a new series at Paramount called *Taking Advantage*, a business magazine in partnership with media giant McGraw-Hill. Pat was a feature reporter on the pilot.

Pat and I had worked together earlier that year on the *World of Entertainment* special I did with Fred Silverman and Gene Kelly, and we had developed a nice work friendship.

I knew she was separated and alone and I was, too. Since I needed someone to take to the Hard Rock, I decided to give her a call. She said "yes."

I really did not think of it as a "date" per se, but in the car on the way home after a fun evening, I guess my deeper inner feelings took over. I reached over and touched her hand. We've been together ever since.

It will be thirty-five years in October. For a guy few (probably including me) thought would ever stay in a long-term relationship..."Holy crap!" Doesn't seem possible that much time's gone by.

Back to that night, October 3, 1982.

I was deeply, madly, head-over-heels in love.

And yes, it was complicated.

It was complicated for a number of reasons. First, Pat was six months out from her marriage to Ed, who had helped me in prior years with my career.

I reached out to Ed and tried to keep a decent relationship. At first he was angry, but in time we patched things up and had lunch a couple times a year; we even sat together at some family events after he remarried and started a second family.

I think he knew how much I loved Pat and, though he had clearly moved on, he still cared about her and her well-being. He was at first concerned I would leave her, as had been my (regrettable) pattern with other women he'd seen me with.

Once he knew I wasn't going anywhere and that I was truly there for Pat, and he was happy in his new family, we developed a comfortable relationship until his passing in 2014. He was a giant in our business and a good man.

Next, as in any family when a parent begins a new relationship after a divorce, it is complicated with the kids. In our case, Pat's son Jon and daughter Ann were grown, in their early twenties, and great, well-adjusted people who adored and were very protective of their mom, as they should have been. That's especially so given she was getting involved with a man considerably younger than she was, with a less-than-stellar rep for dating a bunch of women and at times an excessive '80s "bad boy" image. (Guilty as charged. No excuses except, as I indicated earlier, it was a wild and different time.)

After a couple years they began to trust that I had matured and truly loved their mom, was serious about the relationship, and would be around for the long haul; but on the night three years later when we invited them to dinner to tell them our great news, that we were going to be married, they did not react as we had hoped.

Rather than embracing and supporting the news, they expressed concerns that the marriage might not last and that I would not be there for their mom for the long term.

Words and emotions became a bit heated, especially between Jon and me, and rather than risk some kind of yelling match, or worse, I explained to Pat that I felt it best for me to leave and let things settle down.

I returned a couple hours later and we all calmed down and discussed things in a quiet and sincere way.

By the end of the night, we had their blessing. A few months later, on April 5, 1986, Pat and I were married in a small, family-only ceremony presided over by California Supreme Court Judge Ron George, who would become the chief justice.

Jon, there with his lovely, then-future wife, Marion, made a wonderful toast, and daughter Ann, there with her terrific new husband, Bob Osher, was totally supportive, as was everyone, which meant the world to us. Jon and

Bob went on to become attorneys and highly successful executives in the entertainment industry.

It was a truly warm and beautifully produced (all by Pat) wedding and we were so blessed that Pat's mom, Helen, and my Mom and Dad and "second mom" Ruth were all there along with Pat's sister Ann and almost all my brothers and sisters.

A couple of months later, my wonderful business partner Cliff Perlman and his lovely wife, Nancy Hutson, threw a beautiful party for all our friends and us at Jimmy's in Beverly Hills.

*A family photo from our wedding day*

*(L-R) Seated: my mom, Dorothy; Pat's mom, Helen Crowley; my sister, Lisa Friendly; my "second mom" Ruth Friendly. Standing: California Supreme Court Chief Justice Ron George, who married us; my sister's then-husband, Tim Nicholson; my sister-in-law B.K. Mark; my stepbrother John Mark; my brother, David; my stepbrother Richard Mark and his wife, Maura Mark; me; Pat; son-in-law Bob Osher and Pat's daughter, Ann Osher; my dad, Fred; daughter-in-law Marion Hookstratten; Pat's son, Jon Hookstratten; and Pat's sister, Ann Jones*

It was a truly great night, for which we will always be grateful. Sadly, we lost Cliff earlier this year. Great guy.

As the years went by, Jon and Marion, Ann and Bob and their kids, and our grandkids Eddie, Erin, Kate, Will, and Clare (I skipped the parent part and went straight to grandparent) became a big part of my family as well. I love them all more than words can say.

We were off to a great start, but as I mentioned, there was controversy. Pat was older than me. In our society, a man marrying a woman years younger doesn't raise an eyebrow. But a woman marrying a younger man? That's different. In 1982, when Pat and I got together, it was anathema to some. Nowadays it is a bit more accepted but still controversial, to some folks lacking open hearts and minds.

We were far too in love and far too happy to care, as long as our families and close friends were OK with it, and thankfully they were.

I can also tell you that when you're in a hospital waiting room at 4 a.m., waiting for a surgeon, who is removing a cancerous tumor the size of a tennis ball from your wife's body, to tell you if she will survive, the issue of age is nonexistent. That is exactly what occurred decades later when Pat began her courageous battles with breast cancer and Stage 4 melanoma. A battle she is winning.

Now, thirty-five years after that first date at the Hard Rock Cafe, we both remain grateful to all who stood by us and had the courage to stand up for us against the so-called "haters."

By the time I fell in love with and married Pat, she had already had her children, Jon and Ann, who were in their early twenties. I wanted to have children with Pat and we tried, but it didn't happen. We discussed adopting and had some meetings, but ultimately we didn't.

Although ours was not the traditional family, I cannot imagine a greater one.

I guess I'll always wonder what it would have been like to have my own kids. I think I'd have been a good dad, but who knows. I do know, from watching how well Ann and Jon turned out, and watching Pat with the grandkids, how great a mom Pat was and is. I have so enjoyed being a part of my giant family spread out around the country.

I love them all dearly. They are all unique and wonderful, and watching the younger generation, now in their twenties and early thirties, grow up into smart, caring, community-minded adults, going to and graduating from college and going about their careers, forming their own deep relationships with boy- and girlfriends, and getting married. It's the best. This includes a bunch of my best friends' kids, whom I love like my own family.

There's rarely a day that goes by when I'm not in touch with one or more of them, or a week when we're not doing something with them.

There is no doubt that the most fun, the purest joy, and the best times of my life have been with my family and close friends.

In a video for my 45th birthday Pat made with the kids when I was leaving CNBC for King World twenty years ago, our then-seven-year-old granddaughter Kate Osher (now in her mid-twenties working at Apple) summed it up best in one ad-libbed, spontaneous line only a kid could up with. She yelled out to the camera, while swinging across a zip line in the backyard: "Happy Birthday Andy...how FUN is it?!"

That line has, over the years, has become a kind of family mantra or cheer, repeated at birthday parties and other family events. I had it engraved on the back of a bracelet I gave Pat for her birthday recently.

Kate's now-legendary family phrase "How FUN is it?!" was a potential title for this book, as it truly sums up all the joy of life my family and friends have given me.

Pat and I are so enjoying watching all the kids' bright hopes and dreams coming true from coast to coast. We feel very lucky to be around to witness it all and could not be prouder of them all.

I'm glad I got to tell you about the woman who saved me from a life of being a selfish, immature dope. She has given me the greatest life, love, and family I could ever have hoped for.

That's not to say we haven't had our rough patches. I'm certainly not easy and, as the Sting song goes, my wife can be "all four seasons in just one day." She has very strong opinions on everything from politics to art, culture, and people. If she loves you, she really loves you, and you'll know it. If she doesn't, you'll know that, too.

No relationship or marriage is easy or perfect, and ours certainly has had its roller-coaster ups and downs, but our love was, is, and always will be stronger than any of those challenges.

We've shared her difficult and courageous battle with melanoma and breast cancer over the past decade and a half, including ten separate surgeries we were not sure she'd survive.

Cancer, as you know, is an ongoing, insidious "wolf at the door" that never really goes far away. Every quarterly scan is nervous-making, leading to countless sleepless nights. Every "all clear" is a time of thanks, prayer, and relief. Every "we found something and need to do surgery" prompts ultimate fear and anxiety. Every surgery is endless, waiting to hear if her wonderful surgeons "got it all" or if it's spread to the point of being inoperable.

It's been a roller coaster for our family, Pat, and me, but she has survived all the challenges, and her strength, positive attitude, and sheer will have given us almost fifteen wonderful years we were not sure we'd have, filled with family milestones, graduations, weddings, trips, and an even deeper, greater love and appreciation of our lives together and of life itself.

The cancers, along with Pat's severe, systemic osteoarthritis, which developed over the past five years, have at times been debilitating but are now, thankfully, under control. All of this we battled together with our family and closest friends but primarily through the same strength, courage, and determination that allowed Pat, her mom, dad, and sister Ann to escape their frightening, dead-end lives growing up in the coal mines of Scranton, Pennsylvania.

Pat cooked and ran their little house next to the rail road tracks in Scranton by herself at nine years old as her hardworking, stalwart dad, Vince, left for the coal mine every day at 4 a.m. and her mom and sister were living in New York, helping Pat's talented sister Ann launch her successful Broadway career.

Pat's mom, Helen, courageously took Ann to New York after Ann won a local Scranton singing contest. Helen had the true guts and will to get her girls out of a life around the mines. She gave up all to do it, and she did it. She is a true hero.

Within a few years Pat and her dad were able to join them in a tiny, one-bedroom apartment in Hell's Kitchen, the worst part of Manhattan. It was dangerous and scary, but with a big hand up from her talented and generous older sister, Pat began to get some small parts and modeling assignments, and at sixteen was spotted by a Paramount talent scout and signed to a contract at Paramount. There she starred in dozens of major movies, including *Forever Female*, with Ginger Rogers and William Holden, written by the Epstein brothers, who wrote *Casablanca*.

She also did a number of "road movies," like *Money From Home* co-starring with Dean Martin and Jerry Lewis, as well as some avant-garde serious dramas, including *There's Always Tomorrow* directed by the highly respected New Wave auteur Douglas Sirk. Pat co-starred with the iconic Barbara Stanwyck along with Fred McMurray and Joan Bennett. The film, and Pat's work in it, garnered strong reviews, as did her work on *A Family Upside Down*, a seven-part made-for-TV series in which she co-starred with Helen Hayes and Fred Astaire.

In addition, she starred in her own series, *Please Don't Eat the Daisies*, on NBC along with dozens of top sitcoms and dramas over the next several decades, including *Police Story, Joe Forrester, The Love Boat, Charlie's Angels, Dynasty, Port Charles, Frasier, and Friends.*

After a career of working steadily on Broadway, in more than thirty movies and hundreds of television series, Pat now spends her time taking care of our family, our home, and her many devoted friends, along with her many charitable efforts.

She is as beautiful as ever and loves doing her favorite things—gardening, cooking, decorating, dance classes, theater, and bridge—along with taking care of our great rescue pup, Bonnie, and me, and entertaining and spending time with our family and dear friends.

I feel very blessed to have shared my life with Pat and am thankful each and every day for her. In truth, she's the one who should be writing a book. She got halfway through one a few years ago, and I hope she'll pick it back up. Her stories are truly the ones worth reading

# PAT CROWLEY
# PHOTO GALLERY

*From the Paramount feature film Hollywood or Bust, co-starring with Jerry Lewis and Dean Martin, one of three films she did with them*

"FOREVER FEMALE"
A Paramount Picture

*In her first major movie, Forever Female, starring with Oscar winner William Holden and veteran actor Melvyn Douglas*

*(Love the dark brown hair!)*

*TV Guide cover for Please Don't Eat the Daisies*

*Copyright 2017. TVGM Holdings. 128848:0417RR*

*With Billy Crystal, directing her as Roger Maris's wife in the HBO film 61\**

*Co-hosting A.M. Los Angeles with Regis Philbin and guest Tom Snyder*

*A fan magazine feature with grandkids Erin, Clare,
Kate, Eddie, and Will in the late 1990s*

*Pat's covers for Look and Life magazines, which for decades
were the equivalent of People and Vanity Fair today*

*John Engstead/mptvimages.com*

*With Dean Martin in a fan magazine that devoted an entire issue to Pat*

*They worked together on dozens of shows and movies. I'm not crazy about them being in bed together but I've learned over the years that I'm not the only man who found my wife beautiful and have learned to accept that. Sort of.*

*The Golden Globe Award Pat won for Most Promising Newcomer, Female*

*A great night with family and friends at a 50th-
birthday party Pat threw for me*

*L-R: Christopher Nicholson, Richard Mark, Kate Osher, Bob Osher,
Erin Hookstratten, Anne Osher, Andy Friendly, Jon Mark, Maddie
Friendly, Ruth Friendly, Andrew Friendly, Clare Hookstratten, Jon
Hookstratten, Marion Hookstratten, Pat Crowley, Will Hookstratten,
James Nicholson, Lisa Friendly, Noah Mark, David Friendly.*

*One of my favorite photos of Pat, taken a few years
ago on vacation in Cabo San Lucas*

*At the Western Wall in Jerusalem, on a trip to Israel*

*At S.H. Friendly Hall while visiting granddaughter
Clare at the University of Oregon, 2014*

*Our gang on a bike outing at our vacation home in Palm Desert, 2003*

*L-R: Bob and Ann Osher, Jon and Marion Hookstratten,
Kate Osher, Clare Hookstratten, Eddie Osher, Will
Hookstratten, Pat, Erin Hookstratten, and me*

*At a typical barbecue on our patio with some of our gang*

*L-R: Ramona Orley, Andrew Friendly, Maddie Friendly, Clare and Marion Hookstratten, Jason Orley, Aaron Mark, Catie Mark, Pat, Jon Hookstratten, Noah Mark, Will Hookstratten*

# 22

## RICHARD PRYOR: HERE AND NOW (AND ONE OF THE CRAZIEST NIGHTS OF MY LIFE)

In 1983 I wrote and produced Ralph Edwards' iconic *This Is Your Life* in partnership with the NBC-owned stations for national syndication. While my then-production partner, Bob Parkinson, and I were in the middle of our thirty-nine-episode order, we were asked to a meeting with uber-entertainment attorney Skip Brittenham, David Nochimson and Tom Hansen, who remain close friends to this day.

Skip explained that his client Richard Pryor, whom most top comedians consider the greatest comic of all time and who was a comedy hero of mine, wanted to do another concert film on the heels of his recent, highly successful *Live on the Sunset Strip*.

But this time he wanted to direct it himself and was looking for a TV production team to produce. Richard wanted to shoot on video and then transfer to film for its theatrical release. Richard preferred the "more real" look of TV compared with the slicker, more theatrical look of film for his concert films.

Skip felt that Richard would be comfortable with us, that it would be a good partnership. I think Richard was looking for a new team to go along with his new production company Indigo at Columbia Pictures, which represented a fresh start for Pryor, following a very dark period.

We had heard and read the horror stories about working with the mercurial, temperamental star during his well-documented drug-using (abusing) years. But after nearly killing himself while freebasing cocaine, when his pipe blew up and set his whole body on fire, and a long and painful recovery and rehab, he was now clean and sober. When we met with him at his sprawling estate in Northridge in the San Fernando Valley, he was calm, low-key, and charming, and even played the drums for us as we spent the afternoon listening to him detail his plans for the movie.

It was to be called *Richard Pryor: Here and Now*, and it was to be shot over three nights at the recently restored historic Saenger Theater in New Orleans. But first we would document Richard working out his routines and perfecting the show over several months at the famed Comedy Store in L.A. and a club in Dallas as well.

In addition, we recorded in-depth interviews with Richard as well as his fans in all three locations, shot him working behind the scenes, and used the footage in a brief documentary at the start of the film.

Richard, for the most part, was focused and relaxed, and a pleasure to work with. Any fears we had were quickly gone, and the thrill and absolute joy of being around a true genius in his prime led to one of the greatest experiences of my career.

Except on our first day at the Saenger Theatre.

All had gone well in Los Angeles and Dallas, and there was great excitement as we loaded in our set and equipment and tweaked our huge production trucks during a sweltering summer week in New Orleans.

The day before shooting the first of three concerts, we all were ready to go. Then Richard and the great football legend Jim Brown, who also was the project's executive producer and Richard's partner in Indigo, arrived to do a final prep and tech rehearsal.

Jim was one of my heroes growing up. I remember like it was yesterday, my dad taking me to see him and his Cleveland Browns play my beloved Giants on a freezing winter day at Yankee Stadium. He is widely considered the greatest football player of all time.

Working with Jim was surreal. Here I was at thirty-two, producing a movie for Columbia Pictures with two of my all-time heroes, Jim Brown and Richard Pryor, and having the time of my life.

Until this happened:

Richard was in great spirits as he worked with each of the cameramen, explaining his vision as director of the film about how he wanted them to shoot the concerts. He instructed them on when and how to zoom in and out for close-ups and wide shots to achieve the best comic and emotional effect. He had a clear vision of what he wanted the film to look like, and he communicated it well to his adoring crew. He spent the whole afternoon composing and framing shots, blocking his movements for lighting, camera, and sound. Then he changed into the suit he planned to wear for filming and walked on stage.

*George Hughley, me, and Jim Brown playing ping-pong at my
home. George was a former NFL player and an officer with the
LAPD, and ran security for the film. Both became good friends.*

It was a beautiful, tailored, white silk suit with black pinstripes. It was…
"striking" as Bill Murray says in *Caddyshack* as Carl Spackler. (Favorite
family film, had to get in a reference.)

There was one problem: The bright, white silk and pinstripes would not
work for video. They created a strobe effect that was totally distracting, and
despite our brilliant crew's extensive efforts to adjust the lighting, Chroma,
and video levels, nothing could be done to fix it.

The suit, a last-minute change from one that had been pre-selected to
work with the cameras, had been purchased by our star the day before, and
Richard was determined to wear it all three nights.

He could not accept that he would not be able to wear it.

After an hour or more of trying to change his mind, the suit became our
first crisis; Richard was not budging. He was going to wear it and it was our
job to make it work. Even Jim Brown couldn't get him to budge.

We met again with our crew and the brilliant team that lit and shot most
of the major award and variety specials in Hollywood, tried everything
humanly possible, but there was no way to make the strobe effect from the
suit go away.

It was around 10 p.m. and our night was just beginning.

We consulted with our own wardrobe people and some of the best across the country, even one in Paris. Everyone agreed the only possible solution, and an unlikely one, would be to have it dyed to a more muted shade of "crème," or beige, which might take off some of the sheen and glare. This, combined with bringing the video and Chroma levels down and more muted lighting, might have a long shot at allowing for acceptable video levels that would stop the strobing.

With the help of local crew and wardrobe experts, we contacted dressmakers, tailors, suit makers, dry cleaners, and dye experts—all to no avail. No one felt that we could effectively dye the suit without ruining it.

Several people suggested replacements and offered to open their shops at any hour of the night for Richard to come in, look at alternatives, and be fitted. They promised they would work all day to complete the work in time for the first concert the following night.

At midnight we met with Richard, who would have none of it. He was going to wear his suit and that was that. He appeared irritated and for the first time was acting like the movie star monster we had heard and read about.

At one point I made the mistake of nicely, half-jokingly saying, "You're just fucking with us, right?"

He did not laugh and told me to "get the fuck" out of his suite and that we better fix the problem or he wouldn't appear the next night.

We were exhausted from a long day and week, and our high spirits quickly changed to pure anxiety, fear, and fatigue. Jim Brown was feeling it too and pretty much told us it was our ass and we better get it dyed somehow and make it work.

After more talks with local wardrobe people, dry cleaners, and suit makers, we were tapped out. No one felt they could help us, certainly not in the time frame we had to work with.

Finally, an elderly man who had opened his dry cleaning shop for us told us about a woman he knew who had dyed some dresses for a customer years before, using tea bags in a bathtub. He gave us her number. You can't make this stuff up, folks.

By now we would try anything. We woke the poor woman up at midnight, explained the situation, and begged her to give it a try. She warned us that it would almost surely not work, pointed out that it was the middle of the night, and asked (rightfully so), "Couldn't it wait till morning?"

She must have felt sorry enough for us that she told us to come over and, for an absurdly high fee, said she would give it a try.

So in a surreal and bizarre scene, at about 2 a.m. in a tiny apartment filled with cats and hanging Mardi Gras beads, a bathtub was filled with hot water and dozens of tea bags, and in went Richard's beautiful new, custom-designed, handmade, bright white silk pinstripe suit.

I looked at my partner Bob and he looked at me, and we weren't sure whether to laugh or cry; we did a little of each as we waited two hours for the dye job to be completed. All the while we thought to ourselves, we may never work again.

At 4 a.m. we were handed the now bluish, beige-ish, wet, shrunken, severely wrinkled suit and told to let it dry naturally on a hanger and, when it was completely dry, to have it pressed.

She wished us luck and looked at us with a mix of empathy and pity as we headed back to our hotel to catch a couple hours sleep and say our prayers that somehow the suit would now work for the cameras...and that Richard would go along with the new, definitely-not-white suit.

Around 9 a.m., I was awoken by a knock at the door and our wardrobe person holding the now dried and pressed and severely shrunken, beige/bluish suit. She looked alarmed.

I woke Bob and shared the bad news, and we decided to call Jim and fill him in. We felt like complete dopes. Jim took it in stride, thanked us for trying and staying up all night, and said he'd tell Richard and suggest he wear the original dark green suit that worked perfectly on camera.

Skip Brittenham had thankfully flown in from L.A. for the show and told us not to worry; he'd talk to Richard.

We were nervous and upset all day. We didn't hear back about what Richard was going to do until about an hour before the first show was to begin. We feared the worst as we loaded the excited audience into the theater and awaited Richard's arrival.

Finally his limo pulled up to the theater with our cameras rolling and the crowds cheering. George Hughley, our security guard, stepped out first, followed by Jim, followed by Richard wearing the original dark green suit.

We were able to breathe for the first time in twenty-four hours but were scared as hell about Richard's mood and if we'd survive the night. Bob and I sheepishly went to greet him, not knowing what to expect.

Richard cracked the slightest, wry little smile and went into his concert voice and said, "Y'all motherfuckers done fucked up my shit," as he held the pathetic, shrunken silk jacket out in his left hand for all to see.

We looked at Jim, we looked at Skip, and they were laughing hysterically. The next three nights went off without a hitch, with Richard opening the first night telling the story of the suit and holding it up for the audience to see. Brilliant, hysterical. Pure Richard.

To this day, I'm not sure if he was serious or just having some "fun" with us. He never let on he was anything but serious.

We edited the three nights together into one seamless, brilliant concert with the documentary elements at the start.

At the premiere, Richard took me and Bob aside and thanked us for our work in an emotional and sincere way, and handed us each a check for $75,000 (worth several multiples of that in today's dollars) as a bonus and a thank-you. By far the most money I'd ever received at one time, on top of our very generous producing fees. The film was well received and shot immediately to No. 1 in its opening weekend.

I stayed in touch with Richard for a year or so but eventually lost touch. I was deeply saddened when I heard he had developed multiple sclerosis, which led to his death in the mid-'90s. I wrote to him before his death. I just wanted to thank him.

In the past few years I've read a couple of biographies on Richard, and watched a documentary about him and his challenging life. While I know all about his difficult upbringing, drug use, bad and dangerous behavior, and the rest, I have to say that despite the little suit story, I have never had a more exciting or gratifying work experience or worked with a more brilliant, hysterical, and generous person.

I truly consider myself blessed to have known and produced the great Richard Pryor.

If you haven't seen his concert films in a while, or ever…you owe it to yourself to do so.

The original. The best.

Andy Friendly

# 50 Top-Grossing Films

**(WEEK ENDING NOVEMBER 9)**

Wednesday, November 16, 1983 — *Variety* — 9

Compiled by Standard Data Corp., N.Y.

| TITLE | DISTR | THIS WEEK $ | RANK | LAST WEEK $ | RANK | CITIES | FIRST RUN | SHOW CASE | SCREENS | AVG. PER SCREEN | WEEKS ON CHART | TOTAL TO DATE $ |
|---|---|---|---|---|---|---|---|---|---|---|---|---|
| RICHARD PRYOR – HERE AND NOW | COL | 1,533,815 | 1 | 1,611,845 | 2 | 22 | 15 | 245 | 260 | 5,899 | 2 | 3,141,690 |
| NEVER SAY NEVER AGAIN | WB | 1,377,378 | 2 | 1,745,629 | 1 | 22 | 10 | 256 | 266 | 5,178 | 5 | 12,689,996 |
| THE BIG CHILL | COL | 1,325,020 | 3 | 1,316,504 | 4 | 22 | 13 | 193 | 206 | 6,432 | 6 | 9,760,421 |
| DEAD ZONE | PAR | 1,106,427 | 4 | 1,535,487 | 3 | 22 | 6 | 211 | 217 | 5,098 | 3 | 4,397,920 |
| DEAL OF THE CENTURY | WB | 973,183 | 5 | | | 17 | 10 | 215 | 225 | 4,325 | 1 | 973,183 |
| ALL THE RIGHT MOVES | FOX | 907,142 | 6 | 582,516 | 7 | 18 | 8 | 158 | 166 | 5,464 | 3 | 2,226,449 |
| THE RIGHT STUFF | LWB | 901,396 | 7 | 970,767 | 5 | 22 | 5 | 80 | 85 | 10,604 | 3 | 2,800,294 |
| EDUCATING RITA | COL | 640,821 | 8 | 476,050 | 8 | 21 | 9 | 101 | 110 | 5,821 | 7 | 1,595,785 |
| THE OSTERMAN WEEKEND | FOX | 597,162 | 9 | 266,415 | 13 | 15 | 11 | 135 | 146 | 4,090 | 3 | 496,648 |
| UNDER FIRE | ORI | 373,845 | 10 | 662,834 | 6 | 16 | 4 | 96 | 100 | 3,738 | 3 | 1,834,459 |
| NEVER CRY WOLF | BV | 289,500 | 11 | 118,500 | 20 | 7 | 5 | 9 | 14 | 20,678 | 4 | 621,017 |
| REAR WINDOW | UCL | 284,953 | 12 | 240,458 | 15 | 11 | 14 | 9 | 23 | 12,260 | 6 | 1,385,877 |
| TESTAMENT | PAR | 263,000 | 13 | | | 8 | 3 | 17 | 20 | 13,150 | 1 | 263,000 |
| CITY OF THE WALKING DEAD | 21C | 200,000 | 14 | | | 1 | | 35 | 35 | 5,714 | 1 | 200,000 |
| RUMBLE FISH | U | 188,366 | 15 | 517,391 | 10 | 18 | 10 | 49 | 59 | 3,192 | 5 | 967,631 |
| BRAINS | UA | 154,556 | 16 | 293,251 | 9 | 14 | 9 | 36 | 45 | 3,434 | 6 | 2,967,255 |
| RUNNING BRAVE | BV | 146,700 | 17 | | | 11 | 5 | 46 | 51 | 2,876 | 1 | 147,600 |
| ZELIG | OWB | 93,326 | 18 | 128,565 | 19 | 10 | 7 | 15 | 22 | 4,242 | 17 | 6,715,770 |
| MR MOM | FOX | 90,471 | 19 | 74,817 | 16 | 10 | 13 | 41 | 44 | 2,056 | 16 | 13,458,770 |
| PIECES | FVI | 88,200 | 20 | 82,500 | 22 | 3 | | 19 | 20 | 4,410 | 1 | 1,827,916 |
| THE BEING | or V | 84,000 | 21 | | | 1 | | 18 | 18 | 4,666 | 1 | 84,000 |
| RISKY BUSINESS | GWB | 74,199 | 22 | 292,063 | 11 | 10 | 6 | 21 | 27 | 2,770 | 14 | |
| WICKED LADY | UA | 66,185 | 23 | 121,880 | 18 | 9 | 6 | 23 | 29 | 2,282 | 2 | 240,789 |
| RETURN OF THE JEDI | FOX | 63,604 | 24 | 73,742 | 23 | 7 | 4 | 11 | 12 | 5,782 | 24 | 67,723,687 |
| THE FINAL TERROR | CMW | 59,284 | 25 | 197,100 | 17 | 4 | 7 | 11 | 18 | 3,293 | 2 | 256,984 |
| HEAT AND DUST | UCL | 52,288 | 26 | 67,210 | 24 | 7 | 7 | | 7 | 7,469 | 8 | 466,460 |
| DANTON | TCL | 37,600 | 27 | 38,300 | 25 | 5 | 5 | | 5 | 7,520 | 6 | 185,715 |
| EXPERIENCE PREFERRED | GWN | 37,000 | 28 | | | 2 | 2 | | 2 | 18,500 | 1 | 37,000 |

*I asked Richard to sign the Variety grosses from our opening week, which have since hung proudly in my office.*

# 23

## OPRAH AND *THE ROCK 'N' ROLL EVENING NEWS*

I first met Oprah Winfrey on a riverboat in New Orleans in 1986. We were at the big annual NATPE TV sales convention trying to get our respective new shows on the air.

At the time, Oprah was a little-known local talk show host from Chicago. She was trying to take her show nationwide, and I was exec producing and selling a weekly late-night music series I'd created called *The Rock 'n' Roll Evening News* in association with A&M Records.

King World, which was selling both shows, was at the time a relatively small, family-owned syndicator that had just had its first taste of big-time success. The company had recently convinced Merv Griffin to take his *Wheel of Fortune* and *Jeopardy!* game shows off network TV, where they had been failing after previously successful runs, and try them in the little-known world of first-run syndication.

For the ridiculously low fee of $50,000, the bright, brash, and bold King brothers—Roger, Bob, and Michael—had bought the rights to *Wheel* and *Jeopardy!* They launched *Wheel* to huge ratings success even without clearances in New York and L.A., the two biggest U.S. markets—unheard of for syndicated shows.

Now they were about to launch *The Oprah Winfrey Show*, along with a late-night show with comedian David Brenner and our show.

The New Orleans riverboat was rocking, as the larger-than-life King brothers wined and dined TV station executives from around the country and told them all about the new shows from a giant stage.

All the shows had a buzz, coming off the huge early success of *Wheel* and *Jeopardy!*, and all of them got on the air the next fall, a rarity in syndication.

But the biggest buzz was about Oprah. It's hard to imagine people didn't know who she was, couldn't pronounce her name ("Who is Okra?" was a familiar refrain).

She and I had a couple drinks and a nice conversation about our hopes and dreams for our respective series. She couldn't have been nicer or brighter.

I recall our laughing about the silly way TV shows were sold, like on our rockin' riverboat, but I also remember she was thrilled that the King brothers believed in her and had, in her words, "the guts to be selling an unknown black woman to white station execs from around the country whose template for success in daytime talk was Phil Donahue." Donahue had the No. 1 daytime show at the time. Ten years later, he hosted a show with Vladimir Posner that I executive produced at CNBC.

When Oprah's show debuted the following fall, it quickly exploded and became the biggest daytime talk show ever and the No. 3 show in all of syndication, right behind *Wheel* and *Jeopardy!*. King World became one of the biggest television companies in the world.

Our show, *The Rock 'n' Roll Evening News*, was a critical and modest rating success, doing a solid 3.2 rating, all in "the demo" (desirable young viewers). It aired once a week and was sold on an all-barter basis (stations gave us no cash but allowed us to sell and keep half the advertising time).

We were able to deliver performances by and interviews with Neil Young, Paul McCartney, Elton John, The Go-Go's, Run-D.M.C., Robert Palmer, Nile Rodgers, Michael McDonald, and most of the biggest names in rock; conducted by a great team, including the brilliant *Los Angeles Times* music critic (and author of two major biographies on Johnny Cash and Paul Simon) Robert Hilburn, the *Village Voice*'s Nelson George, and the talented KROQ radio host Richard Blade, along with Adrienne Meltzer, Marianne Rogers, Steve Kmetko, Eleanor Mondale, Marjorie Wallace, and others.

The hugely talented Louis J. Horvitz directed the show, and went on to direct the Grammys, Oscars, Golden Globes, Kennedy Center Awards, and others. When Louis J. directed the Oscars the year my brother David was nominated for producing his wonderful film *Little Miss Sunshine*, he arranged for Pat and me to attend the awards, seated in some of the best seats in the house, and also hosted us at the Governors Ball that evening. That's the kind of guy Louis J. is. Even though my brother's movie didn't win, it was a tremendous night for all.

*The cast and staff of The Rock 'n' Roll Evening News*
*I have my arm around Louis J. Horvitz on my left. Our*
*talented producer Jeff Androsky is on my right.*
*(Once again, nice '80s hair, AF!)*

*With Billy Crystal on the set of The Rock 'n' Roll Evening News*

Louis J. and his wonderful wife Steffanee, Bob Hilburn, Joyce Bogart Trabulus, married to my brilliant doctor and close friend Josh, and many others on the team remain some of my closest friends. Joyce (three to my right in the white shirt) was married to music legend Neil Bogart until his death and played a major role building his company Casablanca with mega stars like Donna Summer, Kiss, and many more.

The young dude kneeling below her in white is her son Evan, who is now a major music producer. He recently married the brilliant singer-songwriter ZZ Ward, whom I first saw perform at Coachella a few years ago with my friend, Grammy producer Ken Ehrlich. She "blew us away" (as the kids say.)

Check out her song "365 Days." As good a song and performance as you're going to hear. Look it up, people, and play it loud.

A prediction: ZZ, already a star, will be a superstar. You read it here.

The *Rock 'n' Roll Evening News* was my dream show, and our director Lou Horvitz made it look like a million bucks, as he does every show he directs, especially Ken's Grammy Awards.

To this day Louis J. (as his friends call him) tells anyone who will listen that I "saved" his career by hiring him when others wouldn't after a publicly self-described bout with substance abuse, following his early success directing *Solid Gold* at Paramount in the early (drug-fueled) '80s. A bout he decidedly won for life.

In truth, we were the lucky ones to have such a brilliant director shooting the biggest music acts in the world at famed Stage 35 at ABC on Prospect Avenue in Hollywood; some of the coolest, most fun shows of my career.

But despite critical and modest economic success, the once-a-week, all-barter show just wasn't making *enough* money for King World to keep it going after our first, twenty-episode season. The Kings were making so much money with their daily, syndicated "strips"—*Wheel, Jeopardy!, Oprah*—that our little late-night weekly show wasn't worth the big effort it took King World to sell it.

So our show and David Brenner's show didn't make it to year two. My team and I were crushed. It was one of several soul-sucking, heart-crushing defeats, inevitable in a career of any length.

When the show ended, I lost touch with Oprah as her series and her brand, including her magazine and book club, grew bigger and bigger through the early part of the 1990s.

Our paths crossed again when I was hired away from running primetime at CNBC to run production and programming for my old friends the King brothers in 1995.

King World distributed Oprah's show, but she and her Harpo Productions produced it in Chicago, so my role was limited.

Once or twice a year I'd fly to Chicago to attend a taping and give her a hug, ask if there was anything we could do for her, and essentially pay my respects to the "queen," as we affectionately called her.

We had a really nice relationship, which began years ago on that riverboat in New Orleans, and despite her huge success, I always found her to be kind, generous, and down-to-earth.

When we launched Roseanne's talk show a few years later in 1998, I asked Oprah if she'd come to L.A. and be a guest on one of the first shows; she instantly agreed.

It was a huge "get" for us, and the ratings went through the roof and got Roseanne's show off to a great start. Ultimately Roseanne's show did not work, but it made a fortune for King World.

I saw Oprah from time to time at other industry events, including her (and my dad's) induction into the Television Academy Hall of Fame. She was a big fan of my dad and vice versa, so that event was a real love-fest.

I left King World in 2001 and lost touch with Oprah until 2014, when I was seated at the same table with her at the United Jewish Israel Appeal annual dinner in New York, which honored my friend David Zaslav, CEO of Discovery Communications, with whom she is partnered on the OWN Network.

They had become and are today very close, and we had a great time that night at a table that also included David's wonderful wife and children, as well as Jackson Browne, Tom Brokaw, Discovery Communications founder John Hendricks, and one of my all-time heroes: Holocaust survivor and author Elie Wiesel, who sadly passed away in 2016. What a true thrill and honor it was to meet and briefly talk with him. He was a giant.

Together Oprah and David overcame some early startup hiccups and have made OWN a vital and successful network.

Industry naysayers doubted it would work, but I never had a doubt with those two in charge.

That night at David's dinner was truly special for David and his family, for me, and all who attended.

As for Oprah, the unknown, African-American, aspiring local talk show host from Chicago with dreams of competing with daytime talk giants like Phil Donahue and Geraldo—all her bright hopes and dreams had come true.

The fun, smart woman I had met on that riverboat thirty years earlier was now a billionaire and the most important woman in television, maybe even the world. And she was partners and dear friends with my close friend.

Here we all were, thirty years after that riverboat ride in New Orleans.

As Jackson Browne, one of my all-time favorite singer-songwriters for over three decades, serenaded David and all of us from the stage, I felt a surreal sense of time through the decades and an awareness of having a very blessed and lucky life.

It was quite the night; one I'll never forget.

*This photo with Oprah was taken in the green room before a taping of Roseanne's show in our studio at CBS Television City, where we had three shows in three separate studios going at once, including Roseanne's, Martin Short's, and Hollywood Squares with Whoopi Goldberg, Tom Bergeron, Bruce Vilanch, and the gang.*

Columbia University in the City of New York | *New York, N.Y. 10027*

GRADUATE SCHOOL OF JOURNALISM                                    Journalism Building

January 22, 1987

Dear Andy:

You know that my philosophy has always been that he prevails
"who can afford to walk away from the table." I never meant
that financially or I'd still be at CBS News. I meant one has
to have the stamina to preserve one's integrity and walk away
from a proposition that just isn't right.

That's what you did, son, and your memo to your staff and your
note to Ruth and me indicates that that's the way you've ordered
your life. I know how much the "Rock 'N Roll Evening News" meant
to you, but I also know you did not want to give up the standards
that you had set. You didn't, and either RREN will find a new
life with you and your organization or you'll move on to bigger
and better things. What your thoughtful and sensitive note to
your staff indicates is that you don't want to water a good
product down to a point where it isn't what it started out to be.

Ruth and I are proud of you. The road is not always smooth and
may have some agony turns in it, but you will prevail, Andy,
because you know what you are. That's all one can hope for in
a son or a daughter.

We know the new show will prosper (I like the brochure), and there
will be many victories along the way as long as you remember who
you are and what you are trying to do.

Good luck and love to Pat.

Always,

*A letter my father wrote me when Rock 'n' Roll Evening News was
canceled. It, too, hangs in a frame in my study and reminds me of
the support my dad always gave me when I needed it most.*

# 24

## DAVID NOCHIMSON, THE FRIEND AND LAWYER YOU WANT IN YOUR CORNER FOR LIFE

I want to tell you about another of my closest friends, David Nochimson. Not because he is a superstar lawyer in our industry, representing many of its biggest stars and top directors including Bill Murray, Norman Lear, Taylor Hackford, Anjelica Huston, and Ridley Scott, but because he is truly special and someone we all can, and should, in my opinion, aspire to be like.

It's fun to tell you about some of the big stars I've been lucky to know and work with but David is truly an inspiration. Pay close attention, young people. You can thank me later, like when you're my age looking back at your life and you remember reading this and how it made you a better person! (smile)

I met David when I produced *Richard Pryor: Here and Now* for Columbia Pictures in 1983.

David, a New Jersey native who went to Yale (where he played on the basketball team) and Columbia Law, was a new partner of uber-entertainment attorneys Skip Brittenham and Ken Ziffren, who brought me and Bob Parkinson in to produce the Pryor project.

After Skip set things up with Pryor and the studio, Columbia Pictures, he turned the project over to David to oversee on a day-to-day basis, and we became close friends as he took on our other projects as well.

A few years later, I went off on my own and David continued to represent me on everything I have done since.

David is a brilliant, highly regarded lawyer, who has guided me and, after I made the introductions, also represented my brother David, and David Zaslav. That's a lot of Davids!

Along with his long list of star clients, as well as his wisdom, grace, calm, and ultimate integrity, he is known for being a "deal maker" and "closer," not a "deal breaker," which, sadly, some big-name, big-ego lawyers can be.

Other lawyers and agents may be louder, more famous, more boisterous self-promoters or appear outwardly tougher or more demanding on behalf of their famous, powerful clients. But no one is better liked, more respected, more trusted, or a better dealmaker than David.

In every difficult, protracted, contentious negotiation we've had at the studios, networks, and syndicators on dozens and dozens of projects, David has found a way to make the deal. And when the negotiation is over, no matter how heated or difficult, the comment I always hear from the other side is: "What a great, nice, smart guy David is."

As great a lawyer as he is, he is an even better person and friend.

Through all my professional and personal triumphs, but especially the battles and difficult times, David has always been there for me and helped guide me through.

David is a highly spiritual and centered person. He is the kind of person *New York Times* columnist David Brooks writes about in his book *The Road to Character*. He's the kind of person who "radiates an inner light" and fits Brooks' description of people of character.

> *"They seem deeply good. They listen well. They make you feel funny and valued. They are not thinking about what wonderful work they are doing. They are not thinking about themselves at all. These are the people we want to be."*

While David's council and friendship have been invaluable in business and my career, he has influenced me in even more important ways.

In 1995, when I returned to L.A. from CNBC to work at King World, David invited me to join the board of his beloved L.A. Free Clinic, now the Saban Community Clinic, which runs three community health centers in Los Angeles.

The centers have become a medical home for people who have fallen through the cracks of the medical and insurance system; it provides more than 100,000 patient visits a year to those who need it most.

In my early forties I was looking to get involved with a charitable organization. I knew of the clinic's work and, thanks to David, joined the board, which was made up of some of the most powerful people in Hollywood, including Les Moonves, Bernie Brillstein, and other top studio and network executives, agents, managers, and lawyers.

I had never served on a powerful board before; I admit I was a little nervous at my first meetings as I tried to watch and learn the process.

As always, all I had to do was watch David as he calmly and wisely did his job as a respected board member and then president of the board.

His quiet, dignified, inclusive leadership style brought out the best of a board full of characters and giant egos. When things got heated or emotional, David's wise and calm demeanor set a tone that kept everyone focused on the important tasks at hand; using his trademark, low-key humor diffused egos and arguments, resulting in positive action and results.

I have never once in thirty-five years seen him lose his cool, even while facing some of the most high-pressure situations imaginable, both personal and professional.

When I became president of the board a decade later, I tried to follow his example, just as I did in everything I did in business and in my personal life.

Even if I rarely rose to his example, David was and is my role model.

Whenever I find myself in a difficult work or personal situation, I think to myself, *How would David handle this situation? What would he say? How would he sound?*

At the annual gala dinner, when the clinic awarded David its prestigious Lenny Somberg Award, named for the clinic's first executive director who started the clinic in the 1960s, I was so proud of him.

Years later, when they awarded it to me and my brother David, we asked if David N. could be the one to present it to us.

Needless to say, his introduction was deeply moving and meant the world to me and my brother and to our assembled family and friends at the dinner in 2007.

Through the many years, David's wife of almost thirty-five years, Gail, and his wonderful mother, Mildred, who recently passed away at 104, became our dear friends as well.

We shared countless dinners, trips, and family events together, including time at their home in Quogue on the beach of Long Island in New York.

After a brave battle with pancreatic cancer, Gail passed away a few years ago.

When she passed, David asked if I would say a few words about her at her celebration of life and memorial. With David's permission, I'd like to share a little of what I wrote and said about Gail that day, as it reflects so much on David as well.

*In a generation when beautiful women were not always taken seriously and often thought of as mere ornaments sitting beside their powerful husbands at dinner parties or charitable events, Gail refused to play that role.*

*Whether the topic at the dinner table was health care and her beloved free clinic, where she volunteered as a family counselor, or our involvement in Iraq or Afghanistan, or global warming, or the latest controversial book, play or movie...*

*Gail always had a strong and informed point of view and she was not shy about stating it.*

*She did not suffer fools.*

*Where we sometimes seek to avoid controversy or confrontation, to be politically correct, Gail always said what was on her mind. She was authentic.*

*Not in an aggressive or hostile way but in a way that made you think and react and that sparked interesting and lively debate and conversation. She always dug below the surface; Gail was not interested in small talk. And she was certainly no ornament.*

We miss Gail very much. And we know how much David does.

But David, as is his nature, remains upbeat. With his new buddy Miles, a handsome golden retriever, he began exploring new adventures, including the monthly hikes he organizes, and at family and holiday events we all invite him to and forever will.

And the best news: In May 2016, at an event put together by our mutual friends Janus Cercone and Michael Manheim, to debut their brilliant spec house in which David and I are investors (dubbed the "Riviera White House," the former home of Ronald and Nancy Reagan, which they rebuilt overlooking Riviera and the Pacific Ocean high up on the crest of a mountain in Pacific Palisades), David met Janice's beautiful, smart, fun friend Laurie Cappello.

Since then they have been inseparable: traveling, hiking, and spending time together at their homes in L.A., New York, and Aspen with their families and many friends.

Laurie is a perfect match and soul mate for David; Pat and I have fallen for her, too.

Aside from being a wonderful skier, golfer, hiker, and home designer/builder, Laurie is a devoted mother to two terrific college-age teenagers who love and have become very close to David.

We knew she was the one when she got him (normally reserved and dignified) dancing like a maniac at our beach club's crazy Fourth of July bash.

And two nights later on top of a table at a Malibu party. (I didn't witness that one in person but saw the incriminating photos.)

We haven't seen David so happy in years. Thank you, Laurie.

For almost forty years, David has been a true blessing in my life.

For me, David is, and will always be, in David Brooks' words: "The person we want to be."

*Janus Cercone, Laurie Cappello, David Nochimson, me, and Michael Manheim, at the Fourth of July bash at our beach club, 2016*

*Pat (holding our pup Lilly), David, and Gail at our home in La Quinta*

# 25

## ALL ROADS LEAD BACK TO NBC, CNBC, SNYDER, RUSSERT, GERALDO AND "ZAS"

On my first day as a consultant at CNBC in Fort Lee, New Jersey, just across the George Washington Bridge from Manhattan in 1990, I was invited to have lunch with network president Michael Eskridge and his senior team at the Red Oak Diner.

The restaurant was a typical Jersey diner in a shopping center across the street from the studios.

Mike, a smart, strong leader and NBC vet, held court with his team there for lunch almost every day to review matters at hand at the startup network, plot strategy, and have a few laughs. Not exactly the 21 Club, but it had a decent tuna sandwich and it was a setting right out of *The Sopranos*.

While I had spent the first decade of my career at various divisions of NBC, that first day after being away for a few years I felt like the new kid at school as Mike and the senior team including Bob Davis, Al Garrity, Mike Reitman, Marc Rosenweig, and the young head of business affairs and general counsel, Dave Zaslav, talked shop and threw a bunch of questions at me, sizing me up as they went.

I had been hired by NBC to help formulate a strategy for CNBC's primetime programming, which was struggling after the markets closed and the business crowd stopped viewing. I wasn't hired directly by Eskridge and his team, so I was viewed a bit circumspectly, and I could feel it.

Mike was a guy who kept tight control and demanded total loyalty, and the fact that I had been brought in by his boss, NBC Cable president Tom Rogers, through Stuart Sucherman's search firm, was not sitting well. *Who is this spy Friendly from L.A.?*

In an effort to make small talk, I asked the young lawyer Zaslav, sitting to my left (he was probably twenty-eight then), where he'd gone to law school. He coolly responded in a sharp voice so Eskridge could hear, "B.U. What's the difference?"

*OK. I can handle this. In time they'll like and trust me. Or not.*

It took a while but over the next few months David and I worked together, did some deals together, and became friends.

I was hired as a full-time vice president of development and programming and later added the title of executive producer of all primetime shows.

After some fits and starts, including battles with the then-heads of business news (CNBC's daytime programming), sales, and distribution, and some initial reticence from across the river at NBC over my plan to take primetime toward day-and-date, topical talk programming, we developed a strong slate of shows. As hosts, we landed my old pal and mentor Tom Snyder, whom I convinced to return to television after a break to do his beloved radio; the newly minted host of *Meet the Press,* the truly great Tim Russert; and Geraldo Rivera and Phil Donahue, both of whom we rescued from the depths of sordid, tacky daytime talk shows in syndication. Both showed they had much more to offer. Phil partnered with the insightful Vladimir Posner. Geraldo, a lawyer before starting his brilliant early career as a reporter at WABC, where he reported on the abuses at Willowbrook State School, focused on the law for us and ultimately the O.J. Simpson trial, where his *Rivera Live* became the show of record on the trial, garnering record-breaking ratings and buzz for CNBC.

At a Quinnipiac Fred Friendly First Amendment Award ceremony this past year, honoring one of our occasional *Talk Live* hosts, Charlie Rose, Geraldo told Ruth Friendly: "Your son Andy saved my career in journalism." Don't know about all that but Geraldo and Phil no longer had to do topics like "Cousins who f**k" for daytime audiences, and both made great use of the opportunity and re-established their careers in broadcast journalism.

We also had Dick Cavett, Al Roker, John McLaughlin, Mary Matalin, Jane Wallace, Dee Dee Myers, Janice Lieberman, Boyd Matson, Cassandra Clayton, and Bob Berkowitz doing terrific talk/informational, issue, and consumer-oriented shows. And Charlie Rose, David Steinberg, Gerry Spence, Arianna Huffington, Cal Thomas, Daisy Fuentes, and many others joined on the weekends as rotating hosts on a series we created called *Talk Live.*

This was at a time when the only other day-and-date, news-oriented talk show in primetime was Larry King's on CNN. Of course, today they are everywhere in primetime on CNN, Fox News, MSNBC, Comedy Central, and elsewhere.

We saw a gaping, underserved programming hole we could run through by providing smart, issue-oriented talk, hosted by some of the best talent anywhere at a relatively low cost, which was a central strategy because we had very little money to spend.

With the faith and full backing of NBC Cable president Tom Rogers, chief executive Bob Wright, and his boss, Jack Welch, at GE, along with NBC stars like the great Tom Brokaw, who believed in us and appeared on our little network regularly, giving us stature and credibility even though he knew no one was watching...we began to achieve liftoff.

The strategy worked, and over a two-year period the network thrived, growing from a 0.2 to a 1.2 rating (over a million viewers) in primetime and from 12 million to 80 million subscribers.

Along the way, I was accepted by the team and grew especially close with "Zas" (David Zaslav's nickname) and Marc Rosenweig, my talented deputy in primetime and later at King World.

We hung out together with our families after work and played a weekly poker game at my rented cottage near the studio.

Here's a poker check from Zas from around that time. I never cashed it but tacked it onto my office bulletin board just to remind him of his butt whupping.

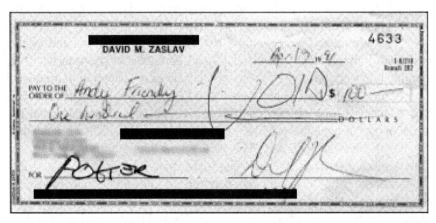

Of course, with his well-reported 2014 payday of $155,000,000 as CEO of Discovery Communications (including stock awards for a new six-year contract a couple years ago), according to a major profile on him in *Time*, I don't think he has to sweat the occasional poker losses these days.

They pay him that because of the tremendous job he's done growing the company around the world in an ever-challenging global media economy, and because he has earned so much money for his stockholders. *Time* recently called him "the most powerful person in media worldwide."

I know he hates that his income is so widely reported, but as CEO of a public company there's nothing he can do to prevent it.

David and his wife of thirty years, Pam, are two of the most down-to-earth, modest people I know, and they give more to charities and friends in need than anyone I know. And not in a public, attention-getting way.

All people hear and read about are the giant paydays and private jets. David and Pam give so much of it back, in so many ways, to so many people and worthy organizations. And with no fanfare.

Twenty-five years ago, in the early building stages of CNBC, we fought side by side on a wide range of battles with our talent and their agents, with fellow executives from other departments who didn't agree with our programming ideas and resented our success within CNBC and NBC.

A few years later, in 1994, a new president of the network, Roger Ailes, became my boss. Roger passed away on May 18, 2017, as this book was going to press, less than a year after he resigned from Fox News amid allegations of sexual harassment.

My working relationship with Roger was reported in Gabe Sherman's best-selling book *The Loudest Voice in the Room* in 2014, and again last fall in a cover story in *New York Magazine* and other media outlets as part of the reporting on Roger's troubles at Fox.

For the record, I did not speak to Sherman or in any way cooperate with his book or any other reporting, but others with axes still to grind did, and leaked confidential internal memos I'd written at the time.

I had long moved on, but in the summer of 2016 I was once again back in the middle of Roger's story because of things that had happened twenty years earlier.

Such is the nature of journalism conducted through unnamed, secret sources and long-held, simmering grudges.

Sometimes it's the only way to get the story, as we're seeing at the highest levels of government today.

It was a critical, invaluable tool in Woodward and Bernstein's coverage of Watergate and many other stories crucial to preserving our democracy, but in this case I became collateral damage in someone else's long-festering war. One I had long moved on from and did not want any part of.

Roger and I had some very tough battles, as documented in Sherman's reporting, but we made it through them and went on with our lives. I do not want to bore everyone by retelling those stories here. But I can't totally ignore this period either.

Roger made a very generous donation a couple of years ago to the project for veterans I helped organize with my friends Steven and Dayna Bochco, as well as the L.A. (now Saban) Community Clinic, on whose board I sit and help run a charity golf tournament, which Roger supported.

He also supported an event Zas and I organized last year for the Shoah Foundation at USC, where David and I are on the Board of Councilors and David has played a giant role.

But in the mid-1990s, in between some very productive and even fun times at the network, we "wrassled" pretty good, and it got nasty at times.

The fights were typical turf and power wars. Not worth dwelling on, but it's not an exaggeration to say that careers and futures were on the line. At times it was a real shit show.

From my perspective, I had spent a few years building CNBC primetime, as described above with Zas, Tom, Marc, and our team. Roger came in as president and my boss. He was smart and talented. He was, like me, an alpha male. Unfortunately he wanted nearly complete control and much of the credit for the success of CNBC. Success we had bled and sweated for, seven days a week, eighteen hours a day, for three years.

Roger did many good things at CNBC. He boosted daytime ratings and the overall marketing and buzz for the network, improved business news and primetime.

I was happy to just keep doing my job running primetime, but that plan just didn't work out. With Roger, there was only going to be one boss and that would be Roger.

When I fought to keep control of the eleven shows I developed and executive produced, the proverbial immovable object met the proverbial brick wall.

I had never met Roger but knew his reputation. Knew people who'd worked with him, including my close pal Tom Snyder, whose *Tomorrow* show Roger had briefly produced, several years after I'd left in 1980.

Snyder and other *Tomorrow* staffers told me stories about him going back years before that. Back to their Philly days when Tom was a top news anchor and Roger was a young producer on *The Mike Douglas Show*. Some pretty wild stuff.

He was a tough guy. A smart guy. A don't "fuck with" guy. He had to control, dominate everything, everyone. He was a Nixon guy. A black ops "will kill you if you're not 100 percent loyal, obedient and don't do everything he wants" guy.

I was wary but open-minded. There was much to like about Roger. I liked his smart, funny producing brain and truly tried to get along with him, and I believe he tried to get along with me at first.

I tried to maintain a mutually respectful, collegial relationship, and for a period we got along, but when there are changes at the top, the knives come out. Even some of my "friends" and top stars aligned with Roger and against me. Most remained loyal, though, which I'll always appreciate.

Fueled in part by others with their own agendas, and in part by our own stubborn, Type-A egos, the rift between Roger and me grew deeper.

It didn't help that Roger was in what many described as a "nuclear" war with NBC cable president Tom Rogers, the man who hired and promoted me.

It also didn't help that in a companywide "Town Hall" meeting Bob Wright conducted from the *Saturday Night Live* studio in 1995, a year or so after Roger joined CNBC, which went to all NBC employees around the world, the company's CEO said the following when it came time in his remarks to talk about CNBC, following his updates on NBC News, NBC Sports, and NBC's huge "Must-See TV" primetime programming, in which he thanked each division president:

> *I'd also like to point out to any of you that don't have the opportunity to see this, that we've had really a big year at CNBC...*
>
> *...And to Andy Friendly, who's in charge of primetime programming for CNBC, my congratulations. The performance there is outstanding. Many of the primetime programs are up 300% in ratings year to year, which is extraordinary. The numbers are obviously considerably smaller than they are at the network, but it's basically just as difficult to increase a ratings performance there as it is anywhere else.*

The director cut away at this point to Roger seated in the first row of Studio 8H at 30 Rock, along with other division presidents. He did not look pleased.

Game over.

The shit got real.

After a few more months of nasty infighting and turmoil, I found a new job at King World, at home in L.A., and was down the road. Soon after, Roger left and started the hugely successful Fox News Channel.

The proverbial silver lining through all of this is that we achieved great success.

David Zaslav, Marc Rosenweig, and I became the closest of friends, and it's fair to say we kept each other going.

We kept each other's spirits up and we fortified each other. And we had a lot of laughs and a lot of fun, too.

At my going-away party when I left CNBC in October 1995 after five years to go to King World (held at Grissini's in Fort Lee, also right out of *The Sopranos*), speakers from Tom Snyder to Charles Grodin to Tim Russert to Geraldo to Dee Dee Myers to Tom Rogers said very kind things in their toasts. Even Roger said some nice, and funny things, which I'll share in a minute.

It was a loud, fun night for my great team and me to raise a few glasses, share some big hugs, and say our heartfelt goodbyes after five years of working together night and day in the trenches.

Here are some excerpts, both funny and sincere, from the toasts that night, for which I remain very grateful, along with a few thoughts about the people who made them.

GERALDO RIVERA, host of *Rivera Live*

*I've been associated with Andy for probably a quarter century now, and I honor him. He was instrumental in bringing me here and I wish him all the greatest success. What greater tribute to a man than to say that he is up for every challenge that the world has for him. To go from Roger Ailes to Roger King, I mean the guy's got balls.*

Geraldo was in my dad's summer program for minorities in broadcast journalism at Columbia University. Dad called him one of the brightest students he'd ever had.

Later Geraldo became a broadcasting legend, reporting on abuses at the Willowbrook psychiatric hospital in New York for WABC-TV. His combination of brave, smart investigative reporting, his long hair and cool style, and his Manhattan social life--hanging around with John Lennon and other top rock stars, fashionistas, and beautiful women at Elaine's, Studio 54, and all the right spots--made him a superstar in my, and everyone else's, eyes.

I was glad I got him to come back to serious quality reporting for us at CNBC after his years in tabloid-oriented syndication and in tacky specials like opening Al Capone's vault only to find nothing there after all the massive hype; that was an embarrassment for him, I know.

I knew how smart he was, and he proved it every night on CNBC.

At first his show struggled to find its way. We covered the war in Bosnia and other important issues, but the breakthrough came when I was sitting at home watching the NBA Playoffs: The network carrying the game broke in to show O.J. Simpson's white Ford Bronco on the 405 freeway in that now famous slow-speed chase on June 17, 1994.

I called Geraldo and his producer, Bob Fassbender, and said: "This is our Iran/hostage story" (which made *Nightline* a successful show on ABC when its producers decided to cover the scandal on a nightly basis years earlier). I made a rather bold prediction and demand: "We're going to cover this trial every night with the best legal minds in America and the world. Geraldo's background as an attorney, knowledge of the law, and reporting skills will make us the No. 1 show in cable news."

That is exactly what we did and that's exactly what happened. Geraldo's ratings soared from a 0.2 to a 2 (over two million homes), helped by Tom Snyder's growing ratings as his lead-in. Geraldo and Tom floated all boats. CNBC primetime was a hit: Zas and his team were able to grow our tiny distribution by tens of millions and the ad sales team hit new records.

Bob Wright, Jack Welch, and the rest of the "brass" at NBC and GE were thrilled as profits soared and the value of their visionary investment, which many at NBC and GE apart from Bob, Jack, and Tom, did not believe in initially, grew exponentially.

It was a heady time and we had fun. Many nights I met Geraldo for post-show drinks at the famous celebrity Manhattan watering hole Elaine's, where there was always a gaggle of writers, movie stars, rock stars, politicians, detectives, mob lawyers, media mavens, top models, famous athletes, groupies, and just about anyone else you can imagine hanging out at Geraldo's table as he held court till the wee hours. One night we were hanging out there with famed New York writer Pete Hamill and the next night with "It Girl" and movie star Ashley Judd. It was always a scene and lot of fun.

On weekends Pat and I visited Geraldo and his vivacious, smart wife, Cece, at their estate in Red Bank in southern New Jersey, or they'd visit our little cottage in Edgewater under the George Washington Bridge on the Hudson River. It was so convenient to our studios in Fort Lee and to Manhattan across the river, Geraldo ended up buying a home there, too.

When we were back in L.A., he'd hang out with us at our home and stayed around the corner at the beautiful Bel-Air Hotel where I had to "rescue" him at 4 a.m., along with his teenage son Gabriel, when the Northridge earthquake rattled through like a freight train at full throttle on the night of January 17, 1994. As tough as Geraldo is, he was pretty freaked out standing with his son in his hotel room with shattered glass, dishes, lamps, and frames crumbled around him on the floor and aftershocks rattling nerves for hours after.

Having lived through these temblors when I first moved to California before college in 1969, I was used to them and so was Pat, so I hopped in my car and made the short trip to the hotel and stayed with them till the sun came up and the seismic thrill ride came to an end.

The same night, my talented senior vice president, loyal deputy, and close friend Marc Rosenweig was also in L.A. for a press event and was on a top floor of the Sheraton Universal hotel near our NBC studio in Burbank when he was awoken by his high-rise tower swaying to and fro like a ride at the Universal Studios theme park. Another New Jersey native, it was his first seismic experience, and he was seriously freaked out as he explained hours later when Tom Snyder interviewed him about his experience on his show. Tom couldn't stop laughing. Marc and Geraldo put on their bravest game faces, but until you've lived through a big one like Northridge, you really can't imagine it.

In later years Geraldo and Cece split up and we got to meet and hang out with his lovely new girlfriend, now his wife, Erica, at their house in Malibu.

I will always consider Geraldo a good friend and a talented reporter, even a "brother" as he called me in a recent email.

One last thing…as my poker buds know, I'm lousy at impressions, but I can do a spot-on Geraldo from his Willowbrook and *20/20* days. It was better when I still had my Geraldo "stache."

So as Carl Spackler (Bill Murray's character) says in *Caddyshack*, "I got that going for me… which is nice."

*With Geraldo and Marc Rosenweig, and our mustaches, 1994*

*With Pat and Geraldo, hanging out at our home in L.A.*

After Geraldo, Roger Ailes spoke and said some nice things:

*When I got there, Andy said he had already made a decision about Geraldo Rivera. I had the option of canceling it at that point, of pulling out and blaming Andy, a trick I've learned at NBC. (laughter)....*

*...Anyway, Andy and I had a lot of conversations about what should happen in primetime and how we should set the lineup up, and he had a lot of confidence in all the talent. He's always been an advocate of the people who are allowed to go up on the air, sit up there, take the shots. He understands that it's not a very easy thing to do, and so every time that he and I had a meeting, he was in there, fighting for the talent, or fighting for the production people, or fighting for money for people.*

*But Andy is, first of all, he's a very funny guy, and he really has a great heart. He's a very gentle guy, he's a very sweet guy; he does fight for other people. He's done a helluva job at NBC and I'm proud of him. I'm sorry to lose him. Andy, we'll miss you.*

*Zas, Roger Ailes, Tom Snyder, and me on a boys' night out at the famed 21 Club in New York soon after Roger arrived at CNBC*

After Roger spoke, Dee Dee Myers, co-host with Mary Matalin of *Equal Time* and former White House press secretary under President Clinton, said a few words:

> *Thanks, as the most recent addition to the CNBC family. I've had the shortest period of time to work with Andy, but I have to say it has been all good.*

> *From the very beginning till the all-too-short end, he has been nothing but gracious and wonderful, and I really thought I understood him when we did the show out in L.A. and there was Andy in his sort of golf togs, looking like he just stepped off the Riviera Country Club and the 18th with O.J. (laughter) Now I get the true essence of Andy.*

> *So speaking for both Mary (Matalin) and I, and all of us at* Equal Time, *sequestered in Washington, you have been fabulous, we love working with you, we miss you, we wish you all the luck, and you always have a home when you come to Washington.*

Dee Dee took over as host after Jane Wallace, the talented former *CBS News* correspondent I hired to co-host *Equal Time* with Mary about a year into the show.

I wanted to do a show from Washington, hosted by two smart women at the opposite ends of the political spectrum, to complement and balance our male- and New York-centric shows. Along with Tom Snyder from L.A., I felt it was important to have a presence in the nation's capital, which we didn't have.

I came up with the title *Equal Time* and knew I wanted former Bush adviser and political insider Mary, whom I'd seen giving all the male experts their money's worth on *Meet the Press*, providing unique insight and sharp-elbowed humor every time.

Jane would be the perfect, smart, wise-ass, and liberal balance to Mary's conservative, no-holds-barred style.

It was the tightest show budget I had ever executive produced, and the ladies endlessly made fun of me on air for being so cheap. But we were proud of our ascetic budget and production values.

*The Washington Post* and other major papers ran rave reviews from the get-go. They likened it to "a drunken sorority party meets *Crossfire*."

That's about right.

Mary, Jane, and later Dee Dee were smart as hell and gave us real credibility in Washington politics, which helped build our credibility and network brand.

It was also fun and interesting for Pat and me to hang out with the Washington crowd on our visits there. We had lunch in the Senate Dining Room with our good friend Bill Cohen, the great senator from Maine who went on to become Secretary of Defense.

*At lunch with Senator Bill Cohen of Maine in the Senate Dining Room*

We attended power dinners in Georgetown at the beautiful home of Senator Cohen and his wife, Janet Langhart, with our friend Dan Rather, the legendary *CBS News* anchor I'd profiled a few years earlier in a documentary for PBS.

We attended the White House Correspondents Dinner and went to Mary's fabulous wedding to James Carville in New Orleans, where Rush Limbaugh followed Pat around like a lovesick puppy telling her she was his all-time TV crush. (I guess there's something Rush and I agree on after all!)

Mary loved Pat and came to dinner at our home in L.A. She was a lot of fun. She and Jane talked about Pat and interviewed her on the phone occasionally, usually asking why I wouldn't buy them the basics like a new coffee table for their set, and why I was so cheap. It was all in good fun, and Pat played along and had fun with them.

*David Nochimson, Pat, Mary Matalin, and I at our home*

It was all a lot of fun until we had some production issues and had to make some changes on the producing team, which Mary was not pleased about. She blamed me and things went south between us.

It didn't help that her old pal and colleague Roger was now my boss, and he and I were not getting along.

Again, my overall memories are positive, and to this day I watch Mary and husband James whenever they appear together on *Meet the Press* and the other Sunday shows. I always learn something and always have a good laugh.

With *Equal Time* established, I soon after approached Tim Russert, who had recently taken over as host of *Meet the Press* on NBC, to host a weekly program for us on the media.

After some serious cajoling on my part, Tim agreed and went on to do one of the best programs I have ever been associated with. It added huge prestige and credibility to our growing network and was an instant success with viewers and critics alike.

Each week Tim brought on the best and brightest print and broadcast journalists, along with leading politicians and leaders in culture and business, to discuss the ever-changing and important role of media in our society. As with *Meet the Press*, he was relentless in his probing, in-depth interview style, never letting his subjects get away with clichéd, stock answers. Always forcing them to be honest and straightforward and to reveal things they might not have wanted to in pursuit of the truth. "The primary role of media is the accountability of government," Tim would say.

I was never more proud to have my name on a program as executive producer.

Here is what my pal Tim said in his toast to me at my going-away party:

TIM RUSSERT, Host of *Tim Russert* on CNBC

*Congratulations, Andy Friendly, and good luck and thank you. Thank you for your support and cooperation. You are something very rare in a television executive: You are user-friendly. And we thank you for that. Take care of yourself.*

I loved working with Tim and still grieve his death from a heart attack at just fifty-eight in 2008.

I feel he was a true heir to Murrow, Cronkite, and Brokaw, and that his unique journalistic voice, credibility, and courage to talk truth to power and the American people are sorely lacking on television today.

I believe he would have had a true and lasting impact on the last presidential election and would have been a continuing beacon of much-needed truth and light for our country.

I miss Tim dearly.

I asked Tim to speak at a Hollywood Radio & Television Society luncheon I co-chaired in February 2003. As always he was brilliant, admonishing hundreds of industry leaders in attendance to do their jobs and not to put profits over Ed Murrow's demand that television must teach and illuminate viewers and not merely entertain.

I keep a picture from the event in my study and hear his strong, clear voice every day when I look at it, saying what he always said to me when I proudly worked with him at CNBC: "Let's go, Andy, let's get this on the air and let's get it right."

*Tim and I at a Hollywood Radio & Television
Society luncheon I produced, 2003*

Back to the party and a funny toast from Tom Snyder from his new *Late Late Show* following Dave Letterman at CBS. Tom had left a year earlier, after a hugely successful run at CNBC that reunited me with my old boss and mentor as his executive producer.

TOM SNYDER, host of CBS' *Late, Late Show*

> *It's going to be strange, I know, for all of you at CNBC to not have Andy Friendly in Fort Lee and in Burbank. He and I go back too far. I met him as a bristling young man, a news assistant at WNBC TV in New York back in the 1970s, and you could tell then that one day he would achieve great things in broadcasting. It's remarkable how this man has matured over the years and I know that you know this as well as I do, and it's why you will miss him and why I miss his presence every day. He is one of the few good men in broadcasting, and I wish him well. I have two wishes for you, Andy, as you go. Number one: I wish for you success and happiness beyond what you've achieved at CNBC, and that has been considerable. And my second wish is...just give me* Wheel! *(King World's top-rated game show). Get me out of here, Andy!! Have a good time, pal.*

# Willing to Be Lucky

TOM ROGERS, president, NBC Cable

*So it was about five years ago, and I thought: We gotta do something about primetime programming on CNBC. So I said: "Do you have any good ideas?" He said, "Talk." I said, "No, you're the guy being interviewed. You talk."*

*(laughter)*

*And I said "Oh, OK. I think I understand. This is the guy who is right for this job."*

*Talk about right decisions, talk was the decision, and if I can be serious for a moment: This company for the last five years has been transformed from an old network to a new-media powerhouse, and when the history of NBC is written, the name right at the top, in terms of driving forces that made that happen, is going to be Andy Friendly. And when we're sitting around twenty years from now, and we're all watching television on some mind-boggling computer contraption that none of us will, in our old age, be able to figure out... (laughter) The golden age of new media at NBC was done right here, and it was done by what Andy achieved: taking CNBC from 0.2s to 2s, taking CNBC to the forefront of the talk niche, making sure information and talk television was being done in a way nobody else had ever done before.*

*When the history of the golden days of CBS was written, it was a guy by the name of Fred Friendly, who was right at the top of the list, that set the standard and I know, I know this very well, when the history of the new media age we're upon is written in its golden days, there's one guy that will be at the top, and it'll be Andy Friendly. Congratulations, you did it, buddy. I'm going to miss you.*

A bit much perhaps (smile), but I truly appreciated Tom's heartfelt remarks and shared them with my then-ailing Dad and my family, who did as well. It meant the world to all of us. Thank you, Tom.

It was quite a night. I was able to get through a little thank-you speech to all of our truly dedicated and talented team, to whom I remain ever grateful.

At the end of my speech I had someone play The Beach Boys' "Do It Again," and some serious drinking, hugging, crying, and dancing ensued.

My CNBC experience, culminating twenty-two years after I first started at WNBC TV news in the summer of 1973 as a temporary summer replacement researcher, remains one of the best of my life, professionally and personally.

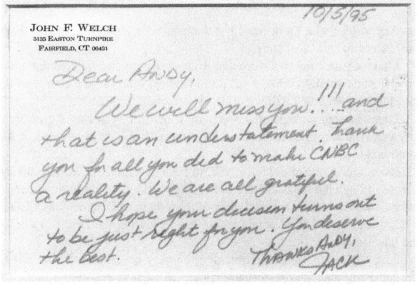

*Here, a note GE Chairman Jack Welch wrote*
*upon my departure from CNBC.*

*I keep it framed in my study, along with a beautiful note from*
*Bob and Suzanne Wright. Suzanne was a truly wonderful woman*
*who passed away in 2016 after a brave battle with cancer.*

It was a great farewell party, but it was a private moment after the party at my house nearby that meant the most to me, as Zas and I shared some twenty-five-year-old single-malt and said our goodbyes.

Before he left, I spontaneously took my favorite watch off my wrist and handed it to him and asked him to wear it once in a while so he'd remember me.

This sounds pretty corny as I write it twenty-five years on, but it was very real and emotional at the moment.

Zas promised he would wear the watch. It became his go-to, day-to-day watch.

We had been through the wars and had become close, close buds. I was happy to be heading home but leaving David, Marc Rosenweig, and our great, talented team was tough.

Fifteen years later, on my 60th birthday, a package arrived at the house by messenger. It was from David. It was a beautiful Rolex watch engraved "Love, D.Z." on the back. I saved the note and attached it to a photo of Pam, Pat, David, and me at a party a few years later at our home.

Anytime I feel a bit down, I put that watch on, and I feel the power of our friendship and I feel strong.

I have a watch my dad wore that Ruth gave me when he died that gives me that same strength when I put it on. I'll pass both on to a couple of the kids someday and they will hopefully do the same for them.

Despite being on separate coasts, my friendship with David grew even stronger. And throughout our lives over the past twenty-five years, it has continued to grow.

It continued long after I left CNBC in 1995 to go to King World/CBS and he rose through the ranks at NBC to become president of cable, syndication, and business development, and onward from there to Discovery as CEO in 2007, a role in which he continues to thrive building the Discovery brand and business worldwide.

At CNBC, our friendship quickly grew way beyond work. Our wives, Pat and Pam, and families became close. We shared everything including the birth of their three great kids, who call me Uncle Andy, and whom I love dearly.

To this day, David and I share everything, good and bad.

These days, as the CEO of Discovery he's too busy traveling and running an international media empire to talk every single day, as we did for twenty years, but not a week goes by where we don't talk, text, and share our lives, and we see each other for a meal whenever I'm back east or he's in L.A. Often with Pam and Pat. And in times of need we're there instantly for each other. Always.

We've celebrated joyous family events, like the bar mitzvahs of all three of his kids, and the most solemn family moments, like my Mom's and Dad's funerals.

We've golfed, been to Super Bowls and Olympics together, and played poker together on trips to Vegas.

Zas is relatively new to golf and doesn't have much time to play, but recently won a tournament with other bigwigs at Augusta National, site of the Masters, where he stayed in the famed Butler cabin.

And this year he "took his talents," to quote LeBron, to play in the AT&T Pro-Am at Pebble Beach with Billy Murray and the boys.

This sandwiched between almost-weekly trips to meet with the Pope to work on saving the planet, with Spielberg to work on the Shoah Foundation, and with heads of state and industry around the world on a wide range of business, environmental, and human rights issues.

But deep, deep down, Zas is about something even greater.

In a business where almost everyone judges you by how important you are at the moment and what you can do for them, it is wonderful to have a friend like David, to whom none of that matters.

When he received the prestigious United Jewish Appeal Leadership Award a few years ago in New York, I flew east for the occasion, where I was seated at his table, along with Pam, the kids, and close friends. I was beyond honored.

After Jackson Browne sang, and Oprah and Elie Wiesel presented the Man of the Year Award to David, he blew me away when he thanked me in his remarks for "teaching me how to make good television."

I was no longer running King World or CNBC and wasn't producing much anymore.

I was nowhere even close to the center of the universe, like my famous tablemates Oprah, Elie Wiesel, Tom Brokaw, Jackson Browne, and John Hendricks, and others at surrounding tables who ran networks, studios, and other major businesses.

I was OK with that and didn't expect David to say what he said, let alone seat me where he did. I just wanted to see him get his award and to visit with him, Pam, and the kids; to celebrate his well-deserved honor.

But that is the real Zas. That's who he is. It's deep, deep down in him. It comes from his amazing mom and dad. It comes from Pam. It comes from so many who love him and whom he has loved back; from Oprah and Spielberg to his earliest childhood buds. All of them are equally important to David.

It is not the public events or proclamations, like at his dinner, that make our friendship so important and precious to me; it's knowing there is someone on this Earth I admire and respect completely. Someone I can always count on and who can always count on me.

A truly good and decent human being who is true and real in a business where that is rare, and who every year on Yom Kippur, as we fast together on different coasts, calls me to say the same exact words year in and year out. For each of the past twenty-five years, and hopefully for the rest of our lives: "Andy, I am so lucky to have you as my best friend." And I say the same to him.

Those words and that friendship sustain me.

It's a powerful force that is always with me, especially in tough times.

Whenever we talk, we always end the conversation with three simple words, "Love ya, buddy." It takes me back to my father's nightly bedtime message when I was a kid, as he switched off my bedroom light and said, "It's good to be your Dad."

I'm a lucky man.

*Pat and I with Pam and Zas at a party at our house, along with a note he sent with a beautiful gift (a fancy watch) for my 60th birthday*

*David and I at Super Bowl XXXII in San Diego*
*on one of our many fun trips together*

*David and I on a golf outing near his beautiful
summer home in East Hampton*

*Zas won the match after getting up and down from the bunker
for par on the 18th hole. He took ten bucks from me.*

*With NBC crew Tom Rogers, Andy Lack, Maria Bartiromo,
David Zaslav, Zas and me at Jordan Zaslav's beautiful
wedding to Ashley in East Hampton September 2017*

# 26

## MY CLUB IS BETTER THAN YOUR CLUB

I'm sure there are other communities besides Hollywood where otherwise highly successful, powerful, rich, middle-aged men brag and bicker passionately about whose golf, tennis, or beach club is better. But I'd bet there's no place where that debate is more dramatic, theatrical, or comedic than here in Tinseltown.

Recently, I overheard two otherwise mature and grounded, highly successful executives arguing like spoiled children over whose beach club had better fireworks on the Fourth of July.

In golf, the at times vitriolic (and highly entertaining) debates center primarily on the country clubs Riviera, Bel Air, L.A., Hillcrest, Brentwood, Wilshire, Sherwood, and Lakeside (the latter being a great track in Burbank where Bob Hope and Jack Nicholson played).

The great golf course architect George Thomas designed Los Angeles Country Club in the mid-1920s, when he also amazingly built Bel-Air and Riviera. All three are in *Golf Magazine*'s top 100 courses.

LACC is famous for not allowing folks from "show business" to join.

LACC will host the U.S. Open in 2023. Riviera has hosted a number of "majors" including the U.S. Open, the PGA Championship, and the L.A. Open, the tour's yearly stop in town.

I have some pals at LACC who, over the years, have been kind enough to bring "the Jewish guy in the business" out for lunch and golf, and it is truly a magnificent course. The prestigious Walker Cup was recently held there.

The vibe is mid-1900s plantation, with older African-American waiters in white gloves serving Rob Roys and mint juleps on the rose-lined porch next to the massive practice putting green.

Tones are hushed and you get the feeling you'd better sit up straight and be on your best behavior at all times. Kind of like you're at Augusta National, or at least my image of it. There are no Hollywood stars, studio heads, producers, or industry leaders to be seen; rather you'll see the leaders of the business community.

Nearby is the beautiful Hillcrest Country Club, which—along with Brentwood—is predominantly Jewish. I find it one of the great anomalies of our times in our modern, socially aware city (New York and others, too) that country clubs are the last bastions of racial and religious separation, as well as different rules and access for women.

There's a men-only club in Palm Desert, where Pat was literally forbidden from driving me up the driveway to drop me off. Normally pretty sanguine on such issues, she was not too happy about that one.

Hillcrest and Brentwood were built in the early to mid-1900s to provide a place for Jewish golfers to play, eat, and socialize. And while the other clubs mentioned have very good courses and amenities, it's the food at the Jewish clubs that in most folks' opinions is far and away the best.

Hands down, Hillcrest, where stars like George Burns and Milton Berle held court daily at the famed "round table," has the best food of any club in town. At least that's my opinion. But what do I know? I like the food at all of them.

My favorite club story is from that famed "round table" at Hillcrest, where for years showbiz legends would meet regularly for lunch and tell stories and "kibbitz".

The story, as I heard it, goes like this:

One day Burns says to Berle and the rest of the guys at the table: "Milton, everyone knows you're famous for having the biggest schlong in town, but I've got a guy out from the Friars Club in New York who says he can beat you."

Milton shrugs and laughs it off. George says, "Seriously, he wants to challenge you to a contest here at the club tomorrow. Can you meet us in the men's locker room at 12? He wants to bet me 1,000 bucks."

The guys are all laughing and urging Milton to accept, but Milton, having heard this kind of crap for years, politely declines.

The guys are needling him and saying, "You're afraid you'll lose," when Burns finally interrupts and says, "Come on Milton, just take out enough to win."

One of the greatest lines of all time was confirmed to me when I sat at a table with the man, Milton himself, along with Billy Crystal (can you imagine how funny that table was?) at my friend Buddy Morra's daughter Ali's wedding a decade or so ago.

I mean, come on! It doesn't get better than that.

Meanwhile, back to our story...

While Hillcrest, Brentwood, Wilshire, and Lakeside are wonderful clubs with great courses, it's amusing to hear members seriously, favorably comparing their courses to the George Thomas masterpieces: L.A., Bel-Air, and Riviera.

Most members are smart and secure enough not to do this but on occasion it'll happen. Usually it's a couple of loudmouth, out-of-shape, lousy golfers who've had too much to drink. It's truly funny. It's like comparing a nice Cadillac to a world-class racecar; both great rides, but really?

On several occasions folks have tried to drag me into the conversation, and I just laugh and avoid the subject.

But it's especially funny when they argue over which has the best food. Invariably, the guys with the biggest waistlines act like, and probably are, the greatest authorities on the subject, and the most prideful and self-assured as they debate which has the best brisket.

I saw two producers nearly come to blows over whose club had the best blintzes.

I could listen to this crap all day. "Only in Hollywood," as they say.

Of the showbiz clubs, Bel-Air is probably considered the best run with a powerful show business membership, including Les Moonves, Jack Nicholson, Dennis Quaid, Greg Kinnear and Al Michaels. Golf legend Fred Couples and tennis great Pete Sampras also are members.

It's a real family club with an active social scene, especially Sunday nights in the Grill Room. Pat and I go often with family and friends. It's always a lot of fun.

It's ironic that we live on the Bel-Air course and are members at Riviera while our family live on Riviera and are members at Bel-Air. The great part is that our family gets to enjoy both regularly. We are very lucky.

As for Riviera, it's hosted four majors, and is generally considered the best golf course in Southern California by all the major golf publications, tour players, and experts.

I joined in 1998 with the help of then-Secretary of Defense William Cohen and then-CBS News anchor Dan Rather, who wrote letters of recommendation on my behalf, along with my friends Jim Hill, Lou Pitt, and others.

My brother David joined at the same time, along with Sylvester Stallone. It has been a great privilege and one of the great joys of my life to play there with my family and friends and even to win the club championship in the net division in 2009. This is especially true since I'm an average golfer with a swing that our grandsons Will and Eddie (great golfers with classic swings) make fun of regularly. I'm a currently a ten handicap. My lowest was a five.

The "Riv," as it is affectionately called, is truly a men's golf club. There are a few women out there playing, including the great champion Amy Alcott, but it's mostly guys.

There's little if any social scene. The food's fine but would never be compared to Hillcrest or Brentwood.

There's a large showbiz contingent including network, studio, and agency heads, and stars like Larry David, who's as nuts and fun as he is on his show. Grandson Eddie Osher (a "stick") and I played with him a couple times; his trademark move is he putts from both sides, righty and lefty, and will often switch from one to the other just before he's about to putt.

For years, "L.D." as we call him was convinced that I dye my hair to keep it dark. I don't, but almost every time I saw him in the locker room he'd say in his classic *Curb* voice: "Yea, you put a little something in the hair, right?"

No matter how many times I'd say, "I'd tell you if I did, Larry," he kept asking. Funny bit.

The Riv's membership has always been home to Hollywood's biggest stars, from Humphrey Bogart and Dean Martin to Spencer Tracy and Katharine Hepburn.

Current stars include Billy Crystal, Mark Wahlberg, Arnold Schwarzenegger, Carson Daly, Christopher Guest, Jamie Lee Curtis, Sugar Ray Leonard, Johnny Mathis, Paul Michael Glaser, Jim Hill, Jim Gray, Joe Regalbuto, and Sylvester Stallone.

Plenty of studio, network, and agency heads, producers, writers, directors, business titans, and owners of sports teams, such as Tom Werner of the Red Sox and Jim Irsay of the Colts.

I'm lucky to have played with and gotten to know many of them, including acting greats Peter Falk and Dennis Hopper (whom I played with regularly before they died a few years ago), along with many guests who've become good pals, like Michael Strahan, the *Good Morning America* and Fox football host and New York Giants Super Bowl champion, who was kind enough to write a blurb for this book.

Michael, whom I met through my good pal and fellow member John Dellaverson, is a major television and sports superstar but an even nicer, down-to-earth, caring, and extremely intelligent person. Not always the case with "superstars." Michael is "for realz." (As the kids say.)

The membership at Riv is diverse, and the atmosphere is fun and at times raucous, with more "characters" than any club in town, which is something I love.

Our dining room after golf on Saturday or Sunday is loud and boisterous, the polar opposite of the stately L.A. Country Club, but that's the way we like it.

David and I and our Riv pals have gone on many truly wonderful golf trips together, to the great, historic courses of Scotland and Ireland (including the 2006 Ryder Cup); Pebble Beach and Bandon Dunes; Torrey Pines in La Jolla; Shadow Creek in Las Vegas; and the greatest courses in Palm Desert.

Some of the best times of my life with some of the best people I've known.

Often we bring family and friends as guests to play the Riv.

The many golfers in my family may as well be members, they've played there so much. All the guys in the bag and locker rooms who work there know them by name.

I will usually back away or change the subject when the eternal "my club is better than yours" debates begin, but I do keep my silver Club Championship trophy displayed proudly on my bar at home. I am proud to be a member at a course that I believe is the best test of golf in Southern California and one of the best anywhere in the world.

I feel very lucky to be a member and to have shared so many great experiences with lifelong friends and family there.

It's kind of my "Cheers," a home away from home where I can hang out, practice, and get a bite to eat anytime, and a place where, as the *Cheers* song goes, "Everybody knows your name."

The people who work there, in the pro shop, dining room, locker room, bag room, and on the course–including the wonderful caddies–are my friends and some of the finest I've known.

They've been very, very kind to me and my family.

I'm not getting in any fistfights with rival club members over our blintzes, but I'd argue that the people at "the Riv" are the best anywhere… and I'd never back down from THAT fight.

**Postscript**: While I'm on the subject of golf, I can't end this chapter without a shout-out to my great teachers: Todd Yoshitake, head pro at Riviera, and Jeff Michealson at Bel-Air Country Club. Nowhere on the planet do there exist two more patient humans.

*My brother David and I at the Riv, 2009*

*I'm holding the Silver Club Championship trophy
I won in the net division that year.*

*At the Riv a few years ago with mega producer-writers Bob Singer and Steven Bochco at the Saban Clinic golf tournament, which my brother David and I have co-chaired for more than twenty years*

*Bob is a poker and golf bud, and both and he and Steven are longtime supporters of the clinic.*

*Standing on the Swilken Bridge at the famed St. Andrews Links with my brother David and my dear friend and fellow Riviera member, the late Allan McKeown*

*Allan was one of the finest gentlemen I have ever known.*

*The man to his left was a local friend of his. We were on a pilgrimage there for my 50th birthday, where we played the course one day after Tiger Woods won the British Open in 2000.*

*With my grandsons Will and Eddie, channeling the famed Jack Nicklaus pose on the 18th tee at Pebble Beach, 2010*

*Golf has always been a big, fun part of our family life.*

*Legendary Bel-Air pro Eddie Merrins presenting our grandson Will with one of his five junior club championships (a title his dad, Jon, won as a teen) in a celebration at our home*

*L-R: Pat, Jon Hookstratten, Eddie Merrins, and Will Hookstratten*

# Andy Friendly

*Following are the letters of recommendation that Dan Rather and Secretary of Defense William Cohen wrote to Riviera Country Club on my behalf when I applied for membership in 1998. I am eternally grateful to Jim Hill, Lou Pitt, and other great members who sponsored me.*

Merlee J. Konecki
Membership Director
The Riviera Country Club
1250 Capri Drive
Pacific Palisades, California 90272

**CBS NEWS**

A Division of CBS Inc.
524 West 57 Street
New York, New York 10019
(212) 975-6677

Dan Rather
Anchor and Managing Editor

19 November 1997

Dear Merlee J. Konecki:

I understand that Andrew Friendly is applying for membership at the Riviera Country Club. I have known Andy since he was a boy, and can vouch for his character and his company without any reservations whatever. He's an extraordinary man, gifted and great fun.

You'll see from his resume that he is already extremely accomplished in the field of television production. But what you may not see, is the intense loyalty he commands among his friends-- and reciprocates fully.

I'm confident Andy will prove an asset to the Riviera Country Club, and I hope you'll give his application your every consideration.

Sincerely,

Dan Rather

THE SECRETARY OF DEFENSE
WASHINGTON

October 27, 1997

Ms. Merlene Konecki
Membership
Riviera Country Club
1250 Capri Drive
Pacific Palisades, California 90272

Dear Ms. Konecki:

I am writing on behalf of my dear and old friend, Andy
Friendly, who wishes membership in the Riviera Country Club.

I have had the honor and good fortune of knowing Andy and
his family personally for over 15 years. Our friendship began during
Andy's tenure at CNBC where his outstanding reputation as an
innovative television program executive propelled him to greater
heights as Executive Vice President for Programming and Production
at King World. He is truly a master in his field.

Without hesitation, I would recommend highly Andy's
membership in the prestigious Riviera Country Club. He is a man of
great intellect, integrity and ingenuity -- a combination, I know, which
will reflect well on your club.

With warm regards, I am

Sincerely,

*With Tiger Woods and our grandkids Will, Clare, and Erin*
*Hookstratten, and Eddie Osher at a party in Palm Desert*
*when Tiger was the No. 1 player in the world*

*With my pal, NFL and GMA host and Super Bowl hero Michael Strahan, and soon-to-be grandson-in-law Will Fay at the Riv*

*Some of my Riv buds and I at Pebble Beach*

*I have my arm around the great Peter Falk, with
whom Pat guest starred in Columbo.*

*L-R: Larry Rivkin, Louis Fishman, Mark Steinman, Barry Smooke,
Ron Herman, Barry Sacks, Peter Falk, me, Steve Chase*

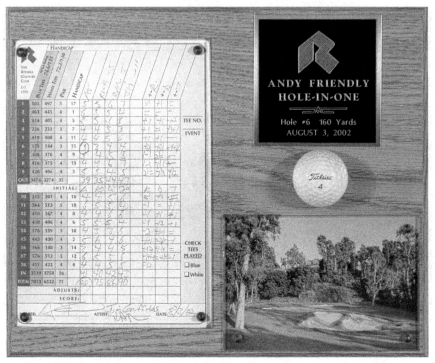

*The scorecard from my first Hole in One on the 160-yard par-3
sixth hole, attested to by my pals Rick Rosen and Jim Griffiths*

*Our fourth player that day was our wonderful friend, the late Dan Blatt.*

# 27

## DIRTY LAUNDRY

*Me, Charles Grodin, and Roger Ailes at the 21 Club, NYC*

I got to know the brilliant actor and writer Charles Grodin in 1994, when we brought him in to fill Tom Snyder's timeslot because Tom was leaving CNBC for CBS late night.

The photo above shows me, Grodin, and then-CNBC president Roger Ailes at the press conference at 21 Club in New York announcing the show.

In 2013, Grodin asked me to write something for a book he was working on about getting even with someone who had done you wrong in your career. Ultimately the book was never published, but here is the story I wrote for him:

*The year was 1995. I had just joined King World, one of the largest television companies in the world (*Oprah, Wheel of Fortune, Jeopardy!, Inside Edition, Hollywood Squares, *etc.) as head of programming and production.*

*For five years prior I had a similar job at CNBC.*

*In both jobs I shuttled regularly between my home in L.A. and New York/New Jersey.*

*At CNBC, where I spent most of my time on the East Coast, I wound up renting a home nearby.*

*But while at King World, I was based in L.A. and spent only a week each month on the East Coast to visit the* Inside Edition *and* American Journal *studios and the King World corporate headquarters in Manhattan. As a King World executive I stayed at a hotel while in New York—usually the Regency on 61st and Park.*

*The Regency was easy, reliable, and centrally located between the studios and corporate offices and walking distance to both. King World had the benefit of a corporate rate—except when it came to laundry.*

*Getting* a pair of boxer shorts laundered in a Manhattan hotel can be *crazy expensive. It was twelve bucks a pair! Maybe more by now.*

*On my first trip to New York in the new King World job,* I ran from show to show, meeting to meeting, *for at least twelve hours a day. I had breakfasts, lunches, drinks, and dinners for a week while getting to know the new production and executive teams. It was a nonstop, whirlwind baptism by fire, which was very productive and a lot of fun. That is, until I got home to L.A.*

Andy Friendly

*I sent in my expense report for that first trip to corporate in New York. Expense filing was normally an uneventful chore done mostly by my assistant, assembling my bills and receipts and submitting them for reimbursement. In five years of similar reports at CNBC, I don't think I was ever questioned about an expense report or ever even thought about one.*

*But at King World, in my second week on the job, I received a phone call about my report. It came not from a clerk in accounting, who in my experience is usually the person processing this sort of stuff, but from a senior executive officer of the company.*

*When I picked up the call I expected a discussion of some business or program matter and maybe even an encouraging "How'd your first week go?" To my great surprise, he only wanted to talk about my underwear.*

*At first I thought he was kidding when he demanded to know how I could spend so much of the company's money having my laundry done on my trip to New York. It honestly struck me as a joke.*

*I laughed along and made some comment about New York hotels "getting you in the shorts," but there was no laughing at the other end.*

*The underwear harangue continued for another five minutes, during which the executive became more and more animated and eventually started yelling. At that point, I was tempted to ask, "Have you considered a prescription?" (I refrained.)*

*He ended the conversation by ordering I take my laundry to a "fluff and fold" place. "I'm sure you can find one in the neighborhood," he exhorted. He then slammed the phone down, hanging up.*

*So much for encouragement and "Welcome to King World."*

*On my next trip to New York I found a small dry cleaner a few blocks away that did fluff and fold, and made two trips to and from during the week to get my laundry done. This went on for months,*

227

*but one week when I was particularly swamped launching a new courtroom series, Curtis Court, I just couldn't get to the place and gave my stuff to the hotel to clean.*

*In my expense report, I attached a note explaining the time crunch. A few days later I received a blistering admonition from the executive (God knows why at his level he was even looking at my laundry bills) telling me that I had already been warned about this and the next time there would be "serious consequences." Woah!*

*About a year later I was meeting Michael King, the CEO of King World, for dinner with a prospective host for one of our shows at the 21 Club in Manhattan and explained I'd be there as soon as I could, but first I had to go pick up my laundry a few blocks away because I'd spilled coffee on my shirt and needed a fresh one.*

*By the time I got out of a late taping at the studio on the Upper East Side, the laundry was closed and I was running late to dinner, so I showed up with a big coffee stain on my shirt.*

*Later after dinner, walking home, Michael asked me why I took my shirts to the laundry instead of having them done at the hotel.*

*Reluctantly, I told him about the back-and-forth with the senior executive.*

*Michael was a brilliant, larger-than-life personality who, with his brother Roger, turned a tiny, one-room operation selling the old* Little Rascals *series into a multibillion-dollar television giant. One can only accomplish such a task knowing how to strategically value and prioritize time and money. He was apoplectic about the laundry situation.*

*"There are two things wrong with that story," he exclaimed. "One, it's a ridiculous waste of your time. I don't pay you what I pay you to spend time getting your laundry done. And worse, it's an even bigger waste of my senior executive's time. I pay him even more than you, and I do NOT pay him to go over senior executives' laundry bills."*

*A phone call between the executive and Michael took place on this topic the next day and I'm told it was rather animated at Michael's end.*

*I was never questioned about my laundry bill again.*

*The moral of the story, as my dear old mom used to say, is never leave the house without clean underwear.*

*And, I might add, if you are a senior officer of a major media company, or anybody's boss for that manner, you may want to reorder your priorities and stay out of other people's "dirty laundry."*

\*\*\*\*\*

> Charles Grodin          8/28/2000
>
> Dear Andy,
>     Thank you for your kind note. Clearly, you don't go from working with a St. Bernard to 60 minutes II, so I know very well I wouldn't be here without you.
>     I will always appreciate all you've done for me,
>                                   Love,
>                                   Chuck

*A note Chuck sent me after he left CNBC to become an essayist on 60 Minutes II*

*Chuck is one of the smartest people I've ever known. Working with him as his executive producer was pure joy.*

229

# 28

## VEGAS, BABY! $1.5 MILLION IN A
## BROWN PAPER BAG

I'm not really a Vegas fan, but in short durations it can be fun. I appreciate garish excess as much as the next guy, and the shows, food, and amenities are "amaze," as the kids say. I've had a lot of interesting experiences there, from attending major prizefights (Holmes-Norton, Haggler-Hearns, and Leonard-Duran in the '70s, '80s, and '90s) to crazy NATPE TV conventions, golf and poker outings, and graduation trips with our grandkids.

One of the more interesting trips I took there lasted less than twenty-four hours.

It started on a Friday afternoon in the spring of 1999, sitting in my then-boss Michael King's office with two other King World executives going over end-of-the-week business. Michael said, "It's been a long week, I'm in the mood for some fun. Who wants to go to Vegas for the night?"

I knew the drill: Probably an all-nighter. It had been a long week, filled with headaches trying to keep Roseanne's talk show from self-destructing to trying to convince the brilliant Marty Short and his famous manager, Bernie Brillstein, that his terrific show aired in the daytime, not late night, which was the vibe they were going for. I tried to beg off but Michael was insistent. As usual, when he wanted to do something, whatever other plans we may all have had pretty much went out the window. He was a hard man to say no to.

I called Pat and let her know that I'd see her the next day. She was understanding, as usual. She had seen this movie before.

The King Brothers were well known as enthusiastic gamblers, "whales" in casino parlance, from Vegas to Atlantic City. There is very little casinos will not do for their whales.

With a phone call, a Gulfstream IV (private jet) was fired up at Santa Monica Airport and a car came to pick us up. Despite my protestations that I had no clothes and wanted to go home to pack a bag, we were in the air a half-hour later to Vegas.

A giant limo met us on the private tarmac in Las Vegas and whisked us to a hidden entrance to the MGM Grand's private palazzo on the grounds of the casino, used only by whales. It's so secret that you enter through a nondescript little fence at the back of the resort complex.

It's called "The Mansion," and for good reason. A winding driveway, lined with beautiful ponds, fountains, and landscaping, leads to a majestic stone villa that is about eight stories high.

Each whale gets a whole floor, complete with four elaborate suites, a grand living and dining area, private pool and spa, and its own complete white-gloved staff, including butlers, maids, bartender, and private chef on call twenty-four hours a day.

Upon arrival around 5 p.m. we were assigned our suites, and a member of the staff asked what clothing and toilet articles we needed for our overnight stay. Anything we wanted. A few minutes later he returned with shirts, socks, underwear, and shaving kits, which were placed in our massive individual suites. Then we all convened in the main living room for drinks and cigars.

A bit later the chef took our dinner orders and presented us with an elaborate feast including caviar, fresh Maine lobsters, and Cristal Champagne.

By 9 p.m. I was urging Michael to go down to the casino to get the gambling part going and hopefully over by around midnight in the hopes of getting a decent night's sleep. But he was in no rush and enjoyed just relaxing and holding court in our super suite. Michael was a great storyteller and was regaling us with stories from the early days of King World and much, much more.

By midnight, I was fading and tried to head to my room to crash, but Michael was having none of it. He was finally ready to hit the tables and insisted I join him and the guys. "Let's go, Andy, we didn't come to Vegas to get a good night's sleep, and besides, I'm feeling lucky."

Again, he was a hard guy to say no to, and off we went.

We entered the casino from the Mansion via a secret hallway and were escorted to a private area of the high-stakes baccarat room. It was an elaborate layout, complete with private croupiers and long-legged cocktail waitresses standing by to grant any food and beverage requests we might have.

After some over-the-top welcomes and greetings from top casino executives, Michael sat down to play his game of choice, baccarat.

At his own private table with croupiers and casino bosses looking on, and with his three executives standing behind him, Michael began playing at the rate of $150,000 a roll. Baccarat is a game played with cards in which players may bet that either or both of the other two hands will beat the dealer's hand.

It was now after midnight and I couldn't keep my eyes open, so I thanked Michael, wished him luck and good night. I went back through the secret hallway to the Mansion and went to bed. That turned out to be a costly decision.

Michael asked the casino to give my fellow executives several thousand dollars worth of free chips so they could gamble along with him. The casino happily agreed.

Over the next forty-five minutes, Michael (and the guys, as they were piggybacking on his bets) got on a major roll.

Michael and his brother Roger, as with all whales, have lost many times and many millions during an outing, but this one went his way. When he got up to $1.5 million in winnings, he calmly thanked the croupiers and said he'd had enough. He requested to have his winnings delivered to our suite the next morning at 10 a.m. and to please have the limo and jet waiting to take us home at 10:30 a.m.

The casino bosses appeared shocked, my colleagues say. The casino staff asked Michael if everything was all right and if there was a problem. He had only played for an hour and he was known to play for many hours typically.

He assured them that all was great, thanked them for their hospitality and went off to bed.

At 10 a.m. the next morning, following some ribbing about how I'd missed out on some real fun and some real cash, the doorbell rang and four huge security guards came in with a casino exec and placed $1,500,000 in hundred-dollar bills, packed in clear plastic, shrink-wrapped blocks, on the dining room table for Michael's inspection.

Michael casually took a look and said, "I'm sure it's all been counted properly." He thanked the executive, who assured us the limo and jet were standing by.

The casino executive asked again if everything was all right. Had the casino done anything wrong? "Are you sure you wouldn't like to stay another day or two?" he asked. Obviously they were hoping to get Michael back to the tables and get some of their money back.

Michael nicely explained that he needed to get home, that all was fine and, again, thanked them for everything.

The slightly incredulous casino executive asked if we'd like the security guards to walk us down to our car or accompany us to the jet, given the large amount of cash we would be carrying. Michael politely declined, at which point the guards put the bricks into four, nondescript brown paper shopping bags and left the suite.

Michael handed each of us one of the bags and we walked out of the Mansion to our waiting limo. On the way down, I asked him why he hadn't kept going on his hot roll. He replied simply, "I'd had enough and knew the roll was at an end."

Before we headed to the Gulfstream, we had a half-hour meeting nearby with a potential partner on an upcoming show. I have to imagine he wondered what exactly we were carrying in the large brown shopping bags, but he never asked. We were home by noon.

While Michael was a whale and enjoyed gambling for big bucks all around the world through the '80s and '90s, in his later years he gave it up, focusing his time and money on his family, his boxing business, and many charitable causes.

As with all gamblers big and small, he realized the casino ultimately wins and big wins like this one are the exception, not the rule.

Like my former partner Cliff Perlman, a wonderful man who once owned Caesars Palace, used to say: "In the casino ownership business, you have good days and better days."

Michael was a wonderful guy who taught me a lot about the television business, about perseverance, and about never compromising. He was beyond generous to our Free Clinic golf tournament and so many other important causes. Michael played a major role in my life for more than thirty years.

I'll always wish I stayed up for the big win that night, but the truth is the lifelong, career-long friendship and collaboration I had with Michael was priceless.

His 2015 death from pneumonia at just sixty-seven was a shock to all who knew and loved him. He was a giant and, as the expression goes, we shall not see his like again.

# 29

## LIFE IN HOLLYWOOD: THE CAR BRAGGER

It's no news flash that cars in Hollywood carry a lot of importance for a lot of people, but over my decades in L.A., what continues to surprise me is how far some people will go to tell you about their fancy new ride. I've heard people work their new wheels into conversation at meetings, parties, the grocery store, a kids' soccer game, the movies, just about everywhere you can imagine. A certain type of Hollywood dweller (and driver) will find a way to spread the word about their big purchase even if it kills them; even if that conversation is totally unrelated.

And it's not just the anxious newcomers to the business. It's an overcompensation reflex that I see even among the veterans. Consider a recent example…

At a pre-event reception for a Hollywood Radio & Television Society (HRTS) luncheon I co-chaired a couple years ago featuring *Saturday Night Live* producer Lorne Michaels interviewed by the great Martin Short, I was chatting with three fellow former execs.

The topic of our conversation: the Russian incursion into Ukraine.

When the chimes were sounded and an announcement made that it was time to head into the main ballroom, we began to make our way from the reception and wrap up our discussion of the Ukraine situation and world politics.

That is, until the former executive, who we had not yet learned had a new car, stopped us. He offered one final point about Russia that was obviously not about Russia at all.

"Hey, my new Jag might not be able to stand up to those Russian tanks but I bet I could beat 'em off the starting line," he said loudly, proudly.

Huh? The only thing I could take from this ridiculous segue was to feel bad for the guy, especially at this point in life.

Really? You're sixty-plus years old, had a successful career, and your identity and self-worth are tied to the car you drive?

As a certain orange politician might say: "Sad."

Or as one late-night comic quipped:

> *"They auctioned off a classic Ferrari last night. It sold for over a million dollars. Earlier that night, the guy who won the bid also was the winner of the small penis award."*

*Saturday Night Live producer/creator Lorne Michaels, Martin Short, HRTS executive director Dave Ferrara, and me at a Hollywood Radio & Television Society (HRTS) luncheon I co-chaired, 2013*

# 30

## COURTING THE "KING OF ALL MEDIA"

I was never a big Howard Stern fan, but I started to appreciate him as his show evolved in the mid-'90s, about ten years after I first heard him doing his NBC show.

Back then it was all sex, strippers, and doody jokes; and while some of it was funny, I found it pretty one-dimensional.

He got much more interesting when interviewing newsmakers or artists, and discussing his own life with a kind of honesty I'd never heard or seen. He went way beyond the expression "warts and all," and I found his often-brutal honesty about his own imperfect life and others' funny and oddly liberating.

He discussed his "small penis," bathroom and masturbation habits, and his insecurities about being feeling inadequate around celebrities. He cut to the truth, probing and getting David Letterman, and other hard-to-get celebs off-script in interviews; they opened up to Howard in ways they would never do with anyone else.

He was a frequent guest on *Letterman*, and my pal Tom Snyder interviewed him one night as well. They got in each other's faces pretty good. Two giants, mentally and physically (Tom was six foot four and Howard an inch taller), going at each other. They didn't like each other much, especially after Howard told Tom, "Talking to you is like talking to a mental patient."

Tom shot back equally hard, and on it went.

On my daily drives from Manhattan to the CNBC studios in Fort Lee, New Jersey, and back, Howard, Robin Quivers, and the gang provided endless entertainment and laughs, and made the soul-sucking boredom of New York traffic much easier to take.

A few years later, when I was in charge of programming and production at King World, I told Michael and Roger King that I thought Howard could do a late-night talk/variety show for us and that I'd like to pursue the idea. They agreed it was worth looking into, albeit a tough sell to conservative TV stations and advertisers.

I arranged a meeting with Howard and his on air-partner Robin Quivers at their agent Don Buchwald's office in Manhattan.

At the time we had the top three shows in the country in syndication with *Oprah, Wheel of Fortune,* and *Jeopardy!*, along with *Inside Edition* also in the top 10.

Howard was already in the TV business and had the sitcom *Son of the Beach* on FX. He was great on every talk show he ever did, from *Letterman* to *Leno*, and every time he showed up, the ratings spiked.

His book *Private Parts* was a huge best seller, and he was working on the movie version of it, which turned out great and was a big hit. He was nice enough to invite the Zaslavs and Pat and me to the giant premiere at Madison Square Garden, which was predictably raucous, wild, and fun. He was exploding.

Our meeting was a hoot. He and Robin were smart, charming, and professional. They were much more low-key than on the radio but still great fun.

The difference between people's personas on camera (or radio) and their personalities in real life has always interested me. Often, as was the case with Tom Snyder and Johnny Carson, they are pretty much one and the same. Although others have said Carson was more withdrawn off-camera, I found him charming and funny. My favorite comedians, Robert Klein and Billy Crystal, both of whom I got the chance to hang out with off-camera, had the same personalities on air as they did off.

Others, such as Robin Williams and Richard Pryor, were much more reserved behind the scenes. Earlier in his career, Letterman was well-known for being morose and even nasty to his staff once the red light went out, though he was always nice enough to me when I had him on *Tomorrow* and when I accompanied Tom to Dave's show a couple times.

Only Howard could get away with calling Letterman out on that while on *Letterman*. Howard was and is fearless and goes right for the most sensitive, embarrassing, never-mentioned taboo stuff in every interview. And when he agrees to be a guest, he takes over the interview and does it to the host; always with humor, but biting and truthful at the same time. It makes for some of the best, most insightful, in-depth interviews anywhere, and this is what I wanted to mine in a talk show with Howard for King World.

I courted him big-time. I even sent him two bottles of Château Lafite Rothschild at the cost of a couple thousand dollars per bottle for his birthday. He mentioned the gesture on his show the next day. Someone had a tape and gave it to me. Here's what he said…

> *Robin and I were sitting and talking to the great Andy Friendly who everybody in the industry loves, he's a good guy. He's beloved by everyone.*

Author's note: This is bullshit but nice of Howard to say. Tons of people think I'm a jackass, though some may think I'm OK.

He went on to say:

> *Andy sent me two bottles of wine for my birthday, which must have been expensive 'cause CBS would not approve the voucher. I'm afraid to drink them; I don't want to just take a swig. His dad was Fred Friendly and it turns out Andy Friendly is friendly. They live up to their name, those Friendlys, they do. Andy Friendly is friendly. They're very friendly.*

> *Fred Friendly was a legendary programming genius. He spawned a son named Andy Friendly who's a very nice guy. Andy used to be with CNBC and now he's with King World. He's like one of the presidents of programming, who the hell knows what he is. But I always like seeing him.*

We had a few more conversations and I got him to appear on *Wheel of Fortune* during a sweeps ratings period. He was a riot. He hadn't done anything like it before, and hasn't since. I'd known Vanna White since we taped *This Is Your Life* in the studio next to *Wheel*'s at NBC fifteen years earlier. (Pat and I still see her at sushi all the time.) She was pregnant then and fully showing. I got her to do a bit with Howard at the top of the show where he hugged her from behind and "revealed" to all of America that "he was the father."

A joke, of course, but the press had a field day with it and the ratings went through the roof. It was the first and only time Howard appeared on *Wheel*.

Unfortunately the talk show idea didn't materialize, mostly because Howard was just too big in radio and was too busy with his movie and other television projects, including a TV version of the radio show, for the E! Network.

As disappointing as it was for me that Stern was the one that got away, I believe radio is the perfect medium for Howard. It's where he's most comfortable and doesn't have to worry about his appearance at all times.

Although he calls himself the "King of All Media," he and his great team have perfected radio and made it an art form. These days I still try to get my fix every day as I tool around L.A.-

Since I only get his show on Sirius XM Radio in the car and not in the house, I often find myself sitting in my garage for an hour or more after I've arrived home, listening to Howard interview James Taylor, Lady Gaga, or Billy Joel. I have other stuff to do but I just can't turn it off. He's just too funny, and the interviews are just too good. Yeah, he occasionally crosses the line into truly gross, mean, and even boring, for sure, but in my opinion he's the best overall interviewer and ranter there is right now.

He keeps threatening to quit the radio show because he has too much work and not enough free time to pursue his painting, guitar, and other interests, but I'm convinced he's just negotiating with Sirius XM. Let's hope he keeps making us laugh for years to come.

Long live the King!

*Howard Stern and me on the set of* Wheel of Fortune, *1997*

# 31

## THREE LEGENDS

### VIN SCULLY – THE MAN WHO SAYS YES

Among the many gifts given to me when Pat and I got together in 1982 was a friendship with her close friends Sandra and Vin Scully. As a kid in the Bronx I grew up listening to the legendary announcer, who retired in 2016 after sixty-seven straight years as the voice of the Dodgers. That's right, sixty-seven straight years!

His is the longest and most revered career in sports and all of broadcasting history. No one in sports broadcasting has received the much-deserved love and respect Vin has.

Bill Plaschke, the award winning *Los Angeles Times* columnist, got it about right in a column I quoted a few years ago when I introduced Vin at a Hollywood Radio & Television Society luncheon.

> *"More enduring than any player, more impactful than any manager, more intertwined with this city than the color blue, Vin Scully is not only the voice of the Dodgers but its soul."* Bill Plaschke, the Los Angeles Times, *July 29, 2009*

Vin's luncheon sold out the Beverly Wilshire ballroom and garnered the most press coverage we'd ever had for an HRTS event. In a speech and then a sit-down interview with our mutual pal, director Ron Shelton, Vin regaled the usually jaded industry heavyweights with perfectly crafted, colorfully told stories from baseball and from life.

A few years earlier, when I asked him to teach my little TV class at USC, he instantly said yes. He came down to campus on a busy day and spent

241

two hours talking to the kids, answering their questions, and giving them tips and advice about how to cover a game, how the best thing you can do as an announcer is "shut up at times and let the moment play out." He took pictures with them and signed autographs and called them by name.

When I asked Vin to be a co-chair for the evening Dave Zaslav, Pat, and I organized last year to raise money and awareness for the Shoah Foundation, he and Sandra instantly said…you guessed it…"YES."

Lending their names would have been more than enough but, to the delight of all those in attendance, the Scullys made the hour-plus drive from their home in rush-hour traffic. As always, they showed up. When they left, they handed us an extremely generous donation to the foundation.

On his last night in Chavez Ravine as the Dodgers announcer, he and Sandra invited Pat and me to sit in his booth with his family. It's one of the greatest treats and honors of our lives.

As the adoring sellout crowd, all the players on both teams, and millions at home celebrated the great man in one emotional tribute after the next, I felt an overwhelming surge of joy and gratitude that transported me back to the Bronx when I was five, driving with my dad while listening to Vin calling a Dodger game on our car radio.

*Pat and I with our friend, the great Vin Scully, in the broadcast booth at Dodger Stadium with our nephew Andrew Friendly and grandson Will Hookstratten, 2014*

I'm not ashamed to admit a tear filled my eye at Dodger Stadium that night.

At our recent holiday dinner, which we share annually with the Scullys, we told Sandra and Vin how proud of them we are and thanked them for all they've done for us, for baseball, for our country, and for always saying "YES" to every charitable and community-oriented request we've ever made of them.

I can assure you this is indeed rare among this town's top stars and celebrities.

There is little wonder why the Scullys are the most beloved couple in Los Angeles.

## MUHAMMAD ALI – THE GREATEST OF ALL TIME

I had many sports heroes growing up: Mickey Mantle, Willie Mays, Y.A. Tittle, Jim Brown, Oscar Robertson, Rod Laver, and Arnold Palmer among many others, but Muhammad Ali was, hands down, my greatest sports hero.

My dad saw him fight Liston. I listened at home on the radio and was mesmerized. Back then, in the early '60s, the heavyweight championship of the world was like game seven of the World Series.

But no one had ever seen the likes of Cassius Clay from Louisville, Kentucky. Young, brash, handsome, and super charismatic. His mouth and wit were as fast as his lightning-fast fists.

In my view he was the first "rock star" athlete. Even The Beatles, who were at the height of their fame, wanted to hang out with the champ. There's a great Harry Benson photograph of them together in Benson's wonderful book *The Beatles*.

Everyone knows Ali transcended sports when, at the height of his career, he refused induction into the army because he was opposed to the war in Vietnam. His famous line: "I ain't got no quarrel with them Viet Cong."

His refusal to serve in 1967, along with his strong stand against racism, which led him to become a Muslim and change his name to Muhammed Ali, landed him in hot water with conservatives and cost him millions in earnings, as he was not allowed to fight for over three years after being convicted of draft evasion.

Ali returned to the ring in 1970 and won the heavyweight title again twice in epic fights with Joe Frazier and George Foreman, but after retiring in 1980 he announced he had Parkinson's disease, which he suffered with until his death at seventy-four in 2016.

I got to meet Ali when I booked him on *Tomorrow* on NBC in 1978. It was beyond thrilling to hang out with him backstage and on set during the taping. Tom Snyder and he sparred (verbally), with Ali refusing to do the normal pre-interview we did with most guests because he insisted on being spontaneous and unscripted. When Tom asked him why, he said: "Because you're a tricky fella and I don't want to fall into your traps. If you don't like it, you can just erase the tape."

Tom laughed his famous laugh and Ali went on, "If I had a lower IQ, I could enjoy this interview." He was the first superstar athlete to "throw rhymes."

I got to meet him again at my dad's induction into the Television Academy Hall of Fame in 1994. Ali was there to induct legendary sportscaster Howard Cosell, his longtime foil. He was in his mid-fifties and shaking a bit from Parkinson's, but he was still in rare form and even performed magic tricks for my then-eleven-year-old nephew Noah.

The last time I got to see him was when he lit the flame at the Opening Ceremony of the 1996 Summer Olympics in Atlanta. Pat and I were lucky enough to be there because King World and *Wheel of Fortune* were sponsors of the Games.

*My brother David Friendly, me, The Champ, and my brother Jon Mark at my dad's induction to the Television Academy Hall of Fame in 1994, where Ali inducted sportscaster Howard Cosell.*

Pam and David Zaslav were there too, with NBC, as were the Kings. We all had tears in our eyes.

I think Bill Clinton said it best in his eulogy to The Champ in 2016. To paraphrase the president, he said that despite all of Ali's greatness, his athletic abilities, even his courageous social stances that cost him three of the prime years of his boxing career, his greatest accomplishment came after he was stricken with the debilitating Parkinson's disease. It was during those years, when he could not use his lightning-fast hands or mouth, that he showed the most strength of all his life through his silent courage, dignity, and unending work to help others.

Ali: not even a doubt. The Greatest of All Tiiiiiiiiiiiiimmmmme!!

## DAN RATHER – "COURAGE"

In 1988 I talked Dan Rather, anchor and managing editor of the top-rated *CBS Evening News,* into letting me put a wireless mic on him so we could follow him and his crew for a full, busy news day and watch, like the proverbial "fly on the wall," as he and his team put the evening news and three other live specials on the air.

The program was a special for PBS and served as on-air pilot for a potential series. It was one of the first projects I did as part of a new overall deal I had with the production studio Todd-AO, which had been brokered by my friend Herbert Hutner.

We followed Rather, executive producer Tom Bettag, Leslie Stahl, Bruce Morton, and other top reporters to Omaha, Nebraska, site of the one and only vice presidential debate that year between Lloyd Bentsen and Dan Quayle.

Yes, the one where Quayle made the mistake of comparing himself to a young Jack Kennedy and Bentsen put him away with the now-famous line: "Senator, I served with Jack Kennedy. I knew Jack Kennedy. Jack Kennedy was a friend of mine. Senator, you're no Jack Kennedy."

Game over.

Dan, Tom, and their team allowed us complete access as we watched them debate and shape their rundown of stories for the evening news, a live radio spot that almost didn't come off due to faulty communication with the network in New York, plus the live primetime debate and post-debate coverage.

With my brilliant cameraman Lynn Rabren, who made a name for himself on CBS' *48 Hours* and other documentaries, where he could make a single camera look like three with his vérité camera style: Always moving, intense, and up close, we were able to capture the sounds and sights of an interesting, intense and long day.

Dan granted us an hourlong interview about his career, which I edited into the footage we'd captured in Omaha.

In addition to writing, directing, and producing the special, I ended up hosting it, for the first and only time in my career.

As with most PBS shows, our budget was extremely tight; we literally didn't have money for a host, so I introduced the program and did the interviews.

*Interviewing Dan Rather for the PBS special "A Day With Dan Rather"*

Shockingly, my mustache and I did OK. The program was well received by the critics, including these famously tough ones.

Now in his eighties, Dan Rather is a broadcast legend and a hero. From his reputation-making, first-on-the-scene reporting of the assassination of JFK in November 1963 (which we watched live on TV in the lunchroom at Riverdale Country Day School, where the president was once a student), to his fearless front-line reporting from the jungles of Vietnam, to his being beaten up and thrown out of the 1968 Chicago convention by Mayor Daley's thug policemen, to his reporting on Watergate, and so much more. Dan Rather, in my view, is in the pantheon of the giants of broadcast journalism.

Sadly, there is an asterisk. In 2004 Dan and his team made a major and life-changing mistake in a report for *60 Minutes* about then-President George W. Bush's service in the National Guard during Vietnam.

Dan later admitted that documents used in the report claiming the president had shirked his duties could not be substantiated. His producer and several others involved in the report were fired. Dan stayed, but a year or so later also left his beloved *CBS News* in a cloud of controversy.

He has remained an active and unique voice in journalism and, in my humble opinion, despite his serious mistake in 2004, is a giant in our industry who lives his famous signoff, "Courage!"

# What Television's Toughest Critics Said About "A Day With Dan Rather"

"...highly watchable."
—**Howard Rosenberg, Los Angeles Times**

"But when Friendly calls Rather "the most talked about and the most private" of the anchors, he couldn't be more accurate, and he could have added that Rather is clearly the anchor most worth spending a day with."

"This program is only a peek into Rather's daily life, but that's all it's meant to be, and it's a candid, satisfying peek."
—**Tom Shales, The Washington Post**

"Friendly's pop culture version of the technique— pictures without commentary—is a lot livelier than the previous day-in-the-lifers."
"...intimate discussion."
—**Marvin Kitman, New York Newsday**

*Here are some quotes from reviews of the Dan Rather program I produced for PBS*

*Cameraman Lynn Rabren, me, Dan Rather, and CBS Evening News executive producer Tom Bettag at the site of the vice presidential debate in Omaha, Nebraska, 1987*

# 32

## FAVORITES

Over the years, I've kept in an informal journal—favorite bits of "wisdom," humor, and the insight of others in the form of literature, films, speeches, poems, songs, theater, jokes, one-liners, and unique, creative expressions of all kinds.

I thought it would be fun to share some of them.

In random order…kind of like they come up in life at dinner with family and friends, in meetings, and just to myself, in my daily musings…here are some of my favorites.

\*\*\*\*\*

### "If"

This is my favorite poem; it's by the 19th-century British poet Rudyard Kipling.

My dad used to recite the last stanza to me growing up. Later I discovered the whole poem and I have it framed in my home and look at it regularly.

The wisdom of it, as noted earlier, has guided me often. For me, it may be the wisest, most insightful collection of words ever assembled on one page.

### IF

*If you can keep your head when all about you*
*Are losing theirs and blaming it on you,*
*If you can trust yourself when all men doubt you,*
*But make allowance for their doubting too;*

## Willing to Be Lucky

*If you can wait and not be tired by waiting,*
*Or being lied about, don't deal in lies,*
*Or being hated, don't give way to hating,*
*And yet don't look too good, nor talk too wise:*

*If you can dream—and not make dreams your master;*
*If you can think—and not make thoughts your aim;*
*If you can meet with Triumph and Disaster*
*And treat those two impostors just the same;*
*If you can bear to hear the truth you've spoken*
*Twisted by knaves to make a trap for fools,*
*Or watch the things you gave your life to, broken,*
*And stoop and build 'em up with worn-out tools;*

*If you can make one heap of all your winnings*
*And risk it on one turn of pitch-and-toss,*
*And lose, and start again at your beginnings*
*And never breathe a word about your loss;*
*If you can force your heart and nerve and sinew*
*To serve your turn long after they are gone,*
*And so hold on when there is nothing in you*
*Except the Will which says to them: "Hold on";*

*If you can talk with crowds and keep your virtue,*
*Or walk with kings—nor lose the common touch,*
*If neither foes nor loving friends can hurt you,*
*If all men count with you, but none too much;*
*If you can fill the unforgiving minute*
*With sixty seconds' worth of distance run,*
*Yours is the Earth and everything that's in it,*
*And—which is more—you'll be a Man, my son!*

**Rudyard Kipling**


## "Cold Mountain"

My favorite novel is Charles Frazier's *Cold Mountain*, about an injured soldier named Inman on a dangerous trek home to his sweetheart through the Blue Ridge Mountains of Tennessee at the end of the Civil War.

My friend Skip Brittenham recommended it to me at lunch one day in 1997.

It was the author's first novel and won many major awards, including the National Book Award for fiction.

It tells the story of Inman's perilous and heart-wrenching journey home, interwoven with his sweetheart Ada's struggle to revive her father's farm with the help of a brave young drifter named Ruby.

Their courageous journeys and struggles against the changing landscape of the devastated South following the war are so brilliantly and movingly captured by Mr. Frazier that I often found myself with tears in my eyes, but also as involved and completely engaged in the exciting action as any book I've read or any film or play I've seen.

I've reread it several times, and it still gives me chills and moves my deepest emotions.

Our son-in-law Bob Osher executive produced a terrific movie for Miramax based on the book when he was running the studio, starring Jude Law as Inman and Nicole Kidman as his sweetheart, Ada Monroe.

## *The Road to Character*

From *New York Times* columnist David Brooks' wonderful book by the same name:

> *We live in the culture of the Big Me. The meritocracy wants you to promote yourself. Social media wants you to broadcast a highlight reel of your life. Your parents and teachers were always telling you how wonderful you were.*

> *But all the people I've deeply admired are profoundly honest about their own weaknesses. They have achieved a profound humility, which has best been defined as an intense self-awareness from a position of OTHER (not self)-centeredness.*

Brooks goes on to talk about two sets of virtues.

> *One set are résumé virtues, the ones you bring to the marketplace. The other set is the eulogy virtues, the ones that are talked about at your funeral--whether you were kind, brave, honest, capable of deep love.*

> *Those are the people we want to be.*

## *New Yorker* Cartoon

I love *New Yorker* cartoons. My favorite is one that my dad kept on his office wall: of a barely clad man and woman sitting on a deserted island after being shipwrecked. The caption has the woman saying, "I'd know, that's who'd know."

He loved quoting it.

## Bertrand Russell

My favorite philosopher is Bertrand Russell. Here's my favorite quote of his.

> *"The whole problem with the world is that fools and fanatics are always so certain of themselves, and wiser people so full of doubt."*

## Quote about the elusive challenge of mastering the famed Riviera golf course

> *"It's like a coquettish woman who winks at you behind her fan. Gives you the come-on. But just when you think she's all yours, wham! You find yourself sitting on the curb with a wilted bouquet, wondering who's kissing her now."*
> --Jim Murray, Pulitzer Prize-winning sports writer,
> *Los Angeles Times*

## Line from Shakespeare evoking the 45th U.S. president

> *"Full of sound and fury, signifying nothing."*
> --*Macbeth*

## Maureen Dowd on Trump

> *"The 70-year-old 7-year-old."*

## Melania Trump line from her speech at the Republican Convention in 2016

> *"We need to stop Internet bullying."*

Honestly, have you <u>met</u> your husband?

**Humorous scene for a potential Fred Friendly biopic (based on a true story)**

On the day in 1966 when Dad confronted CBS chairman and founder William S. Paley and issued his famous ultimatum that he would resign the presidency of CBS News if the network refused to cover the critical Senate hearings on Vietnam live...

He stormed out of the chairman's office in a dramatic final gesture.

The only problem was that instead of walking out of the office, he walked straight into Mr. Paley's private bathroom.

Oops.

**Dad's favorite admonition to his family**

*"Give a damn."*

The "old man" as he loved to be called, had plaques made of this famous 1960s slogan and gave one to each of his kids. These days, I keep it in my bar under a photo of my dad.

**Murrow about television**

> *"This instrument can teach, it can illuminate; yes, it can even inspire. But it can do so only to the extent that humans are determined to use it to those ends. Otherwise, it's nothing but wires and lights in a box."*
> --Edward R. Murrow, October 15, 1958

**Best modern-day example of Edward R. Murrow's powerful use of television to take a courageous stand on an important social issue**

> *If your baby is going to die, and it doesn't have to, it shouldn't matter how much money you make. I think that's something that, whether you're a Republican or a Democrat or something else, we all agree on that, right? This isn't football. There are no teams. We are the team; it's the United States. Don't let their partisan squabbles divide us on something every decent person wants.*
> --Jimmy Kimmel, May 1, 2017

That's from Jimmy Kimmel's opening monologue after his newborn son Billy survived emergency surgery to repair a life-threatening hole in his heart. In the debate over healthcare coverage, Jimmy's comments resonated widely and deeply with congressmen and leaders of both parties, as well as the public.

Having worked with Jimmy on a couple of HRTS events he hosted for us, I wrote to him telling him how grateful and proud of him I was. He emailed back a typically funny and self-deprecating response.

He's one of the smartest, best people I've been lucky to know in our business.

**Japanese proverb**

Fall down seven times. Get up eight.

**Line from *The Sopranos***

My favorite line from my favorite TV series of all time, *The Sopranos*, comes as Tony Soprano's ten-year-old son, Anthony, sits down at the dinner table with his grandmother and entire family for what his mother hopes will be a lovely family dinner and discovers his favorite dish is not being served.

To his dad: *"What, no fucking ziti?"*

***Animal House***

> *"What? Over? Did you say 'over'? Nothing is over until we decide it is! Was it over when the Germans bombed Pearl Harbor? Hell no!"*

From John Belushi's character Blutarsky's pep talk to his fraternity brothers in the face of their house being shut down.

**Adage about the ups and downs of life**

> *"Sometimes you eat the bear, sometimes the bear eats you."*

**Lena Dunham quote**

> *"The thing about me is I don't give a shit about anything, but I have an opinion on everything."*

As her character Hannah on the HBO show *Girls*.

## Carrie Fisher quote

*"Fame is obscurity biding its time."*

## Line from a retired network president

*"It's a lot more fun to watch TV than to make TV."*

From my good pal, retired ABC president Lew Erlicht

## Tom Snyder line about yours truly

On *Tomorrow*, while telling the story of me falling off a horse and breaking my wrist just before the taping of a "big-get" interview with film legend Jimmy Cagney I had arranged for an NBC primetime special…

*"My producer Andy Friendly works in strange and mysterious ways, but he gets the job done."* (followed by the booming Snyder laugh).

## Jimmy Kimmel line while hosting the 2017 Academy Awards

*"Some of you will soon be making wonderful acceptance speeches that the president of the United States will be tweeting about during his 5 a.m. bowel movement."*

## About the red carpet

Funny line about celebrities arriving on the red carpet:

*"The jerk parade."*

--Amy Schumer

P.S.: I produced *Live From the Red Carpet: The 2004 Primetime Emmy Awards* for ABC, and do not necessarily subscribe to Amy's assessment. But it's a funny line, so makes my list.

## Ecclesiastic quote

My favorite and only ecclesiastic quote I know:

*"In the land of the blind, the one-eyed man is king."*
                                        --Erasmus (approximately 1530)

**Martin Luther King**

*"The arc of the moral universe is long, but it bends towards justice."*

**Quote from a Supreme Court justice:**

*"I can't define pornography, but I know it when I see it."*
--Justice Potter Stewart, in a debate on what constitutes porn

**Steve Jobs**

*"It's a lot more fun to be a pirate than to join the Navy."*

**Buddha**

*"Holding onto anger is like holding onto a hot rock. You are the one who gets burned."*

## MOVIES

### *The Godfather*, *Schindler's List* and…yes, *Caddyshack*

As for films, there are just so many to choose from. From *Casablanca* to *Citizen Kane*, to classic war movies like *The Guns of Navarone*, to the great Westerns like *High Noon*, to Billy Wilder's classics *Sunset Boulevard* and *Witness for the Prosecution*, I've always been a huge movie fan.

But the three that stand out most for me are *The Godfather*, *Schindler's List*, and, of course…Harold Ramis' classic *Caddyshack*.

*Caddyshack* is our family favorite. I loved it from day one and made all the kids watch it over and over again on sleepovers at our house to the point where they can, and do, recite almost all of Bill Murray's, Chevy Chase's, Rodney Dangerfield's, and Ted Knight's wildly funny, mostly improvised lines, like this classic from Bill Murray's Carl Spackler character, holding a pitchfork and jabbing it into a young caddy's chest as he delivers the following story about his first time caddying:

256

*So, I tell them I'm a pro jock, and who do you think they give me? The Dalai Lama himself. Twelfth son of the Lama. The flowing robes, the grace, bald head... striking.*

*So, I'm on the first tee with him. I give him the driver. He hauls off and whacks one--big hitter, the Lama--long, into a ten-thousand-foot crevasse, right at the base of this glacier. Do you know what the Lama says? "Gunga galunga...gunga, gunga-lagunga"*

*So we finish the eighteenth and he's gonna stiff me. And I say, "Hey, Lama, hey, how about a little something, you know, for the effort, you know." And he says, "Oh, uh, there won't be any money, but when you die, on your deathbed, you will receive total consciousness." So I got that goin' for me...which is nice.*

To the annoyance of friends and family, the kids and I recite this and other *Caddyshack* dialogue word for word to each other, complete with the goofy Carl Spackler voice impression, on a regular basis.

It was just a silly little comedy no one expected much from, including the studio, cast, and producers, but it has become a classic.

When my brother David and I were honored by the Free Clinic a few years ago at its annual dinner, the family took a full-page ad in the tribute journal with a picture of Bill Murray as the legendary assistant groundskeeper Carl Spackler with the caption "Andy Friendly: Cinderella Story! Congrats on this well-deserved honor." One of his many iconic lines from the film. The ad sits in a frame in my study and makes me smile every day.

The other two are obviously more serious films. I have watched Steven Spielberg's *Schindler's List* at least twenty times.

I'm a proud Jew and was bar mitzvahed, but I'm not big on organized religion and don't attend temple regularly. I probably got that from my dad.

I do fast and atone on the high Jewish holiday of Yom Kippur, and when I was back East at CNBC in the early '90s, David Zaslav and I began watching *Schindler's List* at the end of our fasts and annual hikes. This has remained a yearly tradition and has been shared with some of my other close friends, including my wonderful doctor and friend Josh Trabulus.

I've shared with you my dad's letter to his mother when, as a twenty-nine-year-old, he wrote to her about what he witnessed as an army reporter covering the liberation of the Austrian concentration camp called Mauthausen.

Having been born just a few years after the end of World War II, growing up hearing about it from my dad and reading his letter no doubt brought home Schindler's beautifully told story, shot in black-and-white by master filmmaker Spielberg, in a way that moved me deeply and has done so more and more every time I watch it.

Like most people, I am a huge Spielberg fan and loved *Saving Private Ryan, Close Encounters, Jaws,* and many of his other classics, but for me this is his finest work and in my view the most important film I have ever seen.

If you haven't seen *Schindler's List,* I urge you to watch it. In my view it is a life-altering, life-affirming movie that everyone should watch every few years, and treasure.

In December 2016, Pat and I were at the Shoah Foundation's annual dinner gala at the Dolby Theatre (home of the Oscars and formerly known as the Kodak Theatre), seated one table away from Spielberg, George Lucas with his wife, Mellody Hobson, and *Schindler's List* (and so many other Spielberg and Lucas films) composer John Williams.

The dinner, honoring Lucas on the eve of the premiere of his latest *Star Wars* movie, was truly moving and inspirational, highlighted by Williams performing the themes from *Schindler's List, Raiders of the Lost Ark*, and *Star Wars* with a 100-piece orchestra.

I was lucky enough to meet and chat briefly with Steven and thank him for what he called in his remarks that night "the most important work of my life." That is, the creation and leadership of the USC Shoah Foundation, which has documented more than 53,000 video testimonies of survivors of the Holocaust and other genocides worldwide.

I shared with him my and Zas' Yom Kippur tradition of watching *Schindler's List* and told him how honored I am to play a small part being on his Board of Councilors at the Shoah Foundation. He could not have been warmer or nicer, and gave me his thanks and a hug.

Later, when Williams and his orchestra performed the theme from *Schindler's List*, featuring a hauntingly beautiful solo by a young woman on the violin, I looked over at the film's director just a few feet away and became emotional as I thought about the film, the horrors of the Holocaust, my dad's Mauthausen letter, and the blessing of being involved with the work of the foundation.

Later, Spielberg presented an award to Lucas. Both spoke brilliantly about the importance of the work of the foundation in teaching tolerance to students worldwide through the video testimonies of the foundation, especially in light of the recent U.S. presidential election and the rise of anti-Semitism and Islamophobia, bigotry, and racism worldwide.

Accepting his award, Lucas warned that we must defend truth more than ever; that truth is what the work of the foundation is all about.

Holocaust deniers and others can never refute the truth of the more than 53,000 video testimonies collected by the foundation.

Lucas warned against the dangers of "fake news," which played a major role in the 2016 presidential election. Paraphrasing Yoda from *Star Wars*, he said: "Fake news leads to fear and paranoia, which leads to anger, which leads to hatred, which leads to war and genocide."

It was one of the most important, moving evenings Pat and I have experienced.

The next day I read, from cover to cover, a book Spielberg put together on the making of *Schindler's List* and the founding and mission of the Shoah Foundation, which was given to each dinner attendee. I learned a great deal about what I consider to be the most important movie ever made.

I will never forget that night and am beyond grateful to Zas for getting me involved, and to Steven and the dedicated, inspiring team at the foundation for "all they do, and all they are," to paraphrase one of my dad's sayings.

Perhaps my favorite line from the movie, spoken by Ben Kingsley's character, Itzhak Stern, quoting from the Talmud, will always resonate with me: "Whoever saves one life, saves the world entire."

*****

Finally, my favorite movies of all time... *The Godfather Parts I & II*. I'll never forget the first time I watched the first one. We saw it in the home screening room of real estate magnate and former CBS owner Larry Tisch and his wife, Billie, friends of my parents who screened movies on Sunday nights at their beautiful home on Long Island Sound in Rye, New York.

I remember arguing with my dad about the film on the ride home. I was beyond excited about it and told my dad and Ruth it was the best movie I'd ever seen.

I remember them decrying the graphic violence in the film and saying they didn't enjoy it for that reason. My dad asked me why I loved it so much and I remember saying that they were a family and they truly loved each other and were one hundred percent, unconditionally supportive and loyal to each other despite the madness and violence all around them.

Even if they had chosen that life.

The look, sound, and feel of the films were unlike anything I'd ever seen. Director Francis Ford Coppola had transported me to a place in another time and I felt I was there, witnessing something real.

Of course the stories, the acting, the wonderful writing, and memorable lines and scenes from the first two *Godfather* movies are world-famous. From the opening scene of Marlon Brando petting his cat (a stray that wandered onto the set on the Paramount lot) while sitting in his den listening to requests for vengeance from associates on the day of his daughter's wedding, to the final scenes of Al Pacino in *Part II* as Michael Corleone, a man hardened and alone after consolidating his power and vanquishing his foes, there are dozens of memorable lines and scenes that my friends and I quote at poker.

These are my favorite films. It's a treat to watch them over and over again, year after year, a true gift.

One of my favorite exchanges among dozens in the *Godfather* series, quoted often and perfectly by my poker bud Bob Singer, is in *The Godfather, Part II*, between Michael Corleone and corrupt Senator Pat Geary, who is trying to extort him by demanding a large bribe for a gaming license. Senator Geary says: "I want your answer and the money by noon tomorrow. And one more thing. Don't you contact me again, ever. From now on, you deal with Turnbull." As the senator turns to walk out the door, Corleone responds coolly: "Senator, you can have my answer now if you like. My offer is this: nothing. Not even the fee for the gaming license, which I would appreciate if you would put up personally.'

*****

## MUSIC

My dad's favorite song was "Send in the Clowns," Stephen Sondheim's classic made famous by singer Judy Collins about "losing our timing," as the lyrics go, late in our careers and sending in the clowns when the show finally goes bad.

I have many favorites that have inspired and given great comfort and pure, unimaginable, delirious, almost supernatural joy over the years. I can't begin to cover all the artists who have moved my feet, my heart, and my soul since the day my dad first dropped a needle on a Sinatra track on our old-fashioned record player in the living room of our house on Fieldston Road. In that moment, a lifelong passion was born.

Andy Friendly

Even at my advanced age, I love discovering new bands. I get the same rush I did as a teenager when I fall in love with cool new bands like The xx and The Lemon Twigs. My poker and golf buds make merciless fun of me but, as my nieces, nephews, and grandkids know all too well: I love listening to Taylor Swift, Drake, Gwen Stefani, Charli XCX, Weezer, and Justin Timberlake at top volume on the SiriusXM Radio Hits channel, driving around town like a sixty-five-year-old teenager.

That's right, grizzled boomers; go on and laugh, I can take it.

Gotta keep the musical mind, spirit, and ears open.

I wanted to quote a few favorite lyrics but the lawyers won't let me. Something about paying a lot of money we don't have in the budget for licenses.

I gather those publishers are a litigious group.

Bottom line, if you're around my age and a true fan like me, you already know the lyrics to arguably the greatest rock 'n' roll songs ever written. If you don't…look 'em up, people.

It's impossible to objectively list my top twenty favorite songs of all time. There are dozens to choose from that could and should qualify.

But, in keeping with the rest of this chapter, if I were stuck on that proverbial desert island and could choose only twenty songs to listen to for the rest of my life, these would be my picks, in no particular order:

"Gimme Shelter," The Rolling Stones
"What Does It Take," Junior Walker and the All Stars
"Like a Rolling Stone," Bob Dylan
"The Man Who Sold the World," David Bowie
"A Day in the Life," The Beatles
"The Boxer," Simon & Garfunkel
"(Sittin' on) The Dock of the Bay," Otis Redding
"Pride (In the Name of Love)," U2
"Layla," Eric Clapton
"Secret O' Life," James Taylor
"My Generation," The Who
"Island in the Sun," Weezer
"What's Going On," Marvin Gaye
"Moondance," Van Morrison
"I've Been Lonely Too Long," The Young Rascals
"Mr. Blue Sky," Electric Light Orchestra
"Born to Run," Bruce Springsteen
"God Only Knows," The Beach Boys
"The Pretender," Jackson Browne

# JOKES

**Rodney Dangerfield**

Here's my favorite from the late, great New York comic:

He's asked to speak at the funeral of a dear friend at famed St. Patrick's Cathedral in New York. His departed friend was a devout Catholic, and the priest has conducted a beautiful Catholic ceremony and introduced several of the deceased's friends and family, who have spoken lovingly and said prayers. The priest introduces Rodney (one of the truly great comedians of all time and a Jew), who solemnly strides to the podium, turns to the priest, takes a beat, and begins his remarks…

"Thank you, Rabbi."

The whole place bursts out laughing.

Yes, very silly. Makes me laugh every time.

**Kathy Griffin in a CNN interview lamenting men's reactions to her early standup routines:**

"What's with the jokes, AND the vagina?"

**Elvis joke**

Pat heard this on a radio show about twenty years ago and told it to me…

Elvis was playing the big room at Caesars Palace near the end of his career and had put on a lot of weight. His hair was long and he wore the big gold medallions beneath the famed white leather jumpsuit.

He still had it, and was singing his romantic hit "Love Me Tender" to a sold-out crowd when everyone noticed he was focused on a pretty young woman sitting with her parents in a booth near the stage.

As the song built, Elvis slowly walked toward the young woman; their eyes locked on each other and Elvis crooned his famous love song to her, never taking his eyes off her.

The crowd, especially the women, were caught up in the romance of the moment, and by the time Elvis got to the young lady's booth and the song ended, the crowd fell so silent you could hear a pin drop.

As they stared into each other's eyes, Elvis took a beat and then asked the girl in his inimitable, charming Southern drawl, "Honey, can I ask you something?"

"Anything, anything at all, Elvis," replied the awestruck young woman.

Elvis took another beat, staring into her loving eyes as the crowd watched, and said:

"Honey, are you gonna finish that baked potato?"

**How hot is it?**

"It's so hot I saw a dog chasing a cat and they were both walking."

--Johnny Carson

**How hot is it?**

"It's so hot in here I'm sweating like Mel Gibson at a bar mitzvah."

--David Letterman

**How hot is it?**

"I'm sweating like a poodle at Mike Vick's place."

--David Letterman

Though I don't know the source of these next three, they're among my favorites.

**Wait…exactly how hot is it?**

"I'm sweating like Donald Trump at a Cinco de Mayo party."

**Agent joke**

About a Hollywood agent agonizing over a tough, ethical decision:

"He wrestled with his conscience and he won."

**Favorite poker line**

To a pretentious poker player who thinks and acts as if he's better than everyone else at the table:

"Your poker rep is expanding faster than the universe."

### Second favorite poker line

To a guy at our poker game claiming Ted Cruz had a good sense
of humor:
"Hitler was a lot of fun at a party, too"

--Jonathan Levin

### Favorite faux apology

A pretend apology line after zapping someone with a funny line at a poker
game, staff meeting, dinner, etc.:

"I'm sorry, did I go too far? I was told it was a roast."

--Will Ferrell

### Favorite line about a mustache

Letterman to Tom Selleck about his famous 'stache:
"If I had a mustache like yours, honestly everybody could just kiss my
ass."

### Chris Christie jokes

Letterman has a bunch of gems about this guy; my favorite Chris Christie
jokes by Letterman:
"When he gets on the scale, the scale says, 'Hey, one at a time.'"
"Security at tonight's convention is tighter than Chris Christie's yoga
pants."
"Say what you will, he'd be the first president you could see from
space."
"Chris Christie's blood type? Alfredo."

### Favorite quote on estate planning

"I hope to have some motherfuckers fighting over my money."

--Richard Pryor

**Favorite line to people who always say: "If only…"**

"If we had some ham, we could have some ham and eggs, if we had some eggs."

--Paul Cantor, my lifelong friend whom I shipped out to sea with at 16

**Guy goes to the doctor**

And finally, my favorite joke ever told on *The Tonight Show With Johnny Carson*. The great Bette Midler told this one on the occasion of Johnny's final show.

"An elderly gentleman goes to his doctor and says, 'Doc, I have a terrible and very embarrassing problem. I'm suffering from silent gas emissions.'

"The doc says, 'Tell me more.'

"The older gentleman says, 'Well, just yesterday I took my grandson to the movies and I had a silent gas emission. And last night I took my wife to the opera and I had another silent gas emission. It was very, very embarrassing, Doc.'

"'Yes, go on,' the doc says.

"'And just now sitting here with you I suffered another silent gas emission!!! What the hell are you gonna do about it, Doc?' asked the gentleman.

"The doc took a long pause and said, 'The first thing we're gonna do is check your hearing!'"

Johnny literally fell off his chair laughing.

*****

It's been fun sharing some of my favorites with you.

# 33

## DAD'S FINAL DAYS AND MY EULOGY TO HIM

The decade of the '90s was bittersweet.

It was a decade of productivity and success in my career at CNBC and King World/CBS, along with the birth of many of my nieces, nephews, and grandkids.

But for my dad in his seventies, it was a decade of declining health, including two strokes and a wide range of other health issues. It was tough to watch this giant of a man, a hero to me, struggle.

In my jobs at CNBC and King World, I was back east about half the time, so I got to spend a lot of time with him. That part was a gift. We got to know each other in ways we never had before now that he had more time to sit, talk, and reflect. We did just that on many nights and weekends at our home in Riverdale and at our cottage in Stockbridge, Massachusetts, in the summer.

When Dad passed away on March 3, 1998, at the age of 82, it was a blessing. He had been confined to his bed and unable to function mentally and physically for months. Dad had made it very clear he did not want to live that way.

When my older brother Jon Mark called me in L.A. with the news, I was of course very sad but I knew he was finally at peace. His race had been run and he was no longer in pain.

As Pat and I flew back to New York, we reflected on our last visit with Dad just three weeks earlier, and I started to think about what I wanted to say at his funeral at the Riverdale Temple near our family home in the Bronx in a few days.

Of course it had been on my mind for years as his health declined, but now I had to write and deliver a eulogy that he would be proud of in front of family, close friends, and the assembled priesthood and royalty of broadcast journalism. A truly daunting task in a time of deep sadness.

After days of writing and rewriting, and in front of the likes of network anchors Dan Rather, Peter Jennings, Mike Wallace, Andy Rooney, and Charlie Rose, top media, judicial and education titans, and hundreds of others including family and friends from around the country, and filled with emotion and nerves, this is what I said to begin the many wonderful eulogies to my dad that day.

*On behalf of our whole family, I would like to thank you all for coming today. Dad would've loved that you are all here. And he would've loved the hundreds of calls, letters, and tributes that have appeared in print and on the air over the past couple days. He'd have been deeply moved. So for Dad, and our whole family, a heartfelt thank you.*

*Carl Sandburg used to say my dad "always looked as if he had just gotten off a foam-flecked horse." Dad just loved that.*

*He also loved a line from "the old Abider"–that was Dad and Ed Murrow's term of affection for Sandberg. A line from "Remembrance Rock"–it goes, "The shroud has no pockets... the dead hold in their hands only that which they have given away." By that standard, Dad died with his hands and heart full on Tuesday morning.*

*For Dad gave so much to everyone he came in contact with as a journalist, a teacher, and for Pat and me and all our brothers and sisters, as a father.*

*I was born November 6, 1951, the same week* See It Now *premiered.*

*My earliest memories of Dad are driving with him to see the* See It Now *cutting room in Manhattan, and watching him work. I was too young to understand, but I believe I must have sensed his fear and ultimately his courage putting his career and his young family's future on the line standing up for Milo Radulovich, Annie Lee Moss, Reed Harris, and, ultimately against Joe McCarthy.*

*I also recall all the Saturdays and Sundays driving up and down the West Side Highway from Riverdale to the cutting room where I watched Ed and Dad, Joe Wershba, Dave Buksbaum, Palmer and Millie and the team put* See It Now, Small World, *and* CBS Reports *together. I believe all of that sunk into my subconscious mind, although much of that time was spent shining producers' and editors' shoes at the prevailing rate of ten cents a pair.*

*While many Saturdays and Sundays and most weeknights were spent working, Dad always made time for his kids. One of my favorite memories is waiting at the tiny Martha's Vineyard airport with my mom, Lisa, and David for that single-engine prop en route from LaGuardia on Friday evenings during my first seven summers. On Saturdays we'd catch and then cook swordfish on the open fire on the beach below our house in Menemsha. No lighter fluid allowed! Dad insisted that we kids go round up the twigs and kindling to light the coals. This is a Friendly Family Tradition, along with countless others that continue to this day, and drives our kids nuts because they have to go along with them, too. Like cooking the Thanksgiving turkey on the BBQ grill each year, never in the oven, always with a glass of Scotch in hand, or saying, "I'd know, that's who'd know," or thanking each toll taker at every toll booth, or admonishing us kids, when we'd say, "But we hate spinach," that "the only thing we hate is the word 'hate.'"*

*There are so many "Friendlyisms": keeping a beat-up old copy of the Constitution in his pocket–(he has one with him right now), or his favorite: "My job is to make the agony of decision-making so intense that you can only escape by thinking." Or "Give a damn" or "What the American public doesn't know can kill them."*

*That one comes from my Mom, Dorothy, whose love and support and appreciation for art and culture had a major and continuing impact on Dad.*

*Among my favorite times with Dad were those 4 a.m. fishing expeditions on the lake at Stockbridge. On one cold, damp morning in the summer of '58 we couldn't catch a thing for hours, not even a bluegill. A tired and frustrated seven-year-old whined*

268

*that he was cold and wet and that we'd never catch anything and pleaded to go back and get warm and have some breakfast. The "old man" (he loved to be called that) insisted, "Just one more cast, you're going to catch a big one, I promise."*

*One hour and fifty casts later, and not a nibble. My whining had turned to tears; I was shivering, hungry, and begged my dad to go in. "Just one more cast, I feel it, this is the one, if we don't get one this time, we'll go home." I protested vehemently but had no choice. The "old man" wasn't budging. Now I know this sounds apocryphal, but on my next cast, I felt not one but two strikes and after a rousing fight reeled in a huge bass along with a golden perch on my dual-pronged hook.*

*That incredible Fred Friendly lesson was passed on to five-year-old Will, one of Pat and my "little rascals," on a lake in California just two months ago, and I know that one, along with so many other things Dad taught us, will pass to future generations through so many, in and out of this room, who were, as Ruth would say, in the gravitational pull of my dad.*

*For in the end, his true legacy is that of a teacher.*

*While we were always close and always loved one another, we didn't always see eye to eye. There were things he liked and things he didn't like. And as we all know, he wasn't shy about making both clear. He liked that he taught me to recite all the presidents' names in order in front of company at age five. He didn't like that at age three, in a misguided effort to be helpful and emulate the man at the gas station, I put the garden hose in the gas tank of his brand-new Chrysler and "filled it up." He liked that I began my career at NBC News. He didn't like that I left news to produce primetime entertainment specials, or* Entertainment Tonight, *or a concert film with Richard Pryor; but in time told me he was proud that I had always been my own man.*

*Ruth tells me he was happy and proud that I returned to NBC and helped make CNBC a success, launching programs with some of his favorite students and colleagues like Tim Russert, Tom Snyder, and Geraldo Rivera. And he let me know he was proud when*

Inside Edition *was the only TV magazine, network or syndicated, to win the prestigious George Polk Award, which he had won for lifetime achievement just three years prior.*

*He didn't like it when I grew my hair down to my shoulders in college. In 1973 we actually got in a shoving match after a fight in which I defended my brother's right to wear his so-called Afro as big as he wanted. But in the end he respected all his kids for being ourselves. One of my most prized possessions is a letter he wrote me to that effect in 1984 that is framed in my den.*

*I was lucky to be around him so much from 1990 to 1996 when I came back to work at CNBC. I don't think we were ever closer.*

*With his loving, caring Ruth always at his side (what a hero Ruth has been to all of us), we enjoyed quiet reflective weekends by the lake in Stockbridge, where for the first time we had him to ourselves once in a while. And we were always happy to share him with so many close friends who would stop by–many of you are here today.*

*He loved seeing you all right up to the end. It was a special time, sad in some ways, but happy in others, at least until last year's devastating stroke. There were no speeches to write, no seminars or TV programs to organize, just sweet, bittersweet days and nights filled with simple things we did together when I was a kid. Movies, Knick and Yankee games, quiet dinners, lots of smiles, and animated comments and gestures from the "old man" as always.*

*The last time Pat and I saw Dad was three weeks ago. We flew in to see him and, as weak and disoriented as he was, he was full of love, and his giant hand still felt strong when we shook hands as we always did, since I was a year old. He told Pat how beautiful she looked and asked me, as always, "How's the job?" And he told us that he loved us and he held the back of our hands up to his mouth and kissed them and said: "I love you." But after a short time he asked to go back to his bed. That's where he liked to spend most of his time over the past months. He was "tired."*

*When I was a kid, Dad and I, along with Lisa and David, shared a special custom: Each night, no matter how good or how bad things might have been in our lives or in the world--a bad report card, a tough divorce, a president's assassination, or a frightening war in Asia--Dad came by our rooms before bed, looked us in the eye and told us: "It's good to be your Dad." Our reply was always the same: "It's good to be your son (or daughter)."*

*That day in his room, three weeks ago, I told him, "It's good to be your son," but because of his illness he could not complete his part. But he looked me straight in the eye and smiled and I knew "he got it."*

*I will always cherish those words and that tradition. I will pass them on to my family. I will keep those words in my heart and in my head and then, Dad, you will never be far from me.*

*So long, old man--it's good to be your son.*

I miss and think about my dad all the time. On what would have been his 100th birthday, October 30, 2015, my talented nephew Noah Mark, Ruth, and I collected memories from family and close friends in a video tribute to "the old man" that we shared with hundreds of friends, colleagues, and students of his, along with our families and friends.

His voice and ideas are always with me and guide me along with my brothers and sisters and so many more family members and friends who can still, to paraphrase the big man himself, "hear him now."

I know Dad would be happy to know that we continue to share his Mauthausen letter and so many more lessons he taught us and asked us to live by and pass on to future generations. And that we are all still "willing to be lucky."

A major, lifelong New York Giants football fan, he'd have gotten a big kick out of and been extremely moved by Giant all-pro, Super Bowl hero, and all-around good guy Michael Strahan's foreword to this book, and the fact that each night he tells his kids: "It's good to be your Dad."

Here are just a few of the hundreds of wonderful letters I received after Dad died:

DICK EBERSOL 3/6/98

Dear Andy –

You're dad was one of the few true giants in our history as an industry. And you are one of the *very few* sons of a giant, who have really achieved great and good things as well. He must have been very proud of you and your success. You're in my prayers.

Best –

Dick

*From Dick Ebersol – former chairman, NBC Sports and Olympics*

TOM SNYDER

Dear Andy.

You must know how sad it was to hear of Fred's passing. But we also know he is with the angels now — no doubt perplexing them with so many new hypotheticals they had never considered! And no doubt telling Peter at the gate that even in Eternity the search for truth can never end. Love, Andy.

Tom and Pam

3/6/98

*From Tom Snyder and Pam Burke*

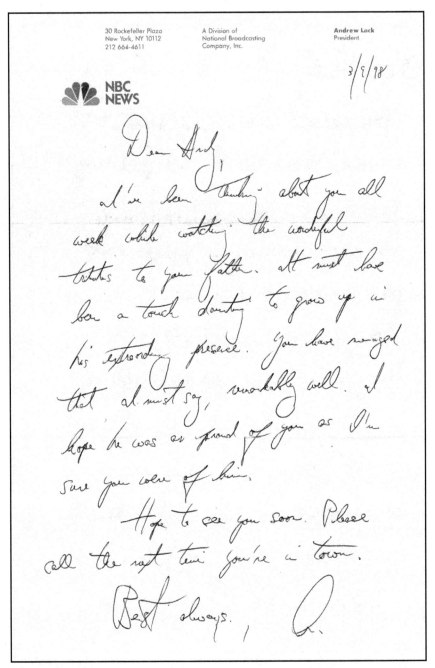

*From Andy Lack – president, NBC News*

Bob Wright

Andy,

   I'm very sad about your father's death. He was a great figure in our business. Please accept my sympathies. I hope all is well beyond this very difficult time.

Bob

3·11·98

*From Bob Wright – former CEO, NBC*

Dear Andy –

   Please accept my heartfelt condolenses on the passing of your father. My thoughts are with you at a time I know they're needed most.

Love
Roseanne

*From Roseanne*

# 34

## BREAKING NEWS...Can Sparky Read??

Every summer Camp Robinson Crusoe brought in a couple of puppies for the campers to play with.

In my first summer of camp at age eight, in 1959, I instantly fell in love with the two adorable black lab pups the camp had brought in, especially the one I called Sparky, with the little white stripe on her chest.

We had a nice cat at home named Green Eyes, but we never had a dog.

About halfway through the summer I learned that the camp would be giving the fast-growing pups away to a couple lucky campers, if their parents allowed.

I wasn't a great writer of letters home but somehow managed with the help of the camp to send a telegram to my parents, who were vacationing in Greece; the telegram is now famous in our family lore. It read simply: "There is a black dog here. Can I have her?"

The return wire said simply: "Yes." Nice going, Mom and Dad!

From that day, to the end of her life seventeen years later, Sparky became a major part of our family.

She was smart, fun, and loving. The only problem was she had a serious case of wanderlust. At night she'd move around from my bedroom, to Lisa's, to David's, and when Jon, Mike, and Richard joined us a few years later in what we call the "merger" following Dad and Ruth's marriage, Sparky added their bedrooms to her nightly rounds.

Everyone craved Sparky time.

The problem was her wanderings did not end at the front door. We constantly got calls from around the neighborhood saying: "This is Angelo's Pizzeria, and we have your dog. Come pick her up," or "This is Mrs. Kheel. We have Sparky, please come get her."

We built a nice, large, fenced pen in the backyard for her to play in when we were away but one day she escaped and found her way onto the IRT subway, heading from our stop in the Bronx at Van Cortlandt Park to Coney Island, the famed amusement park in Brooklyn, two boroughs and dozens of subway stops away, including a line change.

I know what you're thinking…Andy's just making this crap up.

Nope. True story.

Sparky probably followed someone right down to the station and onto the subway, switched trains with him or her, and got off when they did at Coney Island.

When we got the call, we couldn't believe it. Dad and I made the long drive to Brooklyn and retrieved the quite-proud-of-herself pup.

We had her backyard pen reinforced and Sparky's little road trips came to an end.

Soon after the Mark boys joined the family, a heated debate began about just how smart Sparky was. Obviously she had skills. Not too many dogs can go to the amusement park at Coney Island two boroughs away on their own. But just how smart was she?

A lifelong debate began between younger brothers Richard and David as to whether or not Sparky could read *The New York Times*. They were in their early teens and both were determined to win the debate. They dragged the whole family into it.

The question has raged on at family dinners and gatherings for over fifty years.

It started with David Friendly's assertion that he could prove Sparky could read the newspaper and comprehend it.

Richard, who became the Chief of the Civil Division U.S. Attorney's Office for the Southern District of New York, already had a sharp, budding legal mind, and, on purely empirical grounds, rejected David's assertion.

There is not enough paper left in this book to recount the decades-long back and forth, but what better occasion to finally get this thing resolved than in print, for the record, right here, right now. If for no other reason than it's time to move on, people! For the love of God, let it go!

So…I asked Richard and David to write up their final arguments and send 'em in. Furthermore, I asked sister Lisa and brother Mike, both key witnesses at the time, to weigh in with any thoughts.

Finally, I asked our oldest brother, Jon, a longtime partner at the prestigious New York law firm Cahill Gordon & Reindel, who has moonlighted as the mayor of Scarsdale, New York, over the past three years, to serve as judge and make a final ruling on arguments submitted, with Ruth Friendly, matriarch of the Mark-Friendly family having the last word with the option to overrule Judge Jon if she were willing to "hear" the case.

So here now, with the reflection of five decades and endless, granular, borderline-obsessive discussion and debate (welcome to MY world), a unique look into life as a sibling of the Friendly-Mark gang for over fifty years.

Let's begin with younger brother David Friendly, now a successful Oscar-nominated film and television producer who produced *Little Miss Sunshine* and is currently producing *Queen of the South* for USA Network. He started the whole flap at age twelve with his categorical insistence to his new, six-months-older brother Richard that Sparky could, in fact, literally read *The New York Times* and any other printed material.

*Sparky was no ordinary dog. For example, she was "off-leash" and when she wanted to go out, the front door was opened and she was off and running on her neighborhood rounds, through the chestnut trees on Fieldston Road to Indian Pond and then back home. When she came to a stop sign, she did as instructed before crossing the street. This and other observations made it quite clear to me she could read. In addition, as I tried to explain to Richard over and over again, no one could disprove that she could read. So, fifty years later, I still maintain Sparky could and did read. I might add that when I was reading* Old Yeller, *I remember her looking over my shoulder from her perch on the bed and being quite drawn to the material.*

Sister Lisa Friendly:
(Lisa is the senior medical writer and editor, da Vinci Robotic Surgical Systems, at Intuitive Surgical in Sunnyvale, California, where she writes about da Vinci robotic surgery.)

*I recall Richard's justified frustration that the deck felt rather stacked against him. For example, we would lay books in front of Sparky, and if she sniffed around and didn't depart immediately, that was taken as a sign that she was, of course, reading.*

From my brother Michael, a professional singer-songwriter-producer who wrote the theme for *Entertainment Tonight* and has toured for years with Tom Chapin:

*I believe it was around the time of the birth of this controversy that Charles Schulz gave me the guidance I needed on the issue. Schulz was commenting on his own beloved Snoopy, but the problem was the same for Sparky. It wasn't whether she could read or not. It was whether we could train her not to move her lips when she read to herself.*

Richard Mark, now a partner at the prestigious Gibson Dunn law firm in Manhattan, where he does little jobs like supervise the Teamsters elections, is about to make earth-shattering, history-changing BREAKING NEWS. Here now his dramatic, fifty-years-in-the-making statement:

*The controversy over whether Sparks Friendly (aka "Sparky") could read is a question for the ages. It ranks with other imponderables: "Is there a God, and what is its nature?"*

*"How deep is the ocean? How high is the sky?"*

*"With a middling Texas Hold 'Em hand, do you ever take more than two raises before the flop?"*

*And the question of canine cognition has endured for thousands of years. As we are about to read:*

*We are told that Rabbi Eliezer, Rabbi Joshua, Rabbi Elazar - son of Azariah, Rabbi Akiba, and Rabbi Tarfon sat at the Seder table in B'nai B'rak and, the whole night through, discussed whether the domesticated dog could read until their disciples came in and said: Rabbis! It is time now to recite the SHEMA of the morning prayers AND TO TAKE THE DOGS FOR THEIR WALK TO THE CISTERN. (The part in all caps is elided from most Haggadahs.)*

(Author's note: OK Richard, now you're just showin' off!)

*So when the Mark and Friendly families merged about fifty years ago, "Can Sparky read?" became a question of debate at the dinner table, right alongside other Fred-inspired debates on prior restraint, balancing free press vs. fair trial, the evils of the Nixon White House, whether the football Giants would ever have a winning record, and I investigated Sparky's reading skills with the intellectual* *rigor demanded of those other matters. Defining "reading" as the recognition and understanding of printed letters arranged as words on a page, it was evident that no matter the text (*Mad Magazine *to* Moby Dick*), Sparky would literally turn up her elegant nose at books and give us that "wha" sort of look. We never had a discussion of the content of any text–and we all know that Sparky could TALK (she and Ruth would have endless conversations at the dinner table). If Sparky could read, she would have told us.*

*When shown print, I have no doubt Sparky communicated, as in: "This book has no discernible smell and thus is TOTALLY boring. Can I please have a Milk-Bone now?" As a scientific-method-wasn't-the-Enlightenment-the-coolest-thing sort of "scholar," I wanted affirmative proof, not speculation. The lack of evidence did it for me. That and Sparky's score of 250 on the verbal SAT.*

*Perspective does change over fifty years. Expand "reading" to encompass Sparky's acute sensitivity to the doings of the family and she did, indeed, "read" each one of us.*

*So I accept that Sparky could "read." Totally. WITH THE AIR QUOTES.*

HOLD THE PRESSES! WE HAVE A NEW PAGE ONE!
EVERYONE REMAIN CALM.
PLEASE...REMAIN IN YOUR SEATS OR I'LL CLEAR THIS COURTROOM.

## SPARKY COULD READ!!!

And while Richard's historic reversal renders the verdicts of older brother "Judge" Jon Mark and family matriarch Ruth Friendly moot....here for the judicial record is how they weighed in, prior to knowing Richard's shocking reversal.

Jon Mark:

*While I have for decades remained above this particular fray, the newspeak of the current administration in D.C. seems to lend itself to the debate and prompts me to chime in. So, for example, what is meant by "wiretap"? It doesn't necessarily mean tapping into a wire. It also does and might mean surveillance more generally. So too, what is meant by "read"? It might mean reading letters and words the way we do, but it also might more broadly mean reading faces, body language, tone of voice, emotions, etc. Looked at in that way, Sparky certainly could read. For example, she quickly "read" the dynamics of our newly merged families in those early days when we just came together. She then figured out that dividing her sleep time between David's and Richard's beds would make an important statement of inclusion for one newer member of the family. In this sense she could also "speak." When we gave her a bone, she could read us and figure out that if she left the bone on a carpeted floor we would take it away. So into the backyard she would go to bury the bone safely out of our sight. Examples of this sort abound and are low-hanging fruit--and there is no doubt that in this sense, Sparky could definitely read us all.*

*The foregoing being indisputable, I will leave it there, since whether or not Sparky could or could not read the written word is, as I noted years ago, a moot point in light of her passing.*

Ruth Friendly:

*From the very start of Friendlys and Marks joining as a family, rhetoric was a high priority. The two youngest, David and Richard, were quick to learn as they debated with vigor on whether or not Sparky could read. I remember listening carefully the very first time they presented their cases in the dining room and marveling at their fervor as the discussion continued through the years. As a loving parent, there is no way I can come down on either side of this question. So, without a doubt, the right thing to do is to recuse myself, with admiration for the persuasive skills of both. And yes, Sparky lives on.*

No more questions, your honor! The great Sparky debate is now "settled law."

I have at times been asked to weigh in and voice my own opinion, but as my dad used to say: "I prefer to ASK the questions." That said, I think you can guess how I come down on this one. I knew it the day my copy of *The Call of the Wild* went missing when I was fourteen.

What I do know is that Sparky, and every other pet I've had throughout my life, brought nothing but fun, love, and pure joy.

She played a big role in helping our family through some tough times during the breakup of my parents' marriage and then the merger of the Mark and Friendly families.

I keep this photo of Sparky, in all her splendor, in our home and think of her often.

When her huge heart finally gave out at seventeen, my dad wrote us the following very special letter.

*June 3, 1977*

*Sparky was no show dog and wasn't much of a watchdog, but by God she had class. If a Newfoundland mutt can have charisma, she had it. Sparky died in her sleep today and if that makes you cry a little, that's what tear ducts are for. Dr. Bender called to tell me the news just as I was leaving for the office, and I had blurred focus for the next two hours.*

*I spent ten minutes with her yesterday, and then Ruth visited her for fifteen minutes on her way home from school. Although she knew us, her responses were weak and, try as she could, she couldn't even get off her haunches. It may have been our imaginations, but we thought she wagged her tail–just a little.*

Andy Friendly

*We'll all remember Sparky for all the "good times," as the song from our show goes. She was a catalyst in the merger of the two families, and who will ever forget her in that red ribbon (or was it yellow) at the great wedding in the Bernsteins' back yard.*

*We'll each have our special memories of Sparky: Her barking spasms in the middle of the night at the scent of Duke, the raccoon; her scampering off the couch when Ruth caught her in the act; her fabled commute between David's and Rich's beds; Andy's historic letter from camp–"There's a great little black dog here. Can I bring her home?"; Ruth's coaxing her to eat her special diet of cream of wheat laced with hamburger: Ethel or Mike propositioning her, "You want to go for a walk, Sparky?"; all the phone calls from strangers on Waldo Avenue and Mosholu Road and even Broadway–"Have you lost a black dog named Sparky?"; the time she hurt her leg and Dr. Wolff had to invent a new surgery for her; even her special brand of perfume when her digestive system began to deteriorate; her plaintive whimper when a bedroom door accidentally closed on her; her lifelong habit of taking a bone to the laundry; her special alarm system that would cause her to wake up as the long ride from the Berkshires reached the stop-light at 246th Street; the way she would follow Lisa, David, Rich, and anybody else to school; her special relationship with Cliff and Katie; her ability, or at least desire, to catch a dog biscuit in mid-air, even when her aging legs slowed down her reaction time; her waiting by the front door on a late spring afternoon for the family to come home; her special conversations with Ruth, who could make her bark on cue; and David and Rich's endless debate over whether she could read.*

*Dr. Bender told me she was his oldest living patient, and that she was always a good patient. Her collar and dog tag -- "I belong to Fred W. Friendly – KI 9–1750 – Summer: 673-0171," already hang in the study, and are going to stay there. When you look at them, remember what Sparky would have said if she could talk, which Ruth always insisted she could: "Forget that I died: Remember that I lived."*

*Affectionately,*
*Fred W. Friendly*

283

I read Dad's letter often and it always brings smiles and tears.

There's an old saying that if you truly want a friend in this (or any) town, get a dog.

I cannot possibly argue with that one. Pat and I have had three wonderful pups over the decades: Daisy, Lily, and Bonnie.

*Pat with our latest family pup, Bonnie, whom*
*we rescued from a shelter in 2015*

*Like Sparky, she has a huge heart and a great spirit.*

# 35

## TRUMPING TRUMP

In 2003 my friend and fellow Free Clinic and HRTS board member Andrea Wong, who ran unscripted series, specials, and late night for ABC, brought me in to executive produce a special called *Life of Luxury*.

It was pitched by Robin Leach and was pretty much an updated version of the famed *Lifestyles of the Rich and Famous* series he did in the '80s.

Robin was to host and help produce the special, but the network wanted someone to oversee the production, and hired me to do so.

This was instant trouble. Robin was pissed he would not be in full control and immediately tried to wrest control of the project away from me and my talented co-executive producer, Krysia Plonka.

Robin and I had a history. He had worked on the pilot of *Entertainment Tonight* and done a good job. I liked his cheeky, over-the-top style and sense of humor, and decided to keep him on the show when I took over from executive producer Jack Haley Jr., who had done the pilot in 1981.

I came from hard news at NBC and Robin had been toiling in the world of tabloid journalism. We butted heads but I still liked his pieces, and he delivered some big gets for us.

As you know from an earlier chapter, I left *ET* after six months. In the years following, I bumped into Robin from time to time around town and at industry events. He was having great success with *Lifestyles* and I was busy producing a wide range of projects. We got along fine and always shared a laugh.

But this was war. In fairness, I got it. This was his show. He pitched it and thought he was in control of the production. Krysia and I tried to be kind, low-key, inclusive, and collegial, but Robin would have none of it. He fought us tooth and nail on everything.

Somehow we managed to do a great show despite all this, and Robin did his usual great job hosting it, despite the production war going on behind the scenes.

The show featured profiles of some of the richest, most interesting, outlandish billionaires around, including head of Virgin Atlantic Sir Richard Branson, whom we visited on his private Necker Island, where President Obama and wife Michelle stayed after they left the White House.

We also profiled high-living music and fashion moguls Kimora Lee and then-husband Russell Simmons, and finally, yeah, that's right, New York real estate mogul and budding TV star Donald Trump.

One executive at ABC asked us to deliver "garish excess" to viewers, and that's exactly what we did. I had never been given that marching order from a network before, but I guess if you live long enough, you'll see and hear everything.

We kept it slightly tongue-in-cheek and hip; the ratings were strong and the reviews were good. ABC quickly ordered four more shows. Check out Virginia Heffernan's review in *The New York Times*, especially what she had to say about our current president:

### Never-Ending Caviar Dreams and Bling-Bling Wishes

*In short,* Life of Luxury *is a telling, semi-amusing and thoroughly tacky portrait of sated people who manage, against all odds, always to stay starved for more. According to the show, Madonna, for all she has, sometimes can't go on for want of a tea bag. Ms. Simmons, who has a throw pillow embroidered with the never-too-rich-or-too-thin maxim, is impatiently on a waiting list for her next car.*

*Only one of the show's heroes hints that he might be dangerously nearing satiety. Reflecting on past reverses, Donald Trump muses, "How many apartments can you have in New York?" Say what? Mr. Trump, it seems, has recently realized that he need not keep all his buildings' penthouses for himself. He only requires a place for his toothbrush, he says. (All 32,000 square feet of it, but still.)*

*Mr. Trump, scaling back? Mr. Trump, talking about a place for his toothbrush? Mr. Leach, connoisseur of greed, takes the news in stride, but the strange suggestion must have given him pause about this rich man's integrity.*

The network was happy and wanted four more, but there was just one problem…Robin and my team could not work together. The sniping and backbiting was draining, and while we made it through one show, there was just no way to do four more in this state of chaos.

I told the network I'd do the next four but we needed to find a new host. Robin lobbied the network for a deal that would allow him to stay on as host and either produce without me or bring in a new executive producer.

Through multiple, reliable sources, I learned that Robin's pal Mr. Trump had called Lloyd Braun, Andrea Wong's boss and president of ABC, to lobby for my firing so that his buddy Robin could stay.

Tom Snyder and I sat with Trump at a party once in the late '70s and we had some laughs with him, but I barely knew the man.

I kind of enjoyed him on his frequent Letterman appearances, when he allowed Dave to, in Dave's words, "just beat him up," and he'd take it and laugh along.

We had just done a nice profile of Trump for our little special and now the man was telling my boss, Lloyd Braun, to fire me. For all he knew this was my only income, my family's livelihood. According to my sources, he sounded really angry and demanded I be fired.

(Hey Donald, as Letterman told you on his show, if you want to be angry with someone, be angry with your <u>barber</u>.)

Braun, while running the giant management firm Brillstein-Grey Communications, now Brillstein Entertainment Partners, earlier in his career, was instrumental in helping us launch Marty Short's show at King World, and is a fellow Riviera member and a friend. He and Andrea stood up for me and told Trump they were happy with the production team and I would continue on as executive producer.

Ultimately, we hired the iconic, hilarious George Hamilton as host and did four more highly rated specials. Lloyd and Andrea called and asked us to do thirteen more episodes and turn it into a series. To this day, Lloyd teases me about being the only producer in town to ever turn down a firm thirteen-week order.

But there was a reason for that. The problem was: The number of people at the financial and fame levels we needed to profile was quickly running out. Most truly rich and powerful people are quite private, and the last thing they want to do is show off their wealth on television.

We made it through four more shows, but I knew we were running out of great names and starting to settle for the second lead actors on sitcoms showing us their hot tubs in the Valley. (Well, not quite—but almost.)

That was not the show Krysia and I, or the network, wanted to do. Turning it down was the right decision.

I saw Robin at an *Entertainment Tonight* reunion a few years later, gave him a hug, and said I was truly sorry for the way things worked out. And I meant it. He was gracious and we had a drink together. I still get a kick when I hear his famous English accent voicing numerous commercials and comedy bits on television and radio. We just couldn't work together.

As for Trump, I'm going to let Letterman have the last word:

"We elected a president with THAT hair? Let's have an investigation into THAT."

Enough said.

# 36

## MICHAEL KING

Michael's death from pneumonia on May 27, 2015, at the age of sixty-seven was a shock to all who knew and loved him. He died far too soon, leaving behind his wonderful wife, Jena, and four great kids ranging in age from four to thirty-one years old. He was a giant and, as the expression goes, we shall not see his like again.

A magnificent memorial service was held for Michael the following month. Along with a wide-ranging and illustrious group that included Oprah Winfrey, Ted Danson, Norman Lear, and President Bill Clinton, I was one of the few non-stars asked to say a few words.

I do not enjoy speaking before large groups, and especially not at funerals or memorials, but lately I find myself doing it more and more. Sadly, I guess that's what happens when you reach your sixties.

I delivered my remarks at the beautiful ceremony at Skirball Center on Sepulveda Boulevard near Mulholland Drive in the hills above L.A.

I was nervous and at the same time quite emotional as Pat and I took our seats with President Clinton and the other speakers right in front of the stage. Michael's death was so unexpected and such a shock.

As I turned around and looked back at the crowd of hundreds, including dozens of friends, former colleagues, and a wide range of major stars, from Don Henley and Joe Walsh of The Eagles to Sylvester Stallone, I kept reminding myself to breathe deep, focus on my delivery, speak slowly, and look up from my script as much as possible. I wanted to come through for my friend.

Years ago he had said to me, while recounting his dad Charles' early death: "Andy, if I die before you, I'd like you to talk at my funeral about our company and how we did things." I agreed to do it, and the moment weighed heavy on me.

It did not help matters that I'd be directly following Oprah and just one or two speakers behind President Clinton. Arguably the two best speakers on the planet.

They were brilliant and poignant in their remarks. Oprah spoke about Michael's courage; in her own words, "taking an unknown, overweight black woman to the national syndication market in 1986, at a time when that profile did not exist on TV."

The president spoke about the trip he and Michael took to Africa as part of the Clinton Global Initiative, and how generous and deeply committed Michael was to ending AIDS there. He also told some charming and funny stories about Michael.

The president was introduced by Michael's nineteen-year-old son, Teddy, who along with his sisters, Audrey and Ali, led the ceremony with poems and stories about their dad.

They delivered their contributions with remarkable poise and beauty and had all of us in tears.

When it came time for me to get up and speak, all I could think about was that I had to come through for Michael, despite my emotion and nerves.

I carefully climbed the steps to the stage, as I didn't want to stumble.

Looking out at the audience, I took a deep breath, looked at Pat and the president, and decided to go off script for a moment, which actually helped me relax.

I said something like:

*I'm Andy Friendly. I played poker with Michael from time to time, and last night at my weekly Thursday night game I was telling the guys I was nervous because I was going to be speaking about Michael at his memorial along with an amazing lineup of speakers and I wanted to come through for him.*

*I think I'll be OK, I said, as long as I don't have to follow two people…President Clinton and Oprah.*

That got a little chuckle. I turned to look at Cari, Michael's sister-in-law and the producer of the memorial, who had set the order of speakers, and said, "Thank YOU, Cari…it's OK, I have a long memory."

That got a little laugh, and when I looked down at the president he was smiling, so I felt OK.

Andy Friendly

At the suggestion of my poker bud, *Supernatural* showrunner/director Bob Singer, at our game the previous night, I thanked President Clinton for coming. No one had thanked him up to that point. He smiled in response.

I told him how pleased Michael would be to know he had come.

He was in my direct line of eyesight and was very encouraging. I had met him on two other occasions: once at a gathering at Michael's where Pat and I sat with him, along with Barbra Streisand, Bette Midler, and Roseanne, where it was really cool to have a chance to talk with him. I met him again at an HRTS luncheon when he was our featured speaker.

For the rest of my remarks, his smiling, encouraging face became my go-to target. For whatever reason, rather than making me nervous, looking at him just a few feet away somehow helped me relax and feel comfortable.

Here is part of what I said that day:

*I'm Andy Friendly. I was fortunate to be Michael's friend and colleague for over 30 years.*

*Over those years Michael gave me many tough assignments but none tougher than the one* The Hollywood Reporter *gave me recently, to write a tribute to Michael–but to keep it to just three hundred words.*

*That's two small paragraphs to sum up one of the legends in the history of television.*

*Somehow, after much editing, I got it done.*

*Because I have a bit more than 300 words to work with tonight, I have added a few things to my tribute to Michael.*

*Michael had a gift for discovering diamonds in the rough.*

*During the early 1980s, Michael and his brothers, Bob and Roger, ran a fledgling syndication business from the kitchen of their small New York apartment.*

*Somehow these young guys got a meeting with Merv Griffin and offered the legendary creator of* Wheel of Fortune *and* Jeopardy! *the laughable sum of $50,000 for the rights to take the* *soon-to-be-canceled network franchises into the unknown market of first-run syndication.*

*Griffin was amused but thought the guys were smart and had a plan...and with nothing to lose agreed to the deal.*

*Despite lacking clearances in the top three markets, New York, L.A. and Chicago–unheard of when launching a new series– within a year* Wheel *was No. 1, followed by* Jeopardy!

*Then came* The Oprah Winfrey Show, *hosted by the then-unknown Chicago talk show host.*

*After that,* Inside Edition *launched. The show is still in the top ten after more than twenty-five years.*

*Then the long-running* American Journal, *the new* Hollywood Squares, *and* Roseanne *followed.*

*I was lucky enough to run programming and production for King World when Michael was CEO from 1995 until the company was sold to CBS and then Viacom in 2001.*

*Before that I had been an executive producer for the company in the mid-'80s.*

*We had a lot of fun together.*

*I jammed with his band, The Bay Head Bombers, on the Jersey Shore.*

*He jammed with our band on* The Rock 'n' Roll Evening News.

*We fired up the G4 and went to the biggest fights in Vegas, including that of Michael's close friend, the great Sugar Ray Leonard, who is here tonight and who will be speaking later.*

*And more recently the King Sports Fights right here in Santa Monica.*

*We laughed and competed like pit bulls at his legendary poker games with brothers Richie and Bob and close pals Greg, Chuck, Billy, and the wonderful Dick Colbert.*

*Pat and I went on vacation with Michael and Jena and the kids in Hawaii.*

*No one knew how to have a good time better than Michael.*

*But as our leader at work, Michael pushed us harder than we'd ever been pushed.*

*He could be tough, but he was passionate and he cared deeply about everything he put on the air.*

*When other TV magazines went tabloid, he demanded that* Inside Edition *create a serious and expensive investigative unit, headed by network news producers, to cover consumer ripoffs.*

*In 1996, the show won the prestigious George Polk Award for TV journalism, normally won only by major network news organizations.*

*I'd never seen him prouder.*

*Soon after, we scored a worldwide exclusive with Michael Jackson.*

*Soon after that we convinced a red-hot Howard Stern, just after the release of hit film* Private Parts, *to go on* Wheel *during sweeps.*

*He used the occasion to tell the world he was actually the father of Vanna's soon-to-be-born baby. (Just a Howard joke, people.)*

*The press and ratings soared.*

*For years we urged Michael to relaunch* Hollywood Squares, *which he and Roger had brilliantly bought the rights to for a proverbial "song."*

*But Michael wisely waited.*

*"The time's not right, maybe next year."*

*The refrain continued for several years despite our pushing him.*

*When he and Roger finally decided the market was right in 1998, Michael said, "We're gonna do this one big. Bigger than anything's ever been done in the history of television."*

*I can hear his big, booming, determined voice saying those words right now.*

*We announced the show to major fanfare, but Michael decided we'd hold off on the announcement of the critical center square, effectively the star of the show, until our big party at the NATPE convention in New Orleans.*

*At the same time, we would announce our other major new entry for the fall of 1998, starring the No. 1 network star in television at the time, Roseanne.*

*For* Squares, *Michael had only one name in mind for the center square: The Oscar-winning actor and comedian and host of* Comic Relief, *Whoopi Goldberg.*

*After some serious wooing and a lengthy and arduous negotiation, Michael got his center square.*

*In a gesture that is pure Michael, he handed me a pale blue Tiffany box that night and asked me to bring it to Whoopi at her home in Pacific Palisades.*

*It was a beautiful diamond and pearl necklace, and Whoopi cried when she opened it.*

*She told me that no one from a studio or network had ever given her a gift like this before, and she asked me to thank Michael from the bottom of her heart.*

*He didn't have to do it, and she wasn't expecting it. Pure Michael.*

*When it came time to announce Whoopi and Roseanne at NATPE, only one venue would do.*

*While other studios, networks and syndicators rented the best ballrooms and clubs around town for parties to announce their new shows to station execs, Michael had a better idea. A bigger idea. As always.*

*He and Roger decided to rent out the Superdome, home of the previous Super Bowl, and create a giant movie studio set to replicate Times Square, and hire Elton John and his band to perform a full concert live.*

*Needless to say, when word got out, every station exec in the country and from around the world only wanted to come to one party.*

*Other companies literally had to cancel their parties, and competing studio and network heads were calling us and begging for tickets.*

*The green room backstage was overflowing with the biggest stars in the world, from Barbra Streisand to Elton John, as Michael and Roger brought Whoopi and Roseanne on stage and announced our two new shows to thunderous applause and then right into Elton's "Saturday Night's Alright for Fighting."*

*The place went wild. History was made. There has never been, and doubtfully ever will be, another NATPE party like that one.*

*I was lucky to be there; to be his friend, his colleague, and in his gravitational pull for 30 years. He did so much for my family and me.*

*For his 50th birthday Pat and I gave Michael a framed letter written by the great showman P.T. Barnum, along with a photo of the man whom Michael looked up to and to whom he was often compared.*

*Michael, too, was a true showman, a larger-than-life visionary, and a loving and charitable family man.*

*The last time I spoke to him was on April 23, when I called to ask him to come out to our 20th annual Saban Free Clinic golf tournament.*

*My brother David and I wanted to thank him in person at the awards dinner for all his help getting the tournament going in its first few struggling years, when he made King World the presenting sponsor.*

*He told me he was very sick with pneumonia and that he was worried because he wasn't getting better.*

*He explained he could not come to the tournament but wished us good luck.*

*I could hear the fear in my friend's very tough, very brave voice.*

*Before an industry-filled crowd I spoke about Michael's pivotal role and generosity, and a couple days later he sent me an email saying,*

*"Heard you gave me a nice shout-out at the dinner. I really appreciate it."*

*I wanted to come visit him but he was too weak.*

*Two days later I called and learned he was in the hospital. I wanted to visit but Ali told me he needed to stay still and rest.*

*At Ali's suggestion, I sent him a video on my phone telling him he was the toughest guy I knew and that he would beat this and be home soon.*

*Pat and I told him we loved him.*

*I truly believed he would rally, as he always did. But despite some positive reports over the next few weeks, it was not to be.*

# Andy Friendly

*Our hearts go out to you Jena, Ali, Teddy, Audrey, Jessie, and all of Michael's wonderful family and friends.*

*He was truly a great man.*

*A giant.*

*He gave us all so much.*

*Goodbye, my friend.*

\*\*\*\*\*

After I spoke, I walked over to Jena and the kids and gave them each a hug. On my way back to my seat, I passed President Clinton and shook his hand and thanked him again. He said, "Good job," which meant a lot to me.

After me, there were wonderful tributes and musical performances from Whoopi, Ted Danson, California Governor Jerry Brown, Norman Lear, David Foster, and Michael Bolton, among others.

When I returned to my seat, a huge wave of emotion came over me and I clutched Pat's hand tightly.

I turned around and smiled at my beautiful twenty-year-old niece Maddie, who went to school with Michael's kids. We both had tears in our eyes. She gestured me a kiss and I gave her one back. It was a tender and loving moment that spoke volumes about family, love, and the shortness of time. We both knew it without saying a word. It's a moment I'll always treasure.

Later at the reception, I hugged her and my nephew Andrew, a good friend of Michael's son Teddy, for a long time.

We hugged and spoke with Jena and the kids and told them what a great job they had done in their tributes to their dad.

We let them know we would be there for them.

It was a wonderful tribute to Michael. I know he would have been very pleased.

I miss him. It seems impossible, as it does with my dad, Tom Snyder, Ralph Edwards, and others who taught and mentored me, that these giants are no longer here on Earth.

I think of them and find strength in them every day. So they truly are still with me.

How lucky I am to have known them.

*Pat and I giving Michael a signed photo and letter from one of his heroes, P.T. Barnum, for his birthday a few years ago*

# 37

## FLIGHT OR FIGHT: LEARNING TO DEFEND YOURSELF IN LIFE, THE WORKPLACE, AND ON A PLANE AT 35,000 FEET

*The **fight-or-flight** response (also called hyperarousal or acute stress response) is a physiological reaction that occurs in response to a perceived harmful event, attack, or threat to survival. It was first described by Walter Bradford Cannon in 1932.*

Like my father, at an early age I learned I was the kind of guy people either liked or who could rub some folks the wrong way.

I never wanted it to be that way, but that's just the way it's always been. I've had lots of good, deeply rooted, loyal friendships, but there have also been plenty of people who just didn't, and don't, like me. I like to think the majority fall into the former category, but I know there are plenty in the latter.

I've always admired a few of my friends who never seemed to make an enemy or have a negative thing to say or bad feeling with anyone. People who could walk into any classroom, newsroom, corporation, golf club, poker game, or party and just be liked by everyone. For sure, I was not that guy.

Maybe it's because I was tall or opinionated or because of my competitive nature. More likely it was because I was a jerk and a dumbass at times. Maybe it's because I followed my dad and, later at NBC in my twenties, Tom Snyder's occasional "bull in a china shop" examples as my early role models.

They were both tough, larger-than-life guys who didn't suffer fools and subscribed to the philosophy that if you want to be a good leader, you'd better not care about being popular because you're going to have to push yourself and others hard to achieve success.

They believed that you have to fight, and fight hard, for your ideas, principles, and success; and you'll invariably get into disputes with colleagues and friends as well as higher-ups. Or as the great Lakers and Bulls coach Phil Jackson said, "If you want to be loved and popular, don't be a coach or the boss."

As great as they were, my dad and Tom were pretty careless about it at times. Looking back, I wish I'd had the smarts to learn the many valuable things they taught me but not their sometimes undiplomatic, confrontational way of dealing with people and conflict.

As a kid and later a young adult, I did what these giant heroes of mine did, and I ruined some wonderful opportunities and friendships along the way. As an example, I could have handled the turmoil and infighting among the warring partners during the launch of *Entertainment Tonight* much more diplomatically, as recounted in another chapter.

I wish I had some of the insight and coping skills then that I learned later in life from calmer influences like *This Is Your Life*'s creator, the great Ralph Edwards, but I didn't. Life would have been different if I had, but in the big picture I wouldn't trade those two huge giants as early mentors.

My dad used to say, "You have to judge the whole man," and in that sense it wasn't even a close call when it came to these two early influences. I was lucky as hell.

The philosopher Joseph Campbell said, "The privilege of a lifetime is being who you are." These guys and (I like to believe that for the most part) I had that privilege. "Warts and all," as they say. But along the way there were plenty of fights.

Whatever the reason, it's been that way my whole life, although a lot less so now that I've slowed down and am not working as much on shows or as an executive.

When people ask me where I'm from, I still say the Bronx. My wife makes fun of me for that because I'm from a nice section of the Bronx near the Hudson River and grew up in a spacious house on a tree-lined street. Pat chimes in, "He's from Riverdale," as she chuckles.

But the IRT subway line stopped just a few blocks away and I grew up on the playgrounds of Van Cortlandt Park, where some of the toughest kids in the Bronx played basketball and stickball every day, and I was right in the middle of those games and hanging out at the same pizza parlors and bowling alleys and riding the same subway trains to see the Yankees and Giants play baseball or to see the Knicks play basketball. And it was rough at times. You either learned how to handle yourself or you retreated home. I loved playing sports, hanging out, and having fun too much to go home.

It was a different time. We'd take off after school and our parents didn't know where we were or who we were with. Of course there were no cell phones. If we were not going to be home for dinner, we might let our mom know, but otherwise we were on our own from the age of ten or eleven.

And believe me, while I was not a fighter and tried to avoid the local bullies, I had my share of scrapes and had to find ways to defend myself. Not always successfully.

Noticing this, my dad bought some boxing gloves and tried to teach me to fight by bringing some of my buddies over and putting the gloves on us. It was clear early on that my heart wasn't in it. I was much more into sports, girls, cars, and music than fighting.

I never picked a fight and more often than not I'd avoid them, but throughout my life I've had to learn to defend myself. The only times I ever punched someone first was in coming to the defense of a friend who was being bullied and once at camp when a kid threw a rock at a dog; I went off on that guy. To this day, if I see anyone hurt a defenseless person or an animal, it brings out a primal kind of anger in me.

After high school and through my career the battles were more over work, turf, power, and control of shows, companies, fortunes, talent, and office politics. While not often physical, they were intense, and often there was much more at stake than a bloody nose or black eye. Careers and reputations, livelihoods and self-respect were on the line.

No one wins all these battles. If you want to play at the highest levels in the TV business, unless you're one of those rare folks I mentioned earlier who gets along with everyone, you're going to lose and get beat up from time to time, so you'd better develop a thick skin and some reliable and effective battle and coping skills.

As I wrote earlier, I believe the most important of these coping skills are the concepts of under-reacting, staying calm in the chaos of battle, being a "power player," developing an impregnable self-image, having a sharp sense of humor both about yourself and others, and staying on offense, never on defense.

Easy to say, hard to do, but absolutely necessary to survive, and win.

I won some, lost many. But I survived and won enough to achieve much more than I ever imagined in the TV business over a forty-year career. I wish

I had learned these coping and battle concepts in my twenties or thirties, but learning them in time helped a lot and helps to this day.

I try to teach these concepts to the young people in my life, our grandkids, nieces and nephews. I hope they're listening but, like me, they'll probably just have to learn for themselves.

You've got to learn to stand up for yourself, your friends, and the defenseless and for what you believe in without backing down or being intimidated by bullies or thugs. Sometimes it has to be physical, as I learned when Pat and I flew to Hawaii on a vacation in 2005 aboard Northwest flight 91.

At the annual golf tournament my brother David and I have put on over the past twenty years to raise money for the L.A. Free Clinic (now the Saban Community Clinic), we'd raffle off donated prizes. In the spring of 2005 my ticket was drawn from the bowl and we won two tickets to Hawaii, so we decided to head over in early December. I had just finished a few specials for ABC and was in pre-production on a couple of shows for Discovery's new environmental network, Planet Green, along with a bunch of consulting projects; we needed a break.

All was great when we boarded Northwest flight 91 on the morning of December 11. The flight was smooth and uneventful until about an hour in, when Pat noticed some activity in the back of the plane and that the head flight attendant's voice seemed a bit shaky while making a routine announcement on the P.A. system. She was standing near us in the front of the plane, and when she walked by, Pat asked if everything was OK. With 9/11 still fresh in every passenger's memory, we were all on heightened awareness of any potential trouble.

The flight attendant told us she was dealing with a "situation" in the back of the plane but would not elaborate. I got up and walked back to see what was going on.

A man in his late twenties or early thirties was yelling in Spanish and pacing up and down the aisle holding a twisted phone charging cord. A flight attendant was trying to calm him down, with no success.

His focus appeared to be on a young couple in their late twenties holding a newborn baby. The pacing man, according to another passenger, had been threatening to strangle the baby with the phone cord, and he had threatened other passengers and the flight crew as well. This had apparently been going on for ten minutes or so.

After moving his focus from the young couple and their baby, he began threatening to charge the cockpit, and his yelling and taunting became increasingly loud and incoherent.

One of the flight attendants spoke to him calmly in Spanish and after a while got him to sit and calm down a bit. But soon after, he popped up and began walking up and down the aisle again and threatening the couple and the crew.

As I said earlier, I've never initiated a fight and I typically avoid them, but sometimes you don't have a choice, and this was one of those times. Most physical altercations happen in a flash. This one took hours to develop, 35,000 feet above the Pacific, in an airplane traveling at 600 miles per hour.

The fear was of the unknown, of what this guy was up to. Was he carrying a gun, a knife, a razor, or a box cutter like the 9/11 terrorists? Was he planning to rush the cockpit and bring the plane down or crash into a building in Honolulu?

The young doctor sitting across from me with his family and I volunteered to grab him and put him in handcuffs so everyone could relax, but they told us the law was, "Unless he actually attacks the baby or someone else or charges the cockpit, we can't do anything."

So for three hours, a couple hundred passengers sat in terrible fear.

Pat, one of the bravest people I know, was shaking and crying, as were many others. I tried my best to keep her calm but I couldn't. She was a wreck, and with good reason.

While we weren't allowed to handcuff him, the doctor and I took turns standing at the back of the first-class cabin watching his every move, with the understanding that if he did anything we'd try to stop him. He was clearly high on some kind of drug or alcohol. He was agitated, yelling, screaming, and twisting the cord in a threatening manner while staring at the couple and their baby. We just stared at him intently and as menacingly as two middle-aged guys could to let him know we were not going to allow him to hurt that baby or anyone else, and that there was no way he was getting past us to the cockpit if he had designs on that.

After a couple of hours he seemed to calm down with the help of a passenger who was speaking to him in Spanish. As we began our descent, the flight attendant asked us to sit down and put on our seat belts for landing, and we finally did. We were in our final descent when it happened.

While I had relaxed a bit in my mistaken belief that things were under control, the doctor and I remained ready to act if needed.

A few seconds later the guy jumped out of his seat and charged the cockpit. One of the brave flight attendants chased after him. I unhinged my seat belt and in a huge rush of adrenalin grabbed the guy by the neck. The doc soon joined me in wrestling him to the ground, and a couple of young, strong guys from the main cabin joined us about thirty seconds later.

We didn't know if he had a weapon. It turns out he did not, thankfully, but he was kicking and trying to bite us. While he wasn't a big guy, he was strong and wiry and fighting like a wild man.

I smashed my shoulder into the end of a seat arm as we fell to the ground in the galley area. There, after a couple minutes, we were finally able to subdue him, apply the handcuffs given to us by the flight attendant, and strap him into a seat until we landed a minute or two later. Once we were on the ground, several burly federal agents came on board and took him off the plane and into custody.

All we wanted to do was get out of there, but we had to spend the next few hours being debriefed by local police as well as TSA and FBI agents. Finally we got to our hotel, where reporters and camera crews from local and national TV, newspapers, and wire services wanted to talk to us. Just a few years out since 9/11 and anything like this was big news.

My shoulder was banged up from hitting the arm of the chair, but the worst thing was the fear we all had to live with for three hours when we could have subdued this dope an hour into the flight. I still feel bad for that poor couple, the flight crew, Pat, and everyone else who suffered during those three hours.

I get that the rules prohibited us from taking action, but I feel those rules should be revisited and changed so that anyone threatening harm in a situation like that can be restrained immediately.

In the weeks and months following, I was often asked about it by friends and family who wondered if they would have gotten involved and defended the plane. I always responded that I knew they'd do the same, and I believe they would have, but I am still surprised and disappointed by the few able-bodied men sitting near the doc and me who refused to help us when we asked.

I hope I never have to fight anyone again, but to this day I try to be aware of my surroundings and stay alert anytime I'm on a plane or out in public in any setting. It's a violent world and we all need to be ready to stand up and fight, physically or otherwise, for ourselves, our families, and our friends on a plane, in the workplace, or anywhere else.

# Andy Friendly

## Flight 91

# Passengers recount struggle on Flight 91

ANDREW SHIMABUKU | The Honolulu Advertiser

Andy Friendly and his wife, Pat, were among the passengers aboard Friday night's flight. Andy Friendly helped subdue a man who ran toward the cockpit and allegedly threatened a baby on board.

**BY LOREN MORENO**
*Advertiser Staff Writer*

Halfway through his Northwest Airlines flight from Los Angeles to Honolulu, passenger Andy Friendly noticed something was not right.

Another passenger, obviously disturbed and agitated, was furiously pacing the aisles and disobeying the orders of the flight crew, Friendly said.

"We knew something was going on," he said about Friday night's flight. "We had no idea it was serious."

He also didn't know that hours later he would be one of five men who would wrestle and restrain the unruly passenger, who allegedly threatened the life of a sleeping baby.

Santiago Lol Tizol, a 37-year-old Mexican national. is in federal trate today in U.S. District Court in Honolulu, the FBI said.

Friendly and his wife, Pat, of Los Angeles recalled the ordeal aboard Flight 91 during an interview at their hotel in Waikīkī yesterday.

Just moments after Flight 91 was in the air, a flight attendant came on the loud speaker and began making routine announcements. Pat Friendly said she sensed something was wrong.

"Her voice was shaky," said Pat Friendly, an actress.

A little while later, other people onboard began talking about an unruly passenger.

For two hours, Tizol sat across from a Canadian couple, holding a phone cord and staring at their sleeping baby, according to the baby's father, who asked to be identified only by his first name, Jean-Francois. He said on Friday that passengers and flight crew thought Tizol might use the phone cord as a weapon.

Andy Friendly, unaware of the full extent of the matter, wanted to subdue the man before the situation got worse.

"We asked what his issues were, but they (the flight crew) couldn't tell us. They just said he is very agitated," said Friendly, a 54-year-old TV producer from Los Angeles, who was sitting toward the front of the cabin.

By the time the plane was halfway to Hawai'i, Friendly and a doctor sitting across the aisle from him began to plan to restrain the man if he made his way toward the front of the plane again.

Friendly asked flight attendants if he and the doctor could help.

"They (the flight crew) said they are following procedure and

that they were going to handle it," Friendly said.

For about an hour, things remained calm. Flight attendants found another Spanish-speaking passenger who apparently helped to relax the man, Andy Friendly said.

About 10 minutes before Flight 91 was preparing to touch down, Andy Friendly thought "everything was going to be OK."

He was reading a magazine when he saw the man dash past him.

"He went by like a rocket," said Pat Friendly, who added that worst-case scenarios were running through her head.

A flight attendant grabbed the man's collar to prevent him from running toward the cockpit Friendly and the doctor jumped out of their seats and grabbed the passenger's arms. With the help of a third man, the group wrestled the passenger to the ground. Two other passengers joined in.

Other passengers onboard the flight were screaming and panicking, Andy Friendly said.

"He was kicking, biting, jumping up and down. He had super human strength at that point," Friendly said.

After about five minutes o fighting, the group of men wer able to restrain the passenge with plastic handcuffs. He wa strapped into a seat near the exl and was arrested upon arriving i Honolulu.

Andy Friendly said traveler should be prepared for situation like these.

"After 9/11, I think we all nee to have heighten awareness fo these kind of things," Friendl said.

Pat Friendly said the orde will not prevent her and her hu: band from flying.

*Reach Loren Moreno at
lmoreno@honoluluadvertiser
.com or 535-2455.*

*The article about Flight 91 published in the local Honolulu newspaper*

# 38

## SHORT TAKES: TWO BY TEN

A note from my publisher Michael Fabiano: "Hey, Friendly! We're running out of damn paper. Let's wrap this up."

So it turns out there's a limit to how many pages I can write; not in the online version I'm told most people read (you can go on writing forever in that version) but in the printed one.

My otherwise nice publisher Michael Fabiano tells me people don't want to carry around a printed book bigger than 400 pages and that's where we are headed, so in an effort to include at least a few of the dozens more people I really wanted to tell you about, here's a page or two (max) on some of the folks I've been lucky as hell to know or work with.

Not an easy assignment.

### GARRY MARSHALL

The late, great writer, producer, actor, and director of everything from *Pretty Woman* to *Happy Days*.

We did his "life" on *This Is Your Life*, with Ron Howard setting him up and surprising him at the top of the show.

We also honored him and his lovely wife, Barbara, at our long-running Free Clinic golf tourney and annual dinner. A great and longtime supporter of the clinic, he fired off one of the best opening lines ever when he got up to make his acceptance speech before a crowd of Hollywood's biggest stars, movers, and shakers at the gala dinner in Beverly Hills; a line I borrowed, with attribution, many times.

"Hello, rich people…"

*With Garry on New Year's Eve in Hawaii, late 1980s*

## FRANK SINATRA

He was one of Dad's all-time favorites. I heard a lot of Frank Sinatra music growing up but, because I was more of a rock 'n' roller, I didn't develop a love for Sinatra's classic voice, arrangements, and super-cool persona until I was in my thirties.

Pat had guest-starred with him on his TV show, and he was a fan of hers. One night at a party at Kenny and Marianne Rogers' house in the mid-1980s, Pat and I were sitting at the bar at the start of the party when guess who walks up and gives Pat a big hug and asks if he can join us?

Yep, the "Chairman of the Board, Ol' Blue Eyes" himself.

A couple minutes later, a girlfriend of Pat's sat down next to Pat and they started talking, which left me one-on-one with arguably the greatest singer and coolest, most iconic star of all time.

He asked the bartender for his well-known Jack Daniels on the rocks and asked me what I was drinking. Normally a scotch guy, of course I had to join the Chairman in a J.D. rocks. We chatted and laughed together for about twenty minutes until dinner was served. He could not have been nicer or more fun.

Definitely one of the top ten coolest moments ever!

## ROSEANNE

We did a talk show with her for two years at King World. She is famously brilliant and at times difficult, to be charitable, with nine self-admitted personalities.

We had her to dinner one night early on and she was a lot of fun. She adored Pat and included her in her famous "Greatest TV Moms" episode of her No. 1-rated sitcom on ABC.

At dinner, she couldn't have been more fun. She had us belly laughing at her observations of life, including this one from her standup act on women's lib:

"Lots of people don't think I'm feminine enough. I tell 'em they can suck my dick."

## DEBORAH NORVILLE

Pat and I became friends with Deborah when I worked with her and the brilliant team at *Inside Edition*, which is still going strong in the top ten of all syndicated shows after more than twenty-nine years on the air.

During the six years I headed production at King World (now CBS), my senior executives Marc Rosenweig, Rich Cervini, and I worked with Deborah, Charles Lachman, Sheila Sitomer, and the team on many exclusives, including one with Michael Jackson I helped arrange, along with a series of award-winning investigative pieces, including one on insurance scams that won the highly prestigious George Polk Award for broadcast journalism. Normally the province of *60 Minutes* and *20/20*, it was the first time a syndicated newsmagazine had won.

But during my tenure, the story that generated the most attention for the show and Deborah was when I came up with the decidedly "un-friendly" idea to send her to a women's jail in South Carolina for a week during what's called "sweeps" (the thrice-yearly ratings period that determines ad rates for the year, a time when shows promote their biggest stories).

This was not a joke. For four long days and nights starting on February 12, 2000, Deborah bravely endured life as an inmate in cellblock A of the Davidson County Jail in Lexington, South Carolina, in the same extremely harsh and at times frightening conditions as the other inmates, to show what life behind bars was really like: full jail duty and chores, no makeup, clothes, or special perks. She got little sleep in her metal bunk bed due to constant noise and screaming inmates, many with severe mental issues. She was clearly uncomfortable, even scared at times, along with being sleep-deprived and missing her beautiful young kids and husband, but she stayed sharp and did her job, including some sensitive and deeply moving interviews with the inmates.

She was extremely brave, and her reporting won her much praise and several awards along with huge ratings for the show. In an interview on the *Today* show in 2015, she said it was the most difficult, most talked-about assignment of her career and she was glad she did it.

I don't think she was too happy with me about four cold, scary nights into that assignment, but she stuck it out and was a real trooper. We are still good pals and always have a laugh about it to this day.

## ANDY WARHOL

Growing up in the '60s, Andy Warhol was and remains an iconic figure in all things stylish, cool and avant-garde. A true artist and tastemaker who turned a Campbell's tomato soup can, a photo of Marilyn Monroe, and a band called the Velvet Underground into widely recognized international, cultural works of art.

I met him first one night at Studio 54 in Manhattan at the height of that crazy scene where we went almost every night in the mid-'70s after taping *Tomorrow* at NBC.

He was the center of the universe, surrounded by Mick and Bianca Jagger, Halston, Liza Minnelli, and his ever-present Warhol troupe of performance and style artists.

I didn't get to talk to him in-depth until ten years later when his new "it" magazine *Interview* sent reporter Adrienne Meltzer to do a little profile of me when we were producing *The Rock 'n' Roll Evening News*. Apparently he enjoyed it, because I got a call asking if I'd meet him for dinner at the Bel-Air Hotel. Of course I was intrigued, and a couple nights later made the short drive from our home and joined him in the largest booth in the farthest corner of the hotel's dining room.

We were joined by a couple of editors from *Interview* and other business associates, and spent a perfectly pleasant evening discussing everything from our little show to his projects, politics, art, and culture. He was charming, low-key, relaxed, and engaged. No pretense or "I'm too cool for school" attitude. He asked what other projects I was working on and suggested maybe we could work on something together.

He was interested in my life and wanted to know about Pat, as he was a fan. My takeaway was he was a super cool, super smart, unpretentious, nice guy. We agreed to stay in touch but, as that often goes, we did not. I tried but never came up with the right show idea to pitch him.

A couple years later someone sent me an interview he'd done in which he mentioned our dinner. He thought it was funny that at the end of the evening I said: "I'd better get back to my lady." It was very mid-'80s speak; I must have been listening to some Lionel Richie or Kenny Rogers on the way over.

Anyway, super cool.

**Postscript**: Pat and I used to go to the Bel-Air Hotel bar all the time. Just around the corner, it was our local watering hole. We were friends with all the kids who worked there and Antonio, the great piano player. At least once a week, we'd go there for a hamburger and a beer, often meeting or running into friends. Nowadays we never go, as we're boycotting it along with our other local favorite, the Polo Lounge at the famed Beverly Hills Hotel.

When the Sultan of Brunei, who believes in stoning women and homosexuals to death, bought the two iconic hotels, we joined thousands of concerned neighbors, friends and fellow Angelenos in a total boycott.

Full disclosure: We made one exception for our granddaughter Erin's birthday a couple of years ago, as she and soon-to-be-husband Rob love the great food and beautiful atmosphere at the Bel-Air. Only did it for her. Just that once.

## TOM BERGERON

We had signed the brilliant Whoopi Goldberg as center square, and the great production team of John Moffitt and Pat Lee, Steve Radosh, and Jay Redack to write and produce our new version of the classic hit game show *Hollywood Squares* for the 1998 season, but we had yet to find our host.

Time was getting tight; my boss Michael King was getting nervous. We had seen all the usual suspects but hadn't found the right guy. I was a fan of Tom Bergeron's. I loved his sharp mind when he filled in as host on *Good Morning America* and other shows. The Kings weren't sure; maybe a more traditional game show host or stand-up comic or actor would be better.

We organized a mock run-through of the show in a rehearsal hall near Burbank, with ten final candidates culled from a six-month, exhaustive search of hundreds.

The remaining ten were the best and biggest names in the business. They went through their paces and all did a good job, but when Tom went, game over.

Halfway through his mock game, I called Michael King and said we'd found our host. I signed him the next day. He did a spectacular job.

We went on to work on many shows together, including the 2004 *Countdown to the Emmys*, one of the toughest live gigs there is, with all the stars arriving at once and the control room juggling the hosts (Tom co-hosted with Maria Menounos and George Lopez) through an insane, frenzied maze of live and just-taped-for-fast-turnaround interviews with the biggest stars in Hollywood. Then Brad and Jen showed up unexpectedly and we had to go live to them immediately and pure pandemonium ensued.

No one, and I mean no one, could handle that kind of live chaos better than Tom, and he calmly got us through and smoothly onto the live Emmys.

Tom was always there and did a great job when I asked him to host our HRTS network presidents' luncheons and many others. He is a total pro.

When he took on hosting duties of *Dancing With the Stars*, Pat, who danced on Broadway and in countless movies and TV shows, fell in love with the show. Tom was kind enough to invite us to a show and dinner after. He made a big fuss over Pat and we had a great evening.

But the Tom story I like to tell most occurred in 2008, when he was hosting a show for Pam Burke and me called *Supper Club* for Discovery's environmental channel, Planet Green.

Everything about the show was "green," environmentally oriented from the topics discussed by guests like Arianna Huffington and Skip Brittenham, to the food the great chefs made, to the super eco-friendly house in Venice where we shot.

The problem was that Tom and I were still driving gas-guzzling, emission-spewing "muscle" cars. He had a souped-up V8 Mustang and I had a 6 Series BMW, which was even more of an environmental menace. We both had reserved parking spots right in front of the location but were too embarrassed to use them, sheepishly parking blocks away in guilt and shame. Until one morning, and again this story has the added advantage of being true, completely unknown to each other we both pulled up to the location and our assigned parking spots in brand-new, identical, charcoal gray Priuses. We took one look at each other and cracked up, along with the entire crew.

You can't make this stuff up, people.

## AL DAVIS AND MY TRIP WITH THE RAIDERS

In the mid-'80s I became a big Raiders fan when they moved to L.A. They were a breath of fresh air and I liked their outlier, rebel style along with their iconoclastic in-your-face owner, Al Davis ("Just win, baby"), and their great stars like Lyle Alzado, Marcus Allen, and Howie Long.

One day I got a call from an agent at William Morris asking if I'd like to join a group of guys, including the late actor Alan Thicke, and hop on the team plane to a game against the Seattle Seahawks the following Sunday.

As a huge football fan since my days as a kid with my dad watching Jim Brown battle Frank Gifford and Y.A. Tittle in freezing Giants Stadium in the Bronx, I of course said yes. A week later I was sitting on the team plane chatting with Lyle, Howie, Marcus, and some of the other players. It was nothing but fun, laughs, and excitement. There was just one problem: By halftime, the Raiders were getting blown out. The final score was, I believe, 33 to 3.

The mood on the team bus back to the airport was dark, bleak, and angry. Two guys got in a fistfight.

It was the polar opposite of the confident, fun, excited mood on the way up. I took a look at owner Al Davis. He stared expressionlessly out the front window. I've seen guys look happier throwing up.

When we got to the plane, Davis stood at the bottom of the stairway and stared daggers, without saying a single word, toward each and every player and coach as these giant men hung their heads and sheepishly walked past their furious owner and onto the chartered plane.

*With Raider all-pros Howie Long and Lyle Alzado when*
*I accompanied the team to a game in Seattle*

The flight home, needless to say, was deathly quiet and not a lot of fun. I felt bad for these great professionals. The ride up was so full of promise and hope, and now this.

I was pissed at Davis for the ugly, selfish, completely unfair, and unproductive vibe he created.

It's sports. Shit happens. You get to play again next week.

Al Davis and the Raiders had won multiple Super Bowls and were held up as a standard of excellence, but soon after this went downhill, and they have never gotten back to their glory days. I believe this is partly due to the negative impact of their famous owner failing to show leadership when it was most needed.

Just my two cents.

## JACK!

Like everyone, I'm a huge Jack Nicholson fan. Starting with *Easy Rider* in 1969, then *One Flew Over the Cuckoo's Nest* in 1975 and *The Departed* in 2006 and so much more cool Jack stuff; including his decades-long love affair with the Lakers, The Rolling Stones, and everything that is hip. The fact is that Jack defines cool.

So when I found myself standing with him at the patio bar of my next-door neighbors Ed and Mary White's beautiful home five or six years ago, I could barely contain my excitement.

I had chatted with him briefly while golfing once at Riviera, but here I was bellied up to the bar (Sinatra-style) with arguably the biggest movie star in the world.

I wasn't going to miss the chance to have a quick conversation. I introduced myself, told him I was a big fan, and that I lived next door. Blah, blah, blah. He was polite but his eyes kind of glazed over. Unlike the Sinatra scene I described a bit ago, he was not really looking to hang out; probably because Pat wasn't there as she was when Frank came by.

I sensed my time was up but took a shot at extending the conversation by telling him I'd just seen his brilliant 2006 movie *The Departed*, in which he played a character based on Whitey Bulger, the famed Boston mob boss who had recently been arrested living in a small apartment in Santa Monica after a decades-long manhunt by the FBI.

I told Jack how great I thought the movie was and how good he was in it. He smiled and said thanks.

Instead of returning to my table to be with Pat, I really pushed it with a now-lame attempt to get him talking and extend my little moment with one of my idols. "You played Bulger so perfectly, from the voice and mannerisms to his physical look. Did you do a lot of research into him?" I asked.

He took a beat, looked away and then back at me, took off his famous sunglasses and, in that classic Nicholson slow drawl, said the following words to me:

"Research? Really? Research?? I don't DO research, pal."

He smiled, shook my hand, and returned to his table. I sheepishly thanked him for the conversation and returned to Pat's and my table. The conversation was over. I was clearly in way over my head, but this moment ranks in my all-time top ten great Hollywood moments!

My neighbor Ed, who has brilliantly represented Jack (and Vin Scully and other top stars) in business for many years, had a great line the other day as we were walking up the ninth fairway at Bel-Air and I reminded him of my little moment with Jack and how much I'd loved it.

He smiled and said: "Jack's one of the truly great stars Hollywood has seen…and he's lived an extraordinary life. In a sentence: 'He's touched all the bases.'"

Great line. So true.

## THE LATE, GREAT CHUCK BARRIS

We've lost so many friends in the past couple years. Friends we knew and friends we felt like we knew: from Garry Marshall, Jerry Weintraub, and Michael King to close friends and neighbors you may not know, like Warren Forman, Cliff Perlman, and Herb Hutner, to heroes and superstars we'd met like the great Elie Wiesel, Glenn Frey, Carrie Fisher, Debbie Reynolds, and Alan Thicke.

Sadly, I find myself at more and more funerals and memorial services. Sometimes I am asked to say a few words. I find it impossibly sad and difficult, and at the same time each makes me appreciate every precious day left with Pat, my family, and close friends.

As I write this in April 2017, we've just lost another.

I first met Chuck Barris in the mid-'70s when he hosted the outrageous, hysterical daytime game show/mock talent show *The Gong Show*. I fell in love with the show's absurdist humor and its brilliant host, Chuck Barris.

Chuck had already had huge success creating *The Dating Game* and *The Newlywed Game*, which I grew up watching. He'd also written a top-ten hit song called "Palisades Park" and in his spare time was a talented novelist. As if that weren't enough, he claimed to be a secret assassin for the CIA, which he later wrote about in his book *Confessions of a Dangerous Mind*, which

George Clooney turned into a cool movie years later starring Sam Rockwell as Chuck.

In the mid-'70s I turned Tom Snyder on to Chuck and *The Gong Show*, and every day the whole staff would stop whatever we were doing to watch the show, laugh raucously, and carry on like maniacs.

I booked Chuck on the show with Tom and he was great: smart, funny, hip, a great storyteller. Tom loved him.

We began a decades-long friendship, and Chuck extended me the greatest honor by inviting me into his secret and exclusive NFL football pool. He'd been running it for years and its membership included everyone from sportscaster Al Michaels, to major network moguls like Dick Ebersol and Don Ohlmeyer, to the iconic movie director and writer Billy Wilder, and great actors Ben Gazzara and Peter Falk.

How I ever got in the group is a mystery, but I lasted in it for decades and even won the pool one year with my friends Danny Sheridan and Jerry Tanner, whom I brought in as my partners.

The best part was Chuck's weekly newsletter summarizing the week's results and viciously and hysterically lambasting any and all league members who in any of the smallest, ridiculously unimportant, unmeaning ways had irritated "The Commish," as he was famously known.

If you made the slightest error submitting your picks or, God help you, got them in one second later than the Friday noon deadline...you, your family, your closest friends, and everything you stood for, believed in, or cared about in this life were subject to the most extreme, outlandish, highly personal, humiliating, and ultimately hysterically funny diatribes "The Commish" could conjure. And being the brilliant writer and satirist he was, they'd leave a mark. The word "brutal" does not come close. Make two mistakes in a row and he'd throw your ass right out of the league. It didn't matter who or how powerful you were. Your only chance was to appeal to his lovely, longtime assistant, Loretta Strickland, who became a close friend and worked with us on *The Rock 'n' Roll Evening News*. If she felt sorry for you, she was your only chance, but even her appeals were no guarantee of getting back in the league.

Even the famous, powerful stars and moguls in the group shook with fear, as they all recounted when I organized a league dinner for Chuck when the league finally came to an end.

One after another, we all got up and tried to give him back a little of his own medicine, along with our heartfelt thanks for running the league and providing us so much fun for so long.

315

But none of us could really lay a hand on him. And when he finally got up and had his turn at the end of the night, he mercilessly destroyed every single one of us until we were all reduced to uncontrollable tears of laughter. And humiliation.

We loved every second of it.

"I miss you, Chuck."

## JOHN WILLIAMS

I want to end this chapter with something a bit different: a nice little "campfire" to send you off with. Hopefully with a little smile, as it does for me just about every evening.

It's about the great American composer John Williams, who has given us the musical soundtracks of our lives with films like *Star Wars, Raiders of the Lost Ark, Schindler's List,* and countless other classics.

In a recent tribute to director George Lucas for the Shoah Foundation that Pat and I were lucky to attend recently at the Dolby Theatre, Williams led an orchestra of a hundred in portions of those three beautiful scores he'd written, as a tribute to Lucas.

Spielberg, in introducing him, said that both he and Lucas could not have made any of their iconic, award-winning films without Williams' scores. "We simply could not have made them," the director said.

When Williams and the orchestra performed the themes from *Star Wars* and *Raiders*, the distinguished and normally blasé industry crowd stood up and applauded with huge enthusiasm. And when he performed the hauntingly beautiful, highly emotional theme from *Schindler's List,* there was not a dry eye in the house, including Spielberg, who was sitting at the table next to us and whose very real emotion I observed up close.

At the end of the night, we thanked Spielberg and my fellow Shoah colleagues and were about to leave when Pat walked a few feet over to Williams, who was seated with Spielberg and Lucas at the table adjoining ours. She did something I would do but had never seen her do before.

She introduced herself, thanked him for his beautiful performance, and asked him if she could tell him a quick story. He said great. I had joined them and introduced myself and thanked him as well.

Pat said the following. "We live on the golf course in Bel-Air, and almost every night of the year, without exception, we see you walk by our home, usually at dusk carrying a golf club getting in a 'late nine,' as Carl Spackler famously said in our family's favorite film: *Caddyshack.*"

Williams smiled and said: "That's me." He told her that over the years he'd seen us up on our terrace and was happy to finally be making our acquaintance and looked forward to keeping the tradition going for years to come.

It is beyond my imagination as to how another carbon life form breathing the same air, eating the same food –more or less– as me, could possibly hear and write one (let alone the dozens) of truly classic, brilliant scores that John Williams has written.

Each evening when he walks by our house at the most beautiful time of day, as the sun is setting, I marvel at the quiet, spiritual walk he takes to end his day. I wonder if he's hearing notes in his head, composing his next masterpiece, or just thinking about how he pull-hooked his last shot, as I'd be doing.

As Williams passes by, I silently thank him for his incredible music and for his daily spiritual reminder. Usually I have a little single malt in my glass, and I always raise it to him in tribute, even though he has no idea.

It's an honor to have met him.

*****

OK Fabiano. That's it. Just one more chapter to go and we're outta here. I had so much more I wanted to tell you all…

About the time Pat and I sat with Michael Jackson and his little buddy, the chimpanzee Bubbles, at my friend John Branca's wedding.

About our fun times over a forty-year period with the one-of-a-kind, hysterical mega-mogul Jerry Weintraub.

About the time I almost got in a fistfight with Rod Stewart in his suite at the Sherry-Netherland when I was twenty-three.

About drinking beer with Jay-Z and Ken Ehrlich backstage at Coachella.

Or hanging out with Ken and Coldplay's Chris Martin in the latter's dressing room at The Forum.

About my experience developing the movie *Q School* with my friend Ron Shelton, the brilliant writer-director of *Tin Cup* and *Bull Durham*, and executive producing my brother David's documentary *Sneakerheadz* last year.

About the documentary I'm working on now with the Shoah Foundation on the liberators of the concentration camps at the end of WWII, which will include Dad's letter from Mauthausen.

Or some Whoopi, Marty Short, Bernie Brillstein, Dick Cavett, Jackson Browne, Al Roker, and Lorne Michaels stories.

About my poker and golf buddies in L.A., Palm Desert, and around the country.

About so many more brilliant mentors, friends, and colleagues I was so lucky to know and work with.

My nephew James tried to cheer me up the other day when I was explaining I'd run out of time and space: "You can always write another book, Uncle A." I laughed and told him that wasn't gonna happen.

He laughed and said: "You never know." He's right; of course you never do know.

I have truly had fun writing this one, although I'd be lying if I said it wasn't a lot harder and a lot more work than I'd ever imagined.

Ok, almost time to close it up, people.

# 39

## FINALLY....

Time to bring this little clambake to an end.

It's been quite the journey writing this over the past three years, and I truly appreciate you taking a look.

As Springsteen said, writing about yourself is a funny business, but I've tried to be honest.

I hope I haven't bored you to death.

It was fun to relive and share some stories about my heroes, my amazing family, friends, and colleagues. I know I left many out, and for that I am truly sorry. There are so many more stories and people I want to tell you about, and I hope to keep writing in some form or another, so maybe I can tell some more down the road.

Thank you to everyone I ever worked with on every single project: from top writers, producers, directors, talent, and executives to every hard-working production assistant and crewmember. Any success I might have had is largely due to their efforts. I am keenly aware of that fact.

It is fair to say I've had an exciting and eclectic career that was hugely satisfying and rewarding but at times challenging.

When I made the scene in 1951, the president of the United States was a man named Harry Truman. I got to meet him. Now, almost sixty-six trips around the sun later, as I finish this final chapter, the president is a man named Donald Trump. I met and interacted with him, too.

Never thought about this until this moment, but as I write this I can't help but notice both of their last names start with the letters T-r-u-m...

As we used to say in the '60s, "Far out." More accurately: far, far different. About as different as can be.

When I was a little guy in New York and Mr. Truman was president in the early 1950s, life seemed perfect to me. But a few years later, in first grade, we heard an air raid siren go off every single day, at exactly noon, and our teachers made us climb under our desks to prepare us for a nuclear attack. That's right…a NUCLEAR attack.

By Russia.

This was less than ten years after President Truman ended World War II by dropping nuclear bombs on Japan. Images of those bombings and the mushroom clouds they created over Hiroshima and Nagasaki were ever-present in our nation's consciousness, and my own.

Families in our neighborhood were building underground air raid shelters stocked with several months' worth of food and water, blankets, flashlights, and other survival gear.

This went on for years, and those years were the most developmentally formative for the growing childhood brains of my generation.

And they wonder why we "boomers" are NUTZ!

Life was still great thanks to a wonderful, still-happy family: the Yankees, the baseball and football Giants, the Knicks, my bike, camp, and the first musical sounds of Chuck Berry, Elvis, and rock 'n' roll.

Around the age of ten, things got more complicated. My parents' marriage fell apart, and a few years later they divorced at a time when that was uncommon and stigmatizing, especially to a pre-adolescent twelve-year-old trying to fit in.

My mom got sick. Our family was a mess. I had trouble staying focused on my studies in a very strict and academically demanding school.

Somehow, in time and with the love of a newly merged family, a few good friends, and a lot of luck, we survived and even prospered.

If this book has a message, that's it: Hang in there.

At thirty, I first realized my body was no longer the one I had growing up. For the first time I started putting on a little weight, getting tight and sore after sports, things like that.

One day while playing tennis, I pulled a muscle in my back and couldn't stand up for three days.

Over the years I learned to stretch, ice, do insane core exercises, and generally get through a series of back and other relatively small health challenges that occasionally kept me from my beloved sports and workout routines.

But one day about five years ago, after a back injury brought me to my knees on the golf course, I couldn't walk anymore. Time for the dreaded surgery I'd been putting off for years.

My brilliant surgeons, doctors Theodore Goldstein and Rick Delamarter, spent four and a half hours sawing me open and operating on me.

They cut, dug, scraped, and repaired nerves that had wrapped around badly herniated discs and bone spurs. They also repaired something called spinal stenosis, which they explained was like taking off the roof of a building that had collapsed onto my spine and was preventing blood, nutrients, and oxygen from flowing.

Thanks to the tender mercies of the living angels who are the nurses of the Cedars-Sinai hospital here in L.A., and the attentive care of my close friend and doctor Josh Trabulus, I made it through four days and nights of weapons-grade pain, medication-induced nightmares, and utter helplessness, the likes of which I had never known and hope to never know again.

When I got home, all I could do was lie in bed for weeks. I couldn't even get to the bathroom. With Pat's and our family's loving care, I slowly recovered.

When I could finally hobble on a walker to the bathroom a few feet away on my own, I couldn't...pee.

The body was not healed.

I share this not-so-pleasant anecdote to urge the following, somewhat clichéd, life thought:

One word...gratitude.

A few weeks later, when the day finally came I could successfully complete my bathroom functions, an indescribable, life-affirming, soul-soaring wave of gratefulness filled my very being.

Hand to God, I promise to get off the bathroom stuff in a second...but now, each and every morning when I am able to easily take care of that basic function, a big smile comes over my face and I am filled with gratitude.

OK, I'm done. Forgive me.

My parting advice is simple.

Be grateful for the big and the small stuff.

We are all here by the grace of God or nature or whatever higher power we believe in. We are just a split-second electrical heartbeat away from the proverbial "dirt nap," as Letterman calls it.

In 2008, in my late fifties, I had three series on the air, this following an improbably long and successful career starting in 1973. Now, following a number of close but ultimately failed attempts, I have no series on the air.

I won't lie. In a town where one's status is generally determined by how your career is going, I've had to adjust.

The good news is that, through the support and encouragement of close friends and family, I've found other things to do that have allowed me to keep learning, growing, and feeling like I'm, in some small way, contributing to the people and causes I care about. From my ever-growing, talented family and friends to the charities and community organizations I work with, from working on a World War II liberator documentary with the Shoah foundation to continuing my guitar playing and "song-writing.

I continue to enjoy poker and golf, reading, traveling, and exploring new adventures as much as possible. Adventures like writing this little tome, which has reminded me of the value of self-expression. I hope to continue writing, in some form or another, in the future.

As I write this last chapter on April 3, 2017, which happens to be Pat's and my thirty-first wedding anniversary, I'm still excited about it all.

I'm excited to drive up the coast with Pat and Bonnie to play Pebble Beach with my nephew James for his first time, for his thirtieth birthday...

I'm excited to see my favorite band, U2, live with some of the kids in a few weeks, and one of my favorite California bands, Weezer, soon after that.

I'm excited about the upcoming weddings this year and next of grandkids, nieces, nephews, and close friends' kids. I'm still buzzing from the two beautiful weddings in our family last year.

I'm looking forward to the upcoming college graduations of several more of my gang in the months and years ahead.

I'm looking forward to the simple, everyday pleasures, like walking in the park with Pat and Bonnie, and enjoying a good single-malt scotch while watching the sunset from our terrace.

The great CBS news anchor and reporter Bob Schieffer may have said it best on the occasion of his eightieth birthday a couple months ago when asked to sum up his life: "For me it was a great life. I've often said: If my life ended tomorrow, I would have gotten my money's worth."

That's how I feel exactly.

After speaking at the funerals of several close friends who were about my age over the past few years, I think often about how precious our brief time is on the planet.

I deeply miss the close friends and loved ones I've lost.

In these fraught times in the world, I am aware of the irony that I was born into a Cold War and ordered to hide under my desk in first grade every day at noon in preparation for a Russian attack; and that six decades later our country and our precious 240-year-old democracy, was, according to the

FBI, the CIA, and the entire U.S. intelligence community, attacked by Russia in an attempt to influence our most sacred democratic right: the election of the United States president.

You don't need me to tell you that while life is full of promise, joy, and beauty… there is also much to be fearful of.

In my lifetime, I've observed the threat of nuclear war, Vietnam, the assassination of presidents and great leaders, and domestic and international terrorism as on September 11, 2001. Also the fear, pain, and anguish of loved ones and close friends battling serious illness and facing death.

But what I've learned, and what I'll leave you with, is that we will be OK.

As long as we remember to "be brave," as my dad shouted to the firemen driving on their way toward blazing infernos to protect their fellow citizens when I was a kid growing up, and which I repeat to this day when I see firefighters heading to battle fires.

Or as Dave Letterman said the night he returned to his show after 9/11:

"There is only one requirement for any of us, and that is to be courageous, because courage, as you might know, defines all other human behavior."

I don't think you can say it any better than that.

I emailed one of our grandkids about a year ago, relating a eulogy I had given at a close friend's funeral, one of far too many I had recently attended. The event was a magnificent tribute to my friend, attended by hundreds and produced beautifully, and it got me thinking about what I'd like to happen when my own time comes, hopefully many years from now.

In the email, which I ended with one of those smiley-face emoji's, I wrote:

> *When the time comes, I don't want anything big or fancy. Please just have friends and family over, crank up some U2 and Weezer tunes, throw in some Beatles and Stones.*
>
> *Tell everyone: "He had a blast. The bar is open!"*

That's about right, I think.

\*\*\*\*\*

# PHOTO GALLERY

*My sister Lisa and I with President Harry S. Truman in Islamorada, Florida while my dad was shooting a documentary with Truman for CBS News, 1954*

*President Truman autographed the photo to me.*

*Autographs my dad got for me while producing documentaries with President Eisenhower (I was present for this one), the great baseball legend Jackie Robinson, and Robert Oppenheimer, the "father" of the atomic bomb, which ended and allowed the United States to win World War II*

*With President Clinton at a Hollywood Radio & Television*
*Society luncheon where he was the featured speaker*

*With former Secretary of State Colin Powell at
an HRTS luncheon where he spoke*

*My dad in the Oval Office producing an interview
with President John F. Kennedy*

*CBS Photo Archive/CBS/Getty Images*

*Drawing by Ben Shahn, sent to my dad the day he resigned as president of CBS News over the network's refusal to carry Senate/Vietnam hearings live*

*Today it's displayed proudly in my home.*

*Art © Estate of Ben Shahn/Licensed by VAGA, New York, NY*

The Hollywood Radio and Television Society
Recognizes and Honors
Andy Friendly
President 2004 - 2006

*CBS Chairman Leslie Moonves, me, and Charlie Rose at a
Newsmakers luncheon I produced as president of HRTS, 2006*

*My fellow board members presented me with this picture
and plaque upon the completion of my two terms as
president. I remain on the board to this day.*

*With "It Girl" Bo Derek, star of the movie 10, on location for a primetime NBC special I produced with Tom Snyder, 1979*

*The Rock 'n' Roll Evening News house band: John
Fuller, Jeff Androsky, Scott Reynolds, our drummer,
and me performing at a Christmas party, 1986*

*Over the years, I tortured the staff of my various
shows with band performances at parties.*

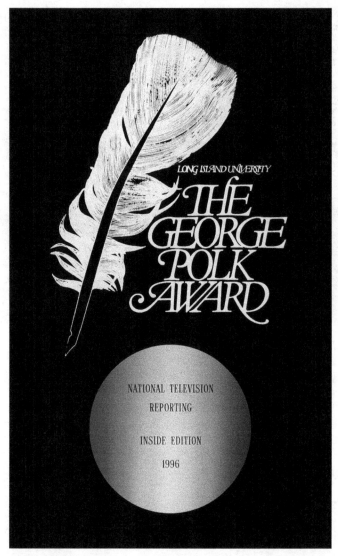

*The prestigious George Polk Award for broadcast journalism
won by Inside Edition in 1996 for its courageous investigative
reporting of insurance companies scamming consumers*

*The award was the first for a syndicated newsmagazine.
It is normally the province of 60 Minutes and other major
network newsmagazines and documentaries.*

*It was one of our proudest moments at King World.*

*Bob Iger, Andrea Wong, Ted Koppel, me, Jordan Levin, and Dave Ferrara at an HRTS luncheon that Andrea and I co-chaired featuring Koppel, the longtime anchor of ABC's Nightline, 2004*

*One of the giants of broadcast journalism, Koppel warned the industry to protect press freedoms at all costs. It was a prescient admonition.*

*Re-creating this book's cover photo, this time with nephew Andrew Friendly on my shoulders following one of the early Free Clinic golf tournaments my brother David and I organized over the past twenty-plus years*

*Grandkids Will, Clare and Erin Hookstratten with "center square" Whoopi Goldberg at a taping of Hollywood Squares*

*Grandsons Will Hookstratten and Eddie Osher with Squares host Tom Bergeron, whom I was lucky to work with on several shows*

*Hanging in the pool with grandson Eddie Osher, nephew Aaron Mark, granddaughter Kate Osher, and niece Ramona Mark (now Orley)*

*That's me as Goose from Top Gun and my niece Maddie Friendly as Wednesday Addams from The Addams Family, at a Halloween party, 2016*

*Some of our gang at University of Oregon, outside Friendly Hall on a recent trip to visit our granddaughter Clare, who attended college there*

*L - R: Jon, Marion, Erin, and Clare Hookstratten, Kate Osher Fay, Rob Kelley, Will Fay*

*With some of the gang at the wedding of Ronen Mark to John Kohn, Chicago, 2012*

*Tomorrow friends and colleagues Patty Mann, Debbie Vickers, Ellen Deutsch, Courtney Conte, and Pam Burke at a memorial celebration of Tom Snyder at our home*

*With "Sipowicz," my all-time favorite TV detective, played by the brilliant Dennis Franz on the seminal series NYPD Blue*

*I asked him to give me his best, famed Sipowicz "perp skunk eye" for this photo in the green room before a taping of Roseanne's talk show at King World/CBS. Great guy.*

*Pat and I with one of our favorite Lakers, Shaquille O'Neal,
on the court at Staples Center at a friend's birthday party,
where we got to shoot free throws with the legend*

*With close friend and business manager Tony Peyrot and my grandkids
Eddie and Will at one of our early Free Clinic tourneys at the Riv*

*Riding the Jon Deere mower volunteering at the VA Golf Course,
which provides recreation and work for veterans in Los Angeles*

*With grandkids Eddie, Kate, Clare, Erin, and Will in Palm Desert
on a golf cart my family gave me for my 50th birthday*

*Close friends Ken Ehrlich, me, Dick Askin, and the late Warren Forman
at dinner with our PGA West buds at awards dinner for Big Fish, a
fishing/golf tourney I dreamed up after one too many scotches*

Andy Friendly

*Sadly, after a long and courageous battle, we
lost our friend Warren to cancer.*

*A talented cameraman who worked on the Grammys and Emmys for Ken,
along with a couple of my shows, Warren, who was born one week and
one block away from me in Manhattan in November 1951, was one of
the best people I've known. He taught us all the true meaning of bravery
in his long battle with cancer. I never heard him complain. Not once.*

*My yearly golf excursions with Warren, Ken, and Dick, to Las
Vegas, Torrey Pines, and other places, are some of the best, most
fun memories I have. All of our gang at PGA West will always
remember Warren fondly as we miss our brave friend.*

*Twenty-seven-year and fifty-two-year (respectively) great
buds David Zaslav and Paul Cantor on one of my annual
summer visits to Stockbridge, Massachusetts*

*With one of my childhood idols, the great New York Giants championship-winning quarterback Y.A. Tittle, whom Pat and I met and spent time with on a cruise to Israel and Egypt*

*Nicest guy ever.*

*With the brilliant Meryl Streep at the birthday party of my dear friend Allan McKeown, given by his loving, talented wife, Tracey Ullman*

*In a town not known for modesty, elegance and grace, Allan had all of those qualities and much, much more. I miss him very much.*

*Pat, Bonnie, and me with cousin Anne Greene, sister Lisa Friendly,
Megan McCarthy, and my nephew James Nicholson in one of our favorite
places: Pebble Beach, celebrating James's 30th birthday, April 2017*

David Zaslav, Pat Crowley & Andy Friendly

and Host Committee:

| | |
|---|---|
| Heather & Skip Brittenham | Julia Franz & Chris Silbermann |
| Harriet & Ken Ehrlich | Jeff Ross |
| Laurie & Jon Feltheimer | Sandra & Vin Scully |
| Shari & Rob Friedman | David Nochimson |
| Rick Rosen | Dana & Matt Walden |

Eugenie Ross-Leming & Robert Singer

*cordially invite you to*

# An Evening in Support of
# USC Shoah Foundation

Monday, February 1, 2016

6:30 p.m. Cocktails & Hors D'oeuvres

7:15 p.m. Program & Discussion

At the Residence of Pat Crowley & Andy Friendly

Address to be provided upon RSVP

*RSVP by Wednesday, January 20, 2016*

*Email Melissa Saragosti at saragost@usc.edu or call (213) 740-3468*

*The invitation for an event Zas, Pat, our wonderful co-hosts, and I put together at our home recently to benefit the USC Shoah Foundation*

Andy Friendly

*It was a moving evening, featuring a Holocaust survivor sharing her memories with many of our family and friends; an evening I will never forget.*

*With Ken Ehrlich and Sandra and Vin Scully at Shoah Foundation fundraiser at our home, 2016*

*Me and my girl at the wedding of our nephew Noah
Mark to Catie Haub, September 2016*

# PHOTO CREDITS

Cover *Andy Friendly on father Fred Friendly's shoulders* (Dorothy Friendly/author's collection)

*"A Friendly Takeover"* (October 1995/Copyright © *Daily Variety*)

*Edward R. Murrow and Fred Friendly* (*CBS Photo Archive/CBS/Getty Images*)

*Edward R. Murrow and Senator Joseph McCarthy*, Ben Shahn (Art © Estate of Ben Shahn/Licensed by VAGA, New York, NY)

*The Beatles at Suffolk Downs* (August 1966, Harry Benson)

*Fred Friendly with daughter Lisa and son Andy, Rockefeller Plaza, 1958* (Dorothy Friendly/author's collection)

*Clint Eastwood, Tom Snyder, and Andy Friendly* (author's collection)

*"Recalling Snyder as Fearless, Peerless Friend"* Andy Friendly (Crain Communications)

*Tom Snyder, Rick Carson, and Andy Friendly at Studio 54* (author's collection)

Johnny Carson *Tomorrow* appearance (Courtesy of Carson Entertainment Group)

Ralph Edwards © 1978 (Bud Fraker/mptvimages.com)

*"Hollywood or Bust"* (© Paramount Pictures. All Rights Reserved)

Forever Female (© Paramount Pictures. All Rights Reserved)

TV Guide cover *Please Don't Eat the Daisies* (Wright's Media)

*A.M. Los Angeles* (Courtesy of KABC)

*LIFE* Magazine (John Engstead, Copyright © TIME/LIFE, John Engstead/mptvimages.com)

Dean Martin Fan Magazine *(NBC)*

*Variety* 50 Top-Grossing Films, November 9, 1983 (November 1983/Copyright © Daily Variety)

Lorne Michaels, Martin Short, Dave Ferrara, Andy Friendly (Courtesy of Hollywood Radio & Television Society)

Television Academy Hall of Fame in 1994 (Photo Credit: Richard Mark)

Colin Powell and Andy Friendly (Courtesy of Hollywood Radio & Television Society)

President John F. Kennedy and Fred Friendly (*CBS Photo Archive/CBS/ Getty Images*)

*CBS Ducks*, Ben Shahn (Art © Estate of Ben Shahn/Licensed by VAGA, New York, NY)

*Leslie Moonves, Andy Friendly, and Charlie Rose* (Courtesy of Hollywood Radio & Television Society)

Back Cover: *Andy Friendly* (Shayne Shnapier)

Tom Rogers, Andy Lack, Maria Bartiromo and David Zaslav (Photo Credit: Sylvia Rogers)

# AUTHOR'S BIOGRAPHY

Andy Friendly is an Emmy-nominated producer, writer, director, and programming executive who has worked with television legends Tom Snyder, Tim Russert, Richard Pryor, Whoopi Goldberg, Dan Rather, and dozens more.

He is currently on the Board of Councilors of the USC Shoah Foundation and is a past president and current board member of the Saban Community Clinic and the Hollywood Radio & Television Society.

He has taught as an adjunct professor at his alma mater, the USC School of Cinematic Arts.

He lives in Los Angeles with his wife, actress Pat Crowley, and their family.

9 781939 961648